AMERICA'S
Ski Book

AMERICA'S

Ski Book

BY THE EDITORS OF **SKI MAGAZINE**
AND **JOHN HENRY AURAN**

WITH AN INTRODUCTION BY **WILLY SCHAEFFLER**

PUBLISHED BY CHARLES SCRIBNER'S SONS · NEW YORK

Library of Congress Catalog Card Number 66-22664

The first issue of *Ski* magazine

FOREWORD

THE story of modern skiing in America really comprises the past thirty years. From 1936, when the first chairlifts were flung up mountainsides and skiers began to adopt modern forms of parallel skiing using vastly improved equipment, the sport has grown to the point where it now encompasses almost two million skiers and some 700 lift-served ski areas in the United States.

Paralleling the development of modern skiing, *Ski* magazine, for thirty almost uninterrupted years, has been a bible of the American ski public. Today, *Ski* is the world's largest ski publication. Between the months of September and March, tens of thousands of skiers religiously search the pages of the magazine for guidance in selecting their equipment, making travel plans, sharpening their technique, and keeping abreast of the racing scene. In *America's Ski Book*, the Editors of *Ski* and Charles Scribner's Sons found the natural opportunity to bring together in a single book the most important of this practical skier information. Truthfully, this is a unique book. For never before has it been possible to encompass within a single publication of this size such a comprehensive presentation of all the major facets of the ski sport . . . its historical development, the equipment, a guide to travel and the ski resorts, instruction and ski competition.

The credit for distilling all of this information into *America's Ski Book* goes to a former editor of *Ski*, John Henry Auran. A lifetime skier, a graduate of the   V

FOREWORD

University of Washington and a former newspaperman, Auran has been a prolific ski author since 1959, covering virtually all of the important developments in the sport including the Squaw Valley Olympics, the revolution in equipment, the rise of the American luxury ski resort, and the formalization of ski teaching technique in the United States. From his home in Boulder, Colorado, Auran spent the better part of a year preparing the material for this book.

Credit for the ski wisdom and expertise in *America's Ski Book* rests with the many authorities who have contributed to the pages of *Ski* magazine. While it is not possible to make mention of all those people whose thinking has found its way into this book, we would like to express thanks to racing authorities Tom Corcoran and Willy Schaeffler, to ski school directors Paul Valar in the U.S. and Ernie McCulloch in Canada, to equipment expert Robert Albouy, to Nordic writer Michael Brady, and to Jakob Vaage, Director of the Ski Museum in Oslo who made important contributions to the chapters dealing with the very early history of skiing.

Mention should also be made of four of the many fine ski photographers whose work appears in this book: Hanson Carroll, Joern Gerdts, Fred Lindholm and Kim Massie.

Special thanks are due to Thelma Slater of *Ski* magazine for her assistance in compiling the scores of illustrations in *America's Ski Book*, and to Donald Hutter of Charles Scribner's Sons who supplied the ingredients of toil and zest to make this book possible.

John Fry
EDITOR-IN-CHIEF
SKI Magazine

New York City
October, 1966

vi John Henry Auran

INTRODUCTION

Willy Schaeffler

MANY fine books have been written on skiing, but with few exceptions their authors have confined themselves to technical aspects of the sport. This is understandable. Skiing in North America is a relatively new sport, one that has had a sizable following only for the last twenty years or so.

But skiing is growing up and growing fast. We are, of course, still concerned with how to ski—and this is not overlooked in this book—but thousands and thousands of skiers have gone beyond the "how-to" stage and have become deeply involved in the many other facets of skiing—its history, its organization, competition, the fine points of equipment and what the skiing is like on the other side of the hill. For those who are concerned with these aspects of skiing, this book answers their needs.

I have had the pleasure to know and work with the writers and editors who created *America's Ski Book*. I can say without reservation that there is encouragement and help in every chapter based on deep professional knowledge. But more important, the writers and editors have not forgotten that we ski to have fun and to enjoy the pleasure of the outdoors in the winter. Even when a chapter goes into technical detail it remains good, light, informative reading and helps us to discover more of the great world of skiing.

As ski coach at Denver University for the last twenty years, I would be remiss **vii**

INTRODUCTION

if I did not mention the importance of skiing for physical fitness and the need for conditioning in skiing. This conditioning does not require violent calisthenics (unless you are a racer or badly out of shape). But it does require consistent exercising throughout the non-ski season. This form of exercise need not be dull. A brisk half-hour walk every day or the regular playing of one or more sports will enable you to get a great deal more out of your skiing.

But much as I like to stress conditioning, we should keep in mind that skis, in the final analysis, are tools to bring us outdoors in winter. The pleasures of nature should not be lost in the technical execution of the sport. As so many of the outstanding photographs in *America's Ski Book* suggest, skiing will always be a fresh, exciting and wonderful sport if we remain aware of the natural beauties of America's ski lands.

Willy Schaeffler
SKI COACH, UNIVERSITY OF DENVER
MEMBER, COMMITTEE FOR ALPINE COURSES, FEDERATION INTERNATIONALE DE SKI
DIRECTOR, COURSE APPROVAL COMMITTEE, UNITED STATES SKI ASSOCIATION
DIRECTOR, PROFESSIONAL SKI INSTRUCTORS OF AMERICA
DIRECTOR, SKI SCHOOL, ARAPAHOE BASIN, COLORADO

CONTENTS

Contents

x

Contents

AMERICA'S
Ski Book

Part One

THE STORY OF SKI

CHAPTER 1

The many joys of the skier

"He saw the pine grove behind and below him, on his right, turned again toward it, and with a quick descent reached the laden trees; they stood in a wedge-shaped group, a vanguard thrust out from the mist-screened forests above. He rested beneath their bows and smoked a cigarette. The unnatural still, the monstrous solitude, still oppressed his spirit; yet he felt proud to have conquered them, brave in the pride of having been measured to the height of surroundings such as these."
The Magic Mountain by Thomas Mann

Enough Americans have become intrigued with skiing in the last ten years to make it this country's most popular winter sport. From a few thousand pioneering devotees before World War II, the sport has grown to where it now can count close to two million enthusiasts in its ranks. And their number grows by about 15 per cent every year.

These figures are cited not to demonstrate what an impressive number of skiers there are, but as evidence of the powerful appeal of this seemingly simple sport. After generations of sticking by their fireplaces during the winter, Americans have discovered, through skiing, a whole new world—a world once 3 thought frigidly forbidding, but now, thanks to skis, at least as enjoyable as the playgrounds of the more temperate seasons.

"It's as if sunspots had altered the climate," skier-philosopher James Laughlin once wrote on the startling growth of skiing. "Winter suddenly became a different season—as exciting as summer—in which we could be outdoors having fun on weekends and on vacations."

There is no question that at least part of skiing's appeal lies in the test it provides for man against nature. Even as we accumulate more leisure time, become ever more proof against the vagaries of wind, sun and storm, we seem to need a certain amount of assurance that we can still prevail without the conveniences provided for us by twentieth-century technology.

The need to be outdoors—whatever its overtones of play—is no small matter. Volumes have been written on the benefits of outdoor recreation, a great deal of which was summed up by the Outdoor Recreation Resources Review Commission, the so-called Rockefeller Commission, in its final report to the President:

"Outdoor activity, whether undertaken lightly or with serious intent . . . is essentially a 'renewing' experience . . . The fact that we live in a world that moves crisis by crisis does not make a growing interest in outdoor activities frivolous . . ."

Skiing provides the "renewing" experience in a special way. As a participant in one of a limited number of winter outdoor activities, the skier does not have to wait until spring or summer to "renew" himself. Whether he tries a few runs on the weekend at a local ski area, takes a vacation at a major ski resort, or goes on a ski tour in the wilderness, skis provide him with a freedom in the snow-covered outdoors that no other activity can match. And with its possibilities of downhill speed, skiing becomes an experience of unusual exhilaration.

Reinforcing this exhilaration is the powerful appeal of the mountains. They can be rolling Midwestern hills or the craggy peaks of the Rockies or the Alps. Snow endows them with a simple beauty few can resist. The reaction of the skier may run from the lyrical to the laconic, but mountain beauty is never dismissed. The fact that a skier is never a mere onlooker at scenery, but

actually comes into meaningful contact with the mountains, heightens his perception and stimulates his appreciation of what he sees.

This very perception which the skier so quickly cultivates also forces him to see the mountains as a challenge to his skill, as an obstacle to overcome, and, particularly in the high mountains, as a possible threat to his survival.

Probing this strange paradox in an article on cross-country racing, *Ski* magazine once noted that "It is one of the ironies of modern civilization that man, in order to remain man, must of necessity make a sport of what used to be of necessity to his survival. The more the products of his genius smooth his path, the more he feels he should walk, should exercise, should run to keep alive those instincts and muscles which enabled him to reach his state of ease in the first place."

That we should get pleasure and satisfaction out of skiing probably defies wholly rational explanation. But Dr. Ernest Dichter, the motivational researcher who originated the term "survival sports" for outdoor activities such as skiing, mountain climbing, sailing and skin diving, says that the benefit of skiing is that it puts the participant on his mettle. And while we are long removed from the Lapland peasant who had to ski to get from place to place, or to hunt, simply to stay alive, nevertheless, "There is a feeling of immediate achievement. At a certain point skiing is self-rewarding. You enjoy it while you are doing it. You know how well you did it. And you don't have to wait for anybody to tell you."

There is no doubt that the challenges of skiing and the feelings of achievement they make possible are tremendously powerful attractions.

The challenges are for all practical purposes unlimited. There are trails and slopes of almost every gradation and with great variations in length, width, steepness and terrain configurations. It is nearly impossible to make the same run twice on the same trail, or even on something as confining as a slalom course. Although most ski terrain seems solid enough, it is constantly being altered by wind, sun and snow, and, above all, by the skiers themselves.

Whatever the challenges of any one area, there is ever greater variety in the challenges of the more than one thousand ski areas in the United States

and Canada, and beyond them the areas of Europe, Japan, Australia, New Zealand and South America. And in addition to the skiing to be found in organized areas, there is the endless terrain open to those willing to dispense with lifts and to tour in the forests or in the high mountains. The possibilities of new challenges of skiing were demonstrated in 1964, when Aspen ski instructor Fritz Stammberger carried skis up Cho Oyu, the 26,600-foot Himalayan peak which is the sixth highest in the world.

It is hardly necessary to seek the challenges of skiing on so grandiose a scale. The average skier finds it challenge enough simply to move himself through the ranks from raw novice, through intermediate, to expert. The technical feat of mastering the variations of parallel skiing under a wide variety of conditions can in itself be a fairly sizable goal. It is one of the charms of skiing that one does not have to be an absolute master to enjoy the sport. Providing the skier is reasonably adept at a few basic fundamentals, there is no reason why he cannot experience most of the sensations of the expert.

It is not uncommon to find many pursuing the sport well into their sixties, and beyond. In Canada, Herman Smith-Johannsen, at ninety, was still endlessly touring Quebec's Maple Leaf Trail. Even without the excitement generated through the clash of competition, skiing simply refuses to get dull.

Underlying the challenges is the need for personal courage, and this applies on all levels of skill. The expert, skiing so flawlessly down a difficult trail, may seem fearless. But one has only to talk to a racer to realize that he is quite conscious of the risks involved. His fear may differ in emphasis from the fear experienced by the beginner, but it is fear nevertheless. Beginner or expert, both have to make a deliberate decision to take the run, and with it all its risks.

What distinguishes skiing from most other risk sports is that it cannot be experienced vicariously. Except for an occasional big race or jumping meet, an Olympics or a World Championship, skiing is not a spectator sport. There is no way of vicariously delegating the risks to someone else, as in auto racing, professional football, or bull fighting, and still get enjoyment and satisfaction out of the spectacle. Ski racing is interesting, occasionally even thrilling, but its excitement, its satisfying sensations, or even its daring are not apparent to the spectator. The very best competitors tend to be the most unspectacular. The only way to experience what skiing has to offer is to try it yourself.

Anyone who has been on skis for a while becomes sharply aware that the challenges of skiing are quite personal. In the absence of a score or other competitive factors, it is up to each skier to determine his objective: what he wants to get out of his day on the slopes or out of a particular run. It may be a modest series of linked snowplow turns or to ski "like Stein." It doesn't particularly matter. No one will ever really know. But this very privacy of decision also demands an honesty with self which allows no rationalizations. It explains why, on the one hand, skiing has been called, despite all the people who crowd the slopes, a lonely sport, and why, on the other hand, skiers as a group are so delightfully ebullient. There are few sensations so thoroughly satisfying as a self-set challenge successfully met.

Skiing is a relatively easy sport to learn and doesn't require a long period of apprenticeship before its thrills and pleasures become apparent. It is an open question as to who gets more excitement from the sport: the expert who makes run after flawless run, or the beginner who for the first time has negotiated the bunny slope without a fall. While the expert has greater expectations, the panorama facing the novice or intermediate is really no less exciting.

While there is no question that challenge and achievement are vital aspects of skiing, there is always the temptation, particularly on the part of skiers themselves, to overstress the sensation of survival. "I crashed," "I was hip deep in powder," and similar notations are common items in the skier's conversation.

Actually, thanks to modern, light-weight insulated clothing, on-mountain shelter, and lifts, skiing is not excessively demanding physically, or even particularly chilling or dangerous. Although skiing can be carried to hazardous lengths, the skier is not basically like the mountain climber to whom high danger and extreme physical effort are stocks in trade. He does not even

require the stoic acceptance of bone-chilling cold of the ice fisherman. While a skier can never ignore the possibilities of extreme cold, heavy storms, or a painful fall, these threats remain for the most part in the background, and are merely part of the spice of his endeavors.

In point of fact, skiing is among the most sophisticated of sports. This applies to its technical aspects as well as the peripheral activities associated with it.

Skiing is not a natural act, such as walking, running or throwing, the basics of most other sports which are usually learned without instruction. There is no such thing as an instinctive skier, because instinctively man dislikes the sensations of falling, of leaning forward on a hill, and of fighting centrifugal force—all of which are essential elements in skiing. To live with these instinctive dislikes, the skier must have a high level of concentration and self-control, even a certain amount of intellectual discipline.

The taste for skiing must be cultivated. Because it emphasizes quick thinking and coordination, and actually defies sheer applications of brute strength, it has a strong appeal to those with a sophisticated turn of mind. It is probably more than coincidental that an overwhelming majority of skiers are college graduates or students.

This sophistication becomes most apparent in the activities that accompany skiing and in the resorts that cater to skiers. As Archer Winsten, ski columnist of the *New York Post*, once wrote, "No matter how good (the skiing) close at hand, skiers have a well-developed yearning for far-away places and strong convictions that the snow is deeper and lighter elsewhere."

It may seem somewhat spurious to claim that skiers receive some special benefit from travel, but comparing them with other tourists, particularly those who journey to Europe, one cannot help but be struck by the difference in the attitudes and impressions they bring back.

The difference is due to having a reason for traveling at all. They go to ski and will spend a week or two at a particular place. Even though their main objective is skiing, the fact that they stay in one place, come into close contact with the natives and really absorb the atmosphere, provides them **11** with a full experience of far greater value than the fleeting impressions of place after place received by the average tourist.

Sir Arnold Lunn, a British philosopher and one of the true pioneers of the sport, has said that one of the main reasons to go skiing is "to absorb mountain culture." This culture may have been diluted by the very internationalism that skiing has fostered and by the many city amenities which have found their way to the mountains. But through travel the skier can still be exposed to a rich variety of experiences.

Even the beginner, making his first turns in some foothill area, quickly becomes aware of the sport's involvement with travel and the international atmosphere that pervades it. The American skier may find that his instructor has an accent—Austrian, German, French, Swiss or even Norwegian. Furthermore, he invariably finds, even if the instructor is native-born or Canadian, that he is being taught in a sort of code, easy enough to understand, but which transcends any language barrier. And it isn't long before he speaks the code himself so that a short exposure will enable him to take lessons in any ski country he chooses to visit. Rink Earle, an American instructor who reversed the usual process by teaching skiing in Austria for a year, once noted: " 'Like so, please! ' is a wonderful pedagogical device."

But the accents are not confined to the instructors. Since the number of topnotch places to ski is relatively limited, it is not unusual to find a scaled-down version of the United Nations at most major ski resorts. And the hotter and more unlikely a place of origin, the more enthusiastic its skiers—which might explain why Texans seem to take to skiing with the same enthusiasm they show for oil wells.

The élan of a high-speed sport, the variety of experiences it has to offer, the sophistication of its milieu, its internationalized language, and its rather sardonic sense of humor—these are the ingredients in the joyful world of the skier. Yet they merely indicate, rather than explain, what skiing is all about.

Many have tried to explain, including some of the world's best writers. All have failed. The reason for this failure was once pinpointed by John Fry, editor-in-chief of *Ski* magazine, who asked his readers to recall a moment when their skiing was absolutely right:

12

The Many Joys of the Skier

"What made that moment of skiing so right? The answers perhaps are many. But one thing is certain in my own mind: the less you talk about it the better. The joy of that original moment lies precisely in its subjectivity; it is valuable because it is private to you. You betray it with each inevitably unsuccessful attempt to describe it to others. After all, they should know; they may have experienced it themselves."

CHAPTER 2

How it all started

ALTHOUGH skiing as a sport is little more than a century old, the origins of skiing can be traced back to the Stone and Bronze ages. These early beginnings have been substantiated by discoveries of skis in bogs and marshes in Finland, Norway, Sweden and Russia, and of rock-wall carvings in Norway and Russia. Archeologists report that some skis found in Finland and Sweden are 4,500 to 5,000 years old—the oldest yet found. Ethnographic experts date a rock carving of a skier on the island of Rodoy, just south of the Arctic Circle in Norway, to be about 4,000 years old. And skis found in southern Norway indicate that there is little truth in the legend that the Lapps were the first skiers.

Most prehistoric skis were more like snowshoes than like the skis we use today. The 4,500 year-old Hoting ski from Sweden is an excellent example of this snowshoe-like construction. The 2,500 year-old Ovrebo ski from southern Norway, however, has a turned-up, pointed tip and resembles a modern ski. These old skis are preserved in museums—the Hoting ski in Umea, Sweden, and the Ovrebo ski in Oslo, Norway. A few other collections can be found in the larger museums of Finland and Russia.

One of the first written mentions of skiing appears in the *Sagas*— the classic literature of the Viking period. The Norwegian Vikings were said

14

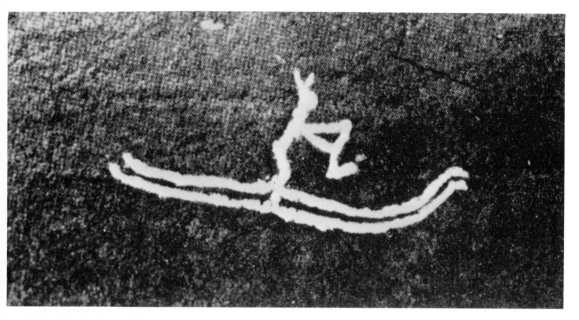

Four thousand-year-old rock wall carving from the island of Rodoy, Norway, showing a man on skis.

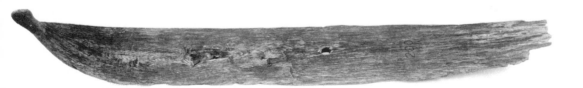

The Ovrebo Ski, estimated to be 2,500 years old, rests in the Ski Museum at Oslo, Norway. It was found in a Norwegian bog.

An 1853 painting by K. Bergslien of the flight of the "Birch-Legs" with the infant King Haakon Haakonsen in the 1206 Norwegian Civil War.

to be excellent skiers, and the *Sagas* describe several kings living around 1000 A.D. as superb skiers. Skiing was so much a part of Viking life that a god and goddess of skiing, Ull and Skade, were objects of worship. The Vikings were not the most peaceful of people, and wars and battles were often described in the *Sagas*, though not employing skis. The first account of the use of skis in wartime occurs in a report of the Norwegian Civil War in 1206. King Sverre sent two scouts, called "Birchlegs" because they wrapped their legs with birch to protect them against the cold, to carry the infant royal son Haakon Haakonson over the mountains in the middle of winter. This feat is commemorated in Norway today by the annual Birkebeinerrennet (Birchleg race), a cross-country event which follows the same 35-mile course taken by King Sverre's scouts more than 750 years ago.

Skiing has played such a large part in Scandinavian life that it is sometimes difficult to separate sport from history. Norway's Birkebeinerrennet has its counterpart in Sweden—the annual 53-mile Vasaloppet cross-country race. In 1521 the Swedish King Gustav Vasa fled from his country to Norway on snowshoes. He was overtaken by his own men, who persuaded him to return to fight the Danes, who were then ruling Sweden. The Vasaloppet race follows the original route, celebrating King Gustav's victory. Today more than five thousand skiers participate in this grueling test, making it one of the great sights in sports as the skiers all surge forward in a mass start.

Skiing is several thousand years old, yet very little improvement occurred in ski technique until the last two centuries. This lack of progress was due mainly to the early bindings and boots. Bindings were just single, loose toe-straps of willow or leather, while boots were usually simple hide or leather shoes. With such a loose connection between boots and skis, it was not possible to jump or turn while in motion. Skis, therefore, were merely a means of transportation and were used chiefly by hunters and woodsmen. They were also used by doctors, midwives, priests and undertakers in nineteenth-century Norway. Norway's first skiing postman made his rounds in 1530.

In 1721 a ski company was formed in the Norwegian army, and twelve years later regular ski drills were held as part of maneuvers. These soldiers were the first to use a leather strap around their heel, in addition to the toe-strap, to keep the skis from falling off when skiing downhill. But even these bindings were too loose to allow for any real control. So a single solid pole was used as a brake downhill and as a "pusher" to increase speed on flat ground. Skis of this period were as much products of local fancy as of technique. Every valley and country village had its own type of ski. The most common type, used in eastern Norway, Sweden and parts of Finland, was one short ski (6 to 7 feet) and one long ski (9 to 12 feet). The short ski was used to push-off or kick (much as one kicks a scooter), while the long one was the gliding ski. In some areas fur was added to the running surface of the short kicking ski to give it better bite. Many areas had special types of skis suitable for jumping or turning.

THE STORY OF SKI

Later in the eighteenth century, ski competition began to appear. Military ski competition began in Norway in 1767, but the development of skiing as a recognizable sport, even in Scandinavia, was slow. The event now known as the Holmenkollen originally started in 1866. In 1879 the jumping meet was moved to Huseby and in 1892 to Holmenkollen in Oslo.

Late in the stick-riding era, skiing was exported from Europe for the first time, specifically to the midwestern United States, California and Australia. Norwegians were much in demand as miners, and their ability to get about in the mountains during winter was an unexpected if highly useful fringe benefit. The man who did most to dramatize the use of skis was John A. "Snowshoe" Thomson. Born Jon Thoresen Rue, he was brought to America from Telemark by his parents in 1837 at the age of ten. He joined the gold rush to Diamond Springs and Hangtown (later Placerville) in 1851, and after a fling at panning for gold he took up ranching.

In 1856, Thomson, recalling the use of "gliding shoes" in his native Norway, responded to a plea by the Sacramento postmaster for someone to carry the mail between Placerville, on the west side of the Sierra Nevada, and Genoa, Nevada, on the east—a distance of ninety miles. Two snowshoers, "Daddy" Dritt and "Cock-Eye" Johnson, had attempted the trip three years

Drawing of a ski jump, 1862. Jumps were often made from walls or embankments.

A 1790 drawing of a Norwegian ski soldier on Osterdal skis (one short, one long).

Lithograph by J. Pettersen, Trondheim, of the Norwegian Ski Company on winter maneuvers in 1822.

earlier, but without success. Yet Thomson was able to reach Genoa in three days and return in two, and he made the trip numerous times during the next thirteen winters, until the Central Pacific railroad was completed in 1869. During the Civil War years, Thomson was the only mid-winter postal connection between California and the Union.

Thomson's feats, in themselves remarkable enough, were further embroidered by the miners. It wasn't long before mountain California was in the grips of the "snowshoe" craze. Competition, a pleasant diversion in the long winters of the isolated mining towns, quickly followed. The rules were simple: the men lined up at the top of the hill and the first man to reach the bottom on both skis was the winner.

As racing grew more popular, ski teams and clubs were organized. The first club in the United States was formed in La Porte in 1867. Port Wine, Poker Flat and La Porte became hotbeds of competitive skiing, and there were numerous entries from other mining communities. It was inevitable that with money and community pride at stake, attempts would be made to coax a little more speed out of the "snowshoes." The first of these innovations was a racing crouch which minimized wind resistance. The miners also developed waxing to the point where the "dope" makers became as important as the racers. Len France of Port Wine and Ed Pike of La Porte were famous throughout the Sierra for their concoctions, and their recipes were closely guarded secrets. "Dope" was usually applied over a coat of burned tar and consisted of bees' wax, sperm, spruce oil and other ingredients. The "snowshoes" so treated made speeds up to 60 miles an hour commonplace.

When gold played out in California after 1875, interest in "snowshoeing" played out with it. In the 1930's, Bill Berry, ski editor of the Fresno *Bee*, started to research the origins of Sierra skiing, and ran into a blank wall when he sought out "skiers" in Plumas county. Only when he referred to "snowshoers" was he able to tap a surprisingly rich vein of newspaper clippings and personal recollections of the era when skis were the major form of transportation in the snow-covered Sierra. A match race was held in 1938 between the best of the new generation of California skiers and the few "snowshoeing"

20

oldtimers left in La Porte. Using skis and a "dope" formula dating back sixty years, white-haired Ab Gould, then in his seventies, had no trouble defeating the youngsters.

While there was widespread use of skis for practical purposes prior to the twentieth century, their recreational potential was circumscribed by lack of a suitable technique for turning and control. Speed was checked by riding the single pole. This lack of a bridge between recreational needs and hell-bent-for-election downhill racing accounted for a temporary decline in skiing once the principal need for skis was superseded by the railroads.

An 1857 engraving of John A. "Snowshoe" Thompson delivering
the mail from California to Nevada.

CHAPTER 3

The turn is born

SKIING AS the widespread, widely practiced recreational and primarily non-competitive sport we know today has its roots as much in mountaineering as in its original Scandinavian form.

Starting in the middle of the nineteenth century, there was a constantly accelerating interest in virtually all forms of sport and recreation throughout Europe and North America. It was this period which saw the emergence of most survival sports.

During this time, the English started to make the Alps, and especially the Swiss Alps, almost their own by systematic assaults on every major peak. As the peaks were scaled and rescaled by increasingly difficult routes, it was only natural for climbers to try to find means to scale them in the winter.

Since 1865 these mountain climbers had been looking longingly at the Alpine summits during the winter. Then one day, four Englishmen were wagered by their St. Moritz host, Andrea Badrutt, that they could not withstand a month of the rigorous Swiss winters. Of course, he knew he would lose. Even before the Englishmen arrived in St. Moritz, they were shedding mufflers and sweaters, and after their return to their fog-bound isle, bronzed and fit after a month of good living, they had little trouble convincing their fellows to accept previously scoffed-at reports of hot winter sunshine and dazzling clear days high in the mountains.

In the latter part of the nineteenth century, the Arctic and Antarctic regions were the last frontiers of man's geographical knowledge. The barriers of ice, snow, wind and extreme cold, and the unavailability of any food, made these regions seem impenetrable. Impenetrable, that is, until in 1888 Fridtjof Nansen showed how to cope with Arctic conditions by crossing the Greenland ice cap with skis in forty-three days. The feat itself generated tremendous excitement as a giant step to the eventual solution of the mysteries of the Arctic and Antarctic, but it was the mountaineers who were to benefit most from the dramatic use of skis in the crossing. The publication of Nansen's book, *Paa Ski over Grönland* (The First Crossing of Greenland), in 1890 inspired mountaineers in every alpine country to experiment with skis with such dedication that skiing rapidly became a movement of international proportions.

Among the young boys playing on skis in the hamlet of Morgedal in Telemark, Norway, in the early 1800's was one destined to be the father of "modern" skiing. As a young man, Sondre Norheim became a master on skis. He could jump farther than the others, and he dared go higher than anyone had thought possible. To add to the fun, Norheim made turning and twisting tracks when he skied downhill. In the dialect of Telemark, these tracks on the hillside were

1881 drawing by J. Berg (Norway) shows Telemark turn and Telemark costume.

The first "stiff" binding made by Sondre Norheim about 1850, mounted on a Telemark ski.

known as Slalom (Sla-slope, Lom-ski track). Norheim soon found that loose leather bindings were of little use, so he fashioned combination toe-and-heel bindings from twisted birch-root, wet-formed to shape, dried and drawn tight. With these "stiff" bindings, he became the first man to control his skis. He could jump and turn. Modern skiing had seen the light of day.

The impulse given by Norheim's binding was all but explosive. As a poor sharecropper, Norheim couldn't afford many luxuries, yet he began experimenting with skis. To make the skis turn better, he made the tips broader than the tails and gave the skis a side camber. With his revolutionary bindings and skis, Norheim became the first man to do a parallel turn in 1850. He also developed a turn with the inside ski in a half plow position; this turn became known as the *Telemark* turn. In 1901, skiers in Christiania (now known as Oslo) again adopted a turn with skis parallel in the fall line. Norheim's 50-year-old turn became the *Christiania* turn.

In 1894 another Norwegian, Fritz Huitfeldt, further improved bindings with the invention of toe irons. Huitfeldt's binding left the heel free to move up and down for walking, but held the toe firmly to allow for a vastly improved control over the skis.

Although this innovation was to be a source of continuing controversy, it opened the field to improvements in the technical aspects of alpine skiing. To Mathias Zdarsky of Austria goes the credit for the first systematic exposition of the dynamics of skis on snow and the possibility of a technique based on these dynamics. Zdarsky was something of an eccentric and lived in hermit-like isolation in a house he built himself near Lilienfeld, not far from Vienna. After reading Nansen's book, he saw skiing as a solution to his annual problem of getting to town in winter. He ordered a pair from Norway, but they came without the benefit of instruction. His subsequent difficulties inspired him to develop a technique.

Sir Arnold Lunn, the British scholar whose own fertile mind contributed greatly to the development of skiing, calls Zdarsky "something of a genius... with the zeal of a schoolmaster and the iron discipline of a Prussian drill sergeant." Zdarsky built his technique on the use of stemmed skis and a single pole. He paid relatively little attention to either the christiania or the telemark. While this limited the scope of his skiing, it did provide the basic mechanics of complete control on Alpine slopes of all types.

Zdarsky didn't have the field to himself for long. Col. Georg Bilgeri, an Austrian army officer, evolved at almost the same time his own stem system; it was based on two poles and a far wider stem. In lieu of stick-riding on the steeper slopes, Bilgeri advocated widening the stem. The resulting controversy, among the followers of the Zdarsky, Bilgeri and the Norwegian schools, and later involving other innovators, was to rage until after World War I.

What tends to be forgotten by those who attempt to evaluate the contributions of Zdarsky and others is that all of these pioneers considered skis as a means to move about in the mountains during the winter. Bilgeri, and to a lesser extent Zdarsky, maintained that the day's sport was the climb, not the

Hannes Schneider combined safety and speed in organizing a logical system of ski instruction.

Charles Proteus Steinmetz, the electrical genius, was often seen trudging on skis in the Mohawk Valley near Schenectady, New York. This photograph was taken in the winter of 1896.

downhill rush. Both stressed the danger of rapid descent and, rightly, the need for safety.

Limited as these techniques were, they resulted in some remarkable ski ascents. All but the most difficult Alpine peaks yielded to skis before World War I. The mountaineer found he had as much freedom in the winter as in the summer. And he discovered there was an added thrill in the run down.

The transformation of skiing from a means to an end, from a mountaineering aid to a sport in its own right, was not the work of one man. But one man looms so large in this evolution that he overshadows all others.

Hannes Schneider was an important innovator, as important as any of his contemporaries. But what distinguished Schneider, a native of Stuben, Austria, from his peers was a far-seeing vision, a deep analytical ability, a colorful sense of the dramatic, and, above all, an ability to put himself in the skier's, particularly the beginning skier's, boots. To Schneider—first instinctively, then consciously—speed was the attraction in skiing. He had barely been exposed to the problems of teaching when he told a companion, "I am going to put speed into everyone's skiing. And I am going to make it reasonably safe. It's speed, not touring, that is the lure."

Schneider solved the problem of safety at high speed by developing a crouch which lowered the skier's center of gravity without putting him back on his heels. Then he added more speed by perfecting the stem christiania, progressively reducing the stemming portion until the skis were almost parallel throughout the turn. Finally, he organized the various maneuvers into a logical system—much as it is taught today—in which the pupil learned one maneuver, then another one more advanced, and so on up the ladder.

What transformed Schneider's Arlberg system from a purely personal method into a universally accepted technique was Schneider's sense of the dramatic. Even as a youth, he participated in races and jumping meets in order to publicize his system. And in the aftermath of World War I, in collaboration with the German documentary film maker, Dr. Arnold Fanck, he pioneered ski movies. The movies were classics of their kind. They made thousands of converts and established the Arlberg technique as a universal ski standard.

CHAPTER 4

Racing Touches off a craze

WITH THE failure of interest in skiing in the California-Colorado mining country, the sport had to be reintroduced to North America. This time the carriers were the Norwegians who provided the manpower for the lumber camps in northern New England, the Midwest and Pacific Northwest, and the iron mines of Michigan. And it was the latter part of this immigration which brought jumping to the United States in the 1880's.

Skiing for these Norwegians was a clannish affair. Their ski clubs—the first in the modern era of skiing—were formed not so much to propagate the sport as to provide means of organizing jumping meets and congenial, ethnic socializing. By 1904, there were enough of these clubs to justify forming the National Ski Association (NSA). The group, however, was dominated by Norwegian members. One of the organizers of the U. S. Eastern Amateur Ski Association recalled in that group's official history that when the Eastern tried to join NSA in 1925, the more or less official philosophy of the National was that only Scandinavians could ski. There was an overwhelming emphasis on jumping, and none at all on recreational skiing.

Norwegian skiers in Red Wing, Minnesota, 1891, the first team in the U.S.: (*left to right*) Paul Honningstade, Mikkel Hemmesteveit, Torjus Hemmesteveit, Ludvig Hjermstad.

Despite this attitude, skiing did manage to become popular. During the 1880's and 1890's, there were reports of skiing in almost every section of the country which gets snow, including one in New York City in 1888. But this activity amounted to little until the infusion of collegiate enthusiasm provided by the outing clubs of the Ivy League colleges.

The outing club idea has a precise beginning. The first club was organized December 7, 1909, at Dartmouth, and the man responsible was Fred Harris. Harris, in suggesting the creation of a ski and snowshoe club to relieve the tedium of Hanover's long winters, wrote to the student newspaper, "Dartmouth might well become the originator of a branch of college-organized sport hitherto undeveloped by American colleges."

28

While the ski activities of the outing clubs had a distinct Nordic character in jumping and cross-country, downhill running quickly found its place thanks to the delightful upper-middle class institution of that period—the *wanderjahr*. This was the custom of the well-to-do sending their sons to Europe for a year between high school and college, and it was these young men who brought back the new message of skiing and a rough approximation of its technique.

These were essentially germinating years. In the absence of formal ski instruction, there was a great deal of trial and error learning, which was further slowed by a complete lack of facilities. But there was noticeable progress. College and community winter carnivals brightened the long winters and gave a boost to skiing. There was enough interest in the sport so that C. A. Lund, a Norwegian immigrant, felt justified in founding the Northland Ski Company in 1911. And across the border, the Canadians, led by the example of McGill University, closely paralleled American development.

For almost two decades after the organization of the Dartmouth Outing Club, American skiing developed without any significant transatlantic influence. A few American competitors were exposed to European skiing in the first two Olympic Winter Games—Chamonix in 1924 and St. Moritz in 1928 —but these games excluded downhill and slalom, and no startling lessons were brought back.

Late in the 1920's North American skiing demonstrated that skiing had commercial possibilities. In the winter of 1926–27 Oscar Hambro of Boston opened the first ski shop—and survived. The Canadian Pacific ran weekend snowtrains from Montreal to the Laurentians and found no difficulty in drumming up customers. American skiing was building up a fair head of steam. All it needed was a good publicist. It found him in the person of Otto Eugen Schniebs.

A watchmaker by trade, a disciple of Hannes Schneider, and the Dartmouth ski coach, Schniebs had a basic message: "Skiing is a way of life." What gave the message special charm and appeal as he delivered it to audiences throughout the Boston area were the Bavarian-accented assaults on the English   29 language that carried it. Much of what Schniebs is supposed to have said is pure fabrication, but his message left its mark and formed the basis for the élan which marks skiers to this day.

Schneider's Arlberg technique did more than establish skiing as a sport in its own right. It created new competitive concepts in the 1930's—downhill and slalom—which divorced skiing from its nordic origins; it established winter tourism as a major economic factor in the Alps; it was responsible for the changing of ski making from a craft to an industry; and it provided a platform for further advances in technique.

The event which established alpine racing and fixed its essential character was the Arlberg-Kandahar. Here, too, Schneider was closely involved, but the original idea for the race came from Sir Arnold Lunn. Sir Arnold had long been irritated by the refusal of the Scandinavian-dominated Federation Internationale de Ski to recognize down-mountain racing, the only branch of the sport at which the British excelled. He also wanted to find a permanent niche

The Canadian Pacific ski train arriving at St. Marguerite Station in the Laurentians in the early thirties.

Otto Eugene Schniebs, a disciple of Hannes Schneider and advocate of skiing as "a way of life." Mr. Schniebs is still active as a ski area designer.

Sir Arnold Lunn originated the Arlberg-Kandahar races. He was knighted for his contributions to skiing and to Anglo-Swiss relations.

for slalom, a personal creation of his. He found a kindred soul in Schneider, who had always objected to the curious double standards that prevailed in the treatment of professionals. Frequently, as a professional, he was asked to give exhibitions—without pay—while the amateurs would not only get trophies, but under-the-table payments too.

The first A-K in March, 1928, featuring most of the top racers in the Alps, had its desired effect. Its success was reflected by imitation in every mountain country, and it created a great wave of interest throughout Central Europe. Within two years the FIS was forced to recognize downhill and slalom as world championship events and, in addition, to accept ski instructors as *bona fide* 31 competitors. This latter concession was to prove a source of serious dispute within the Olympic Committee in future years.

The elevation of Alpine competition to world status had immediate impact. It further stimulated the already growing interest in skiing. Of more immediate importance, however, was the spur it provided for the improvement of equipment and technique.

The invention of the steel edge in 1928 by Rudolf Lettner of Austria was probably one of the most important developments in ski equipment. This simple innovation—which Nansen had originally experimented with in his crossing of Greenland in 1880—had a profound effect on every phase of skiing. While the original function of the steel edge was thought to be merely protective—the reason why Lettner never bothered to patent it—it actually provided the basis for the narrow-tracked, precise running and turning we take for granted today. Before the edge, even the most expert skiers had a constant struggle to hang on to the hill. Control was precarious, and only the fact that most skiing was done on soft snow prevented wholesale disaster. On hard snow, only an awkwardly wide stance could assure that the skier remained upright. The edge had the immediate effect of springing the Arlbergers out of their deep crouch. Control improved and skiing speeds rose, not only for racers but for all skiers who adopted the edge. This was the start of a chain reaction of major developments in equipment and technique which continues today.

CHAPTER 5

The Thundering Thirties

THE 1930's was one of the most fruitful decades in the history of skiing. These years between the invention of the edge and the start of World War II set the groundwork for everything now considered fundamental in skiing. The old ski instructor who today says, "It's been done before," is not really far wrong.

The impetus for these developments was provided by the sport's growing popularity. A rather aristocratic, exclusive and esoteric pastime was being transformed into a mass movement. Skiing changed from being a tool of the winter mountaineer to a sport in its own right, due partly to the proselytizing activities of ski clubs, the impact of the Schneider-Fanck films, and the growing interest in competition. But perhaps as important as all these factors together was the development of uphill transportation.

"One can regard lifts as one will," Prof. Stefan Kruckenhauser, head of Austrian ski teachers, wrote in 1958, "... The fact that skiing pupils can today advance in skill about four times as fast with the help of small lifts as without them is an advantage that cannot be exaggerated. This helps attract thousands to the sport every year." Lifts not only brought more people to skiing, they also changed its dimensions and character.

For the most part the already existing mountain railways of the Alps were useless to skiers. Even the first *téléferiques* were built with summer tourists in 33

THE STORY OF SKI

mind (which explains why many of the older European runs end some distance away from the base terminal). But the lifts were welcomed by skiers, and after 1930 a brisk construction program was underway in most major Alpine ski centers.

By bringing more people to skiing, the lifts also changed the condition of the snow. Where one major run a day used to be par, four, five or more runs were the rule with a lift. The resulting traffic packed down the runs, requiring new technical skills of the skier.

With the popularization of "downhill-only" skiing, there was no longer any need to leave the heel free for walking. The development of bindings with "down-pull," climaxed with the introduction of the Kandahar cable binding in the thirties, allowed unprecedented control over the skis and made further advances in ski technique possible.

The first attempt to change the teaching of ski technique to take advantage of the new control was made by two Austrians, Dr. F. Hoschek and Prof. Friedl

Typical of the early *téléferiques*, this is the aerial cableway at St. Moritz.

Austrian Toni Seelos was the unchallenged master of slalom in the mid-thirties. His technique was characterized by parallel skis throughout the turn.

Wolfgang. They rejected the snowplow and the stem in favor of the "direct way to swinging," emphasizing shoulder rotation and upward unweighting. This approach would not have caused the sensation it did had it not been for the racing successes of Anton (Toni) Seelos, an Austrian ski instructor. Seelos was the unchallenged master of slalom in the mid-thirties, having arrived independently at what Hoschek and Wolfgang essentially advocated. Seelos' technique was characterized by upward unweighting, rotation and vorlage, and, most import of all, parallel skis throughout the turn.

The Hoschek-Wolfgang-Seelos ideas had a cool reception in Austria, but struck a responsive chord in France, then emerging as a major ski power in Europe. Seelos was brought to Chamonix, where he coached the French team, which under the leadership of Emile Allais and Paul Gignoux further refined the parallel technique. It differed from the Austrian version primarily by unweighting with a down-and-forward motion and by what is called the ruade, a lifting of the tails of the skis in a horse-kick type motion.

Even while rotational skiing was reaching its peak, a small but prophetic group of Swiss and Austrian ski technicians were developing a parallel system 35 based on counter-rotation—that is, the twisting of the upper body in a direction opposite to the legs and skis. This is the system which now dominates modern skiing. Based on an analysis of motion, it was invented by the Austrians, Toni Ducia and Kurt Reindl, and by the Swiss, Giovanni Testa and Eugen Matthias. Ducia and Reindl published their counter-rotational thesis, *Le Ski d'Aujourd'hui*, in France in 1935. Testa and Matthias published their first edition of *Natürliches Skilaufen* in Munich the following year.

"What was set forth in these books was for that time fundamentally new, and in fact difficult to grasp," Kruckenhauser wrote. " . . . Looking back, we now realize how far ahead were these four authors and their fellow workers."

Despite the slalom victories of Rudolf Rominger, a powerful downhiller who became the world's best slalom racer with the new technique, an attempt made to institute reverse shoulder in St. Moritz just before World War II was only partially successful. The emphasis of the day was too much on pure parallel, and counter-rotation still based its beginning maneuvers on the *passé* stem and snowplow.

The introduction of new techniques had an important influence on equipment, particularly on boots. Prior to 1930, ski boots were little more than glorified walking or mountain boots. But with the growing need for precise control, boots began to change. They became progressively stiffer, both in the sole and the uppers. The soles were stiffened to bear the growing tensions

The old "bear trap" binding did not allow for release. It was superseded by swivelling toe releases and releasable cables for forward falls.

generated by the new cable bindings, the uppers for rigid support of the ankles so that they could transmit every motion to the skis. The Scandinavian skier of a century or more ago would have had no difficulty in recognizing the functions of the various items of equipment used by skiers in 1930. Just before World War II, he would hardly have recognized any without considerable explanation.

Meanwhile, skiing in the United States and Canada was developing rapidly. Otto Schniebs was giving Americans a taste of the potentials of skiing. The subsequent enthusiasm led Peckett's of Franconia, New Hampshire, to bring over Sig Buchmayr from Hofgastein, Austria, to head the first organized ski school in America in 1929. That same year the Boston and Maine Railroad sponsored a ski train in the United States, running it to Warner, New Hampshire, and Franconia.

The railroads, with their vast publicity power, truly boosted the sport. Another aid was the invention of the rope tow. The brainchild of Alex Foster of Shawbridge, Quebec, the rope tow first saw the light of day in 1932 and was to provide the bulk of uphill transportation for almost twenty years. It was a solution eminently suited for the times—simple, economical and swift. Even in its most primitive form, it had a remarkable hourly capacity, ideal for the huge crowds brought in over the weekend by the ski trains.

With the existence of the rope tow and ski trains, the pattern of the weekend ski trip emerged. Unlike his European counterpart who went to the mountains for a vacation and only coincidentally to ski, the American went primarily to ski.

"The Europeans," said Fred Iselin, the Swiss-born ski school director of Aspen Highlands, "go up on the lift in the middle of the morning, they lie in deck chairs like seals to get brown, or they take a bottle of wine and a salami and go on a picnic. Then they come down on skis. This they call skiing. We don't do that here [in the United States]. The American is geared for technique, for hard sport, and the average American skier is two classes ahead of the European."

37

THE STORY OF SKI

Iselin, who has a reputation as a wit, was only half joking. Particularly in the early days of the rope-tow era, there were no deck chairs at the top of the tows and little to be seen that couldn't be viewed just as well from the bottom. What has often been described as "yo-yo skiing" was primarily brought about by the limited range of the rope tow.

Following the introduction of the rope tow into the United States at Woodstock, Vermont, in 1934, skiing spread swiftly throughout New England and upstate New York. Snowtrains to these regions became commonplace. For the first time, skiing could boast of a substantial following outside the small hard core of super-enthusiasts.

Skiing, and winter sports in general, benefitted greatly when the third Olympic Winter Games were held at Lake Placid in 1932. Lowell Thomas, who skied occasionally, broadcast an account of the Games, and was to write

The world's first rope tow at Shawbridge, Quebec, 1932. Powered by an old four-cylinder Dodge with a jacked-up wheel, it was invented by Alex Foster and was originally referred to as "Foster's Folly."

Governor Roosevelt conducts opening ceremonies at the 1932 Winter Olympics, Lake Placid, New York.

later that "it was the Olympics at Lake Placid that sold me on skiing." His frequent broadcasts about skiing and ski areas in subsequent years were important publicity for the sport.

All skiing needed at this point was a touch of glamor. It was provided in 1936 with the opening of Sun Valley. Modeled after an Alpine village, Sun Valley was the inspiration of W. Averell Harriman, then president of the Union Pacific Railroad. The atmosphere, however, was the creation of Steve Hannegan, the famous publicist who later was postmaster-general under Franklin Roosevelt.

Much of what is today standard equipment at major ski resorts was first introduced at Sun Valley. Chairlifts, swimming pools, private cottages, high style dining and entertainment, and a clientele studded with society names and movie stars, gave skiing a prestige previously reserved for yachting and polo. More important, although it wasn't stressed in Hannegan's promotion, 39

Averell Harriman, founder of Sun Valley, Idaho.

One of the first two chair lifts in the world was built at Sun Valley in 1936.

Enthusiastic crowds attended ski exhibitions at Madison Square Garden in the late thirties.

Sun Valley offered ski terrain and snow conditions few European resorts could match.

There was a need in the mid-thirties for competent instructors. With Europe teetering on the edge of war, many Swiss and Austrians, inspired by the example of Buchmayr and Schniebs, emigrated to the United States. Sepp Ruschp came to Stowe, Hans Hauser and Friedl Pfeifer to Sun Valley, Luggi Foeger to Yosemite, Benno Rybizka to North Conway, Walter Prager to Dartmouth, Fritz Loosli to Quebec, Hans Georg to Southern California, and Hans Thorner to Franconia. There were also many others a good deal less competent. These were the ones who gave rise to the phrase, "Bend zee knees, two dollars pleez." By 1937 skepticism about ski instruction had reached such a point that the Eastern Amateur Ski Association ordered the first certification examinations. These were held at Suicide Six at Woodstock in February, 1938. Of the seventeen candidates who took the certification examinations, six passed, ". . . showing all too clearly," as reported by certification chairman Ford K. Sayre, "that many of those now giving instruction need further training in skiing as well as in teaching." The certification idea spread rapidly. It thrived in great part because no attempt was made to establish a unified system of ski instruction. The only demand was that an instructor show skiing competence in his chosen system and an ability to explain it to his pupils. Each system had its own strong advocates. Louis Cochand and Hans Georg had brought over the reverse shoulder of the St. Moritz School. Loosli was an early advocate of the all-parallel school of Emile Allais. Thorner and Prager taught traditional Swiss methods. Yet, despite these various heresies, Schneider's Arlberg method remained the accepted standard of what good ski technique was supposed to be. His personal lieutenants—Foeger, Lang, Pfeifer, and Rybizka—were not only superb skiers and teachers, they were also highly articulate, and their message during this era of technique confusion was strongly supported by a number of influential American skiers.

42   North American skiing made impressive strides from 1936 to 1939. Major

The 1936 Olympics Ski Team thirty years later: *(left to right)* Clarita Heath Bright, Grace Lindley McKnight, Helen Boughton-Lee McAlpine, Betty Woolsey, Marian McKean Wigglesworth, and Mary Bird Young.

lift installations were built at Alta, Sugar Bowl (California), Belknap (New Hampshire), Stowe (Vermont), Franconia and Mt. Tremblant (Quebec), and hundreds of rope tows were installed on less imposing hills in every snow region of the United States. Thousands were learning to ski under competent instructors, and being rescued from occasional follies by members of the National Ski Patrol System, an organization inspired principally by Minot Dole, and formally recognized in 1938. And American racers were closing in on the Europeans. A remarkable group led by Dick Durrance planned to go to the FIS World Championships in Norway in 1940. As it turned out, most of them, as well as hundreds of others, volunteered for the ski troops instead. 43

CHAPTER 6

The war and the post-war boom

THE RAPID-STRIKE capabilities of the Finnish patrols in the Russo-Finnish war made a deep impression on certain tacticians in the U.S. War Department. In the bitter winter of 1939–40, the Finns, taking maximum advantage of the mobility of skis, were able to bring the Russian Army to a dead stop, using hit and run raids on vulnerable supply and communication lines. Not until the snow left the ground were the Russians able to bring superior fire and manpower to bear and to break the Finnish resistance.

But the point had been made. At the urging of Minot Dole and a few other American skiers who saw that the United States might shortly be involved in the European war, the Army activated the Eighty-seventh Mountain Infantry Regiment at Fort Lewis, Washington. For the first time in American military history, the Army had a unit specializing in mountain and winter warfare. Initially composed only of volunteers who had demonstrated ability on skis, the Eighty-seventh drafted a good portion of the best skiers in the country. And even though this quality was diluted when the regiment was

Colonel Rolfe of the Tenth Mountain Division and "Minnie" Dole; Dole argued for the formation of the Tenth and was a founder of the National Ski Patrol System.

The Tenth Mountain Division specialized in mountain and winter warfare, and contained most of America's best skiers of that time.

expanded into the Tenth Mountain Division, throughout the war the unit remained one of the Army's elite corps.

The Tenth saw its first action in the Aleutians in 1943 when it was used to regain the island of Kiska from the Japanese. The operation was carried out in a dense fog and all the division casualties were self-inflicted. An intelligence lapse had failed to note that the Japanese had abandoned the island.

The division was in training for two more years before it saw action again, this time in Italy during the closing phases of the war. The Germans were firmly entrenched along the Gothic Line, guarding the agriculturally rich Po Valley. The anchor point of this line was Riva Ridge on Mt. Belvedere, a 1200-foot rock ledge which blocked entrance to the Po Valley. By scaling Riva Ridge without artillery preparation, members of the Eighty-sixth were able to surprise the defenders in a dawn attack. The following day, led by the Eighty-seventh, the division took Mt. Belvedere and despite many casualties held the position against heavy counter-attacks, thus opening the way to Rome.

On the home front, skiing remained at low throttle "for the duration." Gas rationing precluded much travel, material shortages discouraged expansion of facilities. Skiing might well have died out had it not been for the concentration of skiers in the Tenth Mountain Division. The division assured continuity, providing much of the manpower for the expansion of the two decades following the war. Many of the leading names in skiing today were on the personnel rosters of the Tenth Mountain Division.

Equally important to skiing immediately after the war was the vast amount of surplus ski equipment available. Originally intended for the division, it was of remarkably high quality and, with virtually no modification, was adaptable to civilian sport. Availing oneself of this equipment, it was possible to take up skiing for about $25, and that was including oversized parkas and pants. Thousands seized the advantage.

An indirect result of mechanical lifts, moguls are caused by large numbers of skiers making turns in the same spots.

The post-war decade was a curious mixture of status quo and experimentation. A comparison of racing styles, for instance, showed little difference between pre-war and post-war masters. In many cases, they were the same men. Only among the German and Austrian ski masters did the war take a substantial toll. Nor was there much change in ski instruction. The Austrians, while using many of the foundation maneuvers of the Arlberg technique, had adopted sideslipping and a great deal of rotation from the French. And while the French emphasized their no-stem approach, they were not nearly as dogmatic about it as in former years. The rivalry between the two systems flared briefly after the war when Emile Allais came to the United States, but generally there was little difference between the top practioners of the two systems.

Equipment changed slightly, but initially the plastic bottoms made little impression and an overwhelming number of skiers followed the waxing ritual as before. And with few exceptions, skiers as a whole spurned the few release (then wrongly called safety) bindings coming on the market.

What was changing radically, however, was the sport's popular acceptance. And the growing number of skiers brought about changes in technique. The effect of a large number of skiers on a slope gave rise to a condition called "moguls," probably a Tirolean or Bavarian corruption of the German word *hügel,* meaning small hill or hillock. Moguls are caused by skiers turning continuously in the same spot. Whole fields with these bumps began to appear in the late forties, requiring tighter turning instead of the long, swooping curves skiers were used to cutting. Particularly on trails carved out of the forests and on steep narrow slopes, the skier's choice of turn became more limited. Theoreticians began to talk about a phenomenon called *gegenschulter,* an application of reverse shoulder used with occasional success by racers, allowing them to get as close as possible to the inside pole of a slalom gate. However, there were few instructors who took it seriously, believing it to be meaningless for recreational skiers. Two men who did not take this attitude were Dr. Stefan Kruckenhauser of Austria and Georges Joubert, a physical education professor at the University of Grenoble.

48

The very number of skiers also influenced changes in ski areas. Rugged outdoorsmen became a decreasing percentage of the ski population. The new skier began to demand better facilities—better lodging, better food, better entertainment. And to cope with the growing liftlines, high capacity-high speed lifts were developed, of which the double chairlift was the first. It was also during this period that slopes were first mechanically groomed. Less experienced skiers found the going much easier at those areas which cleared and packed their slopes, and flocked to them.

Finally, a note of fashion began to make itself noticed in ski clothing. Baggy pants became less baggy and the parkas—they were still called jackets then—were almost fit to wear in public. While the potato-sack-tied-in-the-middle look was still widely in vogue, a few skiers who had been to Europe started to appear in closely tailored Kaltenbronner pants from Davos or, a rare skier, with Bogners from Munich.

Howard Head of Baltimore, Maryland, designer of the world's first successful metal ski.

Professor Stefan Kruckenhauser of St. Christoph, Austria, directed the creation of the official Austrian ski teaching system in the post-war era.

The International Congress of Ski Instructors meets periodically to demonstrate ski techniques from around the world.

Even before the mid-fifties, people were finding they had not only more time for leisure, but also more money. The socio-economic force of the leisure boom changed skiing in less than a decade from a slightly eccentric pre-occupation of a few thousand people to a mass participation sport with the number of participants exceeding a half million. Between 1954 and 1957, skiing found itself with a new image in the eyes of the non-skiing public.

During these years, skiing also became a more graceful sport. By 1954, *gegenschulter* was no longer a stylistic abberation of a few top racers. Not only were all of the good racers using it, but a large number of expert recreational skiers as well. These sinuous dance-like movements were officially endorsed the following year with the introduction of the New Official Austrian Ski System at the International Ski Instructors' Congress held in Val d'Isere, France. Its ultimate form—continuous turning down the fall line—was called *wedeln*.

The new system, although seemingly more complex than the older rota-

50

tion, spread like wildfire throughout the ski world. The reasons for this rapid propagation are several. A growing number of skiers had advanced sufficiently to be capable of *wedeln*. Metal skis, easier to turn than the old skis, were seen on the slopes in increasing numbers. Furthermore, precise control of the skis had been considerably enhanced by the improvement in boots. Double boots, developed by the French during World War II, were introduced into the United States in the late forties. By the time *wedeln* became official, even the lowliest skier had a better linkage with his skis than the super experts of the old era.

Adding greatly to the glamour inherent in the new technique was the introduction of stretch pants in 1955. These made the technique more obvious and attractive, particularly to women. What before had been a sea of navy, tan and black, suddenly became a pallet of every conceivable color. This fashion factor along with the new socializing possibilities of the sport are frequently underestimated as contributors to the startling growth of skiing over the last ten years.

Ski racing too underwent important changes. Winning racers in international meets were acclaimed with world-wide publicity. Toni Sailer, Stein

A lift line at Mt. Snow in the 1960's.

Eriksen and the ill-starred Buddy Werner became household names. The trials and tribulations of American racers—Tom Corcoran, Penny Pitou, Ralph Miller, Betsy Snite, Brookie Dodge and Sally Deaver—were widely covered as they made their lonely assaults on the great racing trails of Europe.

Every year provided new evidence of the booming growth of skiing. For the 1959–60 season, for instance, more new lifts were built than were in existence throughout the United States and Canada in 1950. And the pace has been at least as hectic since then. The money it cost to build the resort of Vail, Colorado, for the 1962–63 season (about $5 million to start) in all likelihood would have bought all of the major American ski areas in operation at the start of World War II.

In these short chapters we have attempted to record the evolution of skiing from its dark beginnings to its full blossoming as the great participant sport we know today.

Our account is by no means complete.

But what it does show is the incredible dynamism of the sport, a sport which has captured the imagination of twentieth century man.

Part Two

THE EQUIPMENT

This rental shop at Stowe, Vermont, offers beginning and occasional skiers wide selection of equipment. Once caught by the "ski bug," skiers will go on to purchase their own equipment.

CHAPTER 7

To rent or to buy?

THE QUESTIONS asked about ski equipment, particularly by beginning skiers, are difficult to answer since ski equipment has become highly specialized and is available in a wide price range. There are a great many ifs, most of them arising out of the questions, "Is it really suitable for me?" and "Is it really worth it?"

Unlike equipment for many other activities, skis, boots, poles and bindings are really basic to the sport. You can run track without track shoes, or play baseball without owning a bat, shoes or glove, but it is impossible to go skiing without certain items. Once on the slope, you cannot trade off equipment, or borrow for a few minutes one or several items. Whoever wants to ski must come fully prepared either by borrowing, renting or buying.

Ski equipment is not cheap. Just for skis, boots, poles and bindings, plan on spending a minimum of $100. What you get will not be the best, or even what is considered average today. Between $150 and $200 will put you in the average bracket, and it is easily possible to spend $300 or more for these items. For the beginner, particularly, this poses real difficulties. There are limits to anyone's pocketbook, and the beginner isn't even sure he will like the sport.

55

THE EQUIPMENT

BORROWING

SINCE most new skiers are introduced to the sport by their friends, the easiest and most economical solution is to borrow equipment from them. If the equipment is suitable—and beware of the friend who assures you that you can get by with an over-size pair of skis or boots—well and good. But keep in mind that the usual reason there is a spare pair of skis around is because they aren't worth trading in or selling. If the equipment needs minor repairs, go to the nearest ski shop and have them made, along with any needed adjustments. It is irritating to all involved if, once on the hill, you find that your boots don't fit into your bindings, that you are missing Arlberg straps, or have a broken edge.

It is possible, though more difficult, to borrow ski clothing. Most stores don't rent ski clothing, but one can get away with long, preferably thermal, underwear under blue jeans and a couple of sweaters. While this kind of outfit will draw a few smiles, it isn't unusual. The younger set quite frequently use blue jeans or cords, particularly in spring when it can get surprisingly warm.

Even if you are not sure of how you feel about skiing, a small investment in ski clothing will not be wasted. Parkas, sweaters and stretch pants are acceptable wear for many activities and can serve for various kinds of informal, social occasions.

RENTING

IF equipment cannot be borrowed from friends, it can be rented. Many kinds of shops are in the ski rental business, but a ski shop is your best bet because it will often credit the rental cost if you decide to buy. It is a good idea to check on this point before renting.

Rental fees run anywhere between $3.50 to $7.00 a day, depending on the kind of equipment you rent and the region you live in. Rentals tend to be slightly lower in cities than in ski areas, but keep in mind, particularly if you are going to a distant resort, that you will be paying for the equipment while you are transporting it back and forth. Of course you may find that the rental equipment at the resort is not suitable to your needs, particularly when there is a large demand for it during the so-called "high seasons"—the two weeks over Christmas, and from mid-February to mid-March.

It should be stressed that beginners are not the only ones who rent. Experienced skiers who live in regions where there is no weekend skiing and who take an annual ski vacation are often renters. So are casual skiers—those who ski fewer than three or four weekends a year. The decision whether to rent or buy often hinges on the amount of skiing you plan to do in any given season.

BUYING

I<small>F</small>, after an outing or two, the rank beginner finds that he enjoys the sport, it is time to consider the purchase of equipment. Your budget should bear some relation to the amount of skiing you plan to do. For instance, lift tickets, lodging and meals must be taken into consideration in determining how many ski trips are feasible each season. Figuring an average of $5 a day for meals, $7 for lodging and $6 for lifts, for a total of about $18 a day, how many such days can you afford?

It is safe to say that if you ski ten days or more a season, it will pay you to buy your own equipment. Assuming that a $175 outfit, consisting of metal skis, medium-high quality boots, good bindings and poles, has a life of at least five years, you will save $75 over this period by buying instead of renting. Furthermore, you have something to trade or sell if you want to get out of skiing or step up to more costly equipment.

Even if you ski fewer than ten days a year, you should definitely consider an investment in boots. Rental boots are not always of high quality, and the fact that they are worn by dozens of different feet in the course of a season is bound to stretch them out of shape. Foot shape is as personal as fingerprints, and a boot not broken to a particular foot will never be truly comfortable. For this reason, rental boots never really provide a perfect link between skier and skis, the one justification for the price and construction of ski boots.

57

THE EQUIPMENT

In buying boots, it is essential that maximum leeway be allowed in the budget. In order to get that perfect fit, it may be necessary to go into a price bracket not originally anticipated.

Only after boots have been bought is it time to decide on skis, bindings and poles—preferably in that order.

In buying skis, keep in mind that metal skis, while more expensive than wood skis, have a longer life and are virtually impervious to humidity. Furthermore, metal skis can be reconditioned after several years of use and can be counted on to have a trade-in value, even after five or six years. However, if you have any doubts about your attachment to skiing, settle for a pair of medium-price woods.

In bindings, buy the best you can afford. Bindings can last a lifetime and can be taken off when changing skis. Even the best are not excessively expensive, and their release features, when properly adjusted, can save you from serious accidents.

The purchase of poles gives your budget the widest latitude. While it is a distinct joy to handle a modern, lightweight pole, such a pole is not essential for the average skier. There is a wide selection of perfectly adequate poles in the $12–15 price bracket.

In buying equipment you should not overlook such items as Arlberg straps, boot trees, goggles and ski racks. Their cost is relatively small, and they should be considered even by the budget conscious skier.

Needless to say, equipment should be bought from a reputable ski shop. Selling ski equipment not only requires a lot of specialized knowledge about the equipment itself, but also about its suitability for each individual skier, its servicing and its maintenance. For instance, mounting a pair of bindings is not merely a matter of putting some screws into a pair of skis; it is a precision operation if the binding is to function properly.

Don't be talked into buying "hot shot" racing equipment that is beyond your capabilities. The glamor of name-brand racing skis is totally lost on the slope if you are not equipped to handle them. You will only hurt yourself by trying to make the salesman believe that you are better than you really are.

Finally, a few thoughts on children's equipment. There is a tendency, even on the part of experienced skiing parents, to skimp on children's equipment on the grounds that "they'll grow out of it by next year." This is a mistake. Generally speaking, the price spread in children's equipment is a good deal narrower than in adult equipment. For very few dollars extra, you can get the equipment they should have, particularly good boots. And one of the advantages of getting better than average skis, boots, bindings and poles for children is that they can be sold after the children have outgrown them. There are lots of parents in a similar situation.

Another good source for equipment are the annual ski swaps staged by many ski clubs just before the start of a new season. It is a good idea to get to these swaps early because the best items go fast.

If you are operating on some sort of budget, keep in mind an overall balancing of costs between skis, boots, bindings and poles, even though boots have the first priority. The table below can be used as a rough guide, whether you are buying for adults or children.

TOTAL EXPENDITURE	BOOTS	BINDINGS°	SKIS	POLES
$ 75	30	15	25	5
$100	40	15	40	5
$125	50	15	50	10
$150	55	20	65	10
$175	60	20	85	10
$200	65	25	100	10
$225	70	25	120	10
$250	75	30	130	15
$275	80	35	140	20
$300	90	35	150	25
UP TO $410	135	40	200	35

° Includes installation.

CHAPTER 8

All about boots

SKI BOOTS are essentially a corrective device to remedy an oversight of nature. Man's feet and ankles did not evolve with modern skiing in mind. If they had, they would have been a great deal stronger, with much better circulation.

Ski boots have three basic functions: to transmit the motions of legs and feet to the skis; to give support to feet and ankles when they are under stress, as in a turn; and to keep the feet warm. The modern ski boot fulfills these functions admirably, although at a relatively high cost. Even the cheapest boots cost as much or more than a good pair of shoes.

There is no other footwear like a ski boot. Although fashion has invaded skiing in force, the boot remains completely functional. It is not a thing of great beauty, yet it is the topic of more ski conversation than any other item of equipment. "I love my boots. It feels so good when I take them off," is only one of the many jokes about boots, whose "clump, clump" heralds the arrival of the skier long before he comes into sight.

Ski boots were known as such with the coming of alpine skiing, but they did not develop as a species distinct from mountain boots until the development of cable bindings in the 1930's. Even the rigid box toe was developed as much for mountaineering as for skiing. The box toe not only helped keep **61**

THE EQUIPMENT

toes warm, but prevented them from being squeezed and chafed by the straps of toe irons and crampons.

One of the first consequences of the cable binding was that its tension buckled the soles of existing ski boots. And so, the heavy half-inch sole was developed. But this was only the beginning. With full control over the ski established by the cable bindings, skiers began to demand more support from their ski boots, a demand that developed the high, stiff boots of today. In addition, the rapid increase in the number of lifts made walking an almost incidental adjunct of skiing.

The trend toward the modern boot was sharply accelerated with the introduction of sideslipping as a formal part of skiing technique. This required strong support of wobbly ankles.

As boots got higher and stiffer, they also became more uncomfortable and harder to fit. In response to this problem, European bootmakers developed the double boot consisting of a soft inner boot and a stiff outer shell. This solved the problem of comfort and fit, but raised the problem of lacing; women particularly had difficulty lacing the hard outer boot. This in turn gave rise to the development of the buckle boot.

In its basic parts a boot is quite simple. It consists of a heavy sole, usually made of a series of leather layers, and an upper, which includes the shaft for ankle support and a closure of either laces or buckles. The sole, beyond sustaining the high tensions of cable bindings, must have a groove in the heel so

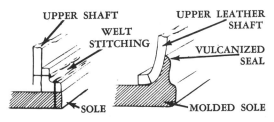

62 Traditional welt construction (*left*); sealed sole of rigid plastic material vulcanized to shaft (*right*).

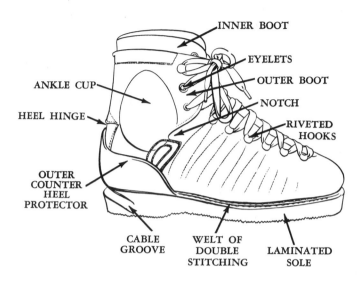

INNER BOOT

EYELETS

ANKLE CUP

OUTER BOOT

NOTCH

HEEL HINGE

RIVETED HOOKS

OUTER COUNTER HEEL PROTECTOR

CABLE GROOVE

WELT OF DOUBLE STITCHING

LAMINATED SOLE

Knowing names for parts of boots lends authority to buying.

that the heel release unit of the binding or the cable can hold the boot in position. The bottom of the sole is usually made of rubber or rubber compound with a ribbed surface to allow easier walking on snow or ice.

The last few years have seen some changes in sole construction. Instead of laminated leather a one-piece wooden sole enclosed in plastic has been substituted. This sole is completely moisture resistant and can be "sealed" instead of stitched to the upper. Another recent development is the canted sole, which counters the tendency of most people to put their weight on the outside of their foot rather than the inside. By raising the inside edge of the sole by about $\frac{3}{16}$th of an inch, this tendency is neutralized. This is important in skiing because most ski maneuvers are done on the inside edges.

The construction of the upper is much more complex. Because the upper provides the essential ankle support, it must be stiff and rugged and must maintain these characteristics over a number of years. This requires the best leathers, carefully tanned. Chrome tanning, while expensive, is best for ski boots **63** because the leather stiffens with repeated wettings and dryings. Vegetable tanning, while cheaper, is not suitable for ski boots because it turns the leather spongy, allowing it to stretch and lose its support and protective qualities. There are also several methods of combination tanning. While more satisfactory for the occasional skier, the leathers from these processes are not desirable for rugged ski use.

One of the drawbacks of chrome-tanned leather, particularly as used in the heavy, stiff outer boot, is that it will not readily "break" to the shape of the foot. This is why the double boot was developed.

The inner boot is made of soft leather and is padded. It helps transmit leg and foot action to the skis because it is sewn to the sole, but its main function is to allow comfort and a snug fit. And because it provides another layer of leather, it makes the double boot warmer than the single boot.

As boots became higher to provide more and more lateral support—to keep the ankles from rolling from side to side—the hard outer boot was also modified. Although lateral movement of the ankles was undesirable, a certain amount of freedom to move forward and back was essential. This has been made possible by the development of the hinged shaft, accomplished in two basic ways. One is to notch the upper at the point where it turns into the shaft and to cut an opening into the back of the upper just above the heel. This allows front-back movement while preserving the lateral integrity of the shaft. The other method is to separate the shaft from the upper completely and to use a mechanical hinge.

One popular design variation is ankle cups, indentations in the leather at ankle joint level. They accommodate the ankle joint protrusions at the sides of the foot and in this way make the boot more comfortable.

LACE CLOSURE

Closure by lacing the right and left sections of the uppers is the oldest method of tightening the boots to the feet. By using eyelets and hooks spaced from three-fourths of an inch to an inch apart, it is possible to lace the boot in such a

Criss-cross lacing (*left*); non-loosening lacing (*right*).

way that it spreads the tension evenly around the foot and thus forces the leather to conform to the shape of the foot.

An advantage of lacing, and particularly of non-slip lacing, is that it allows adjustment of the tension at any point. Further, the lace system spreads the pressure over so wide an area that the chances of discomfort are greatly reduced. But the system also has disadvantages. Lacing is more time-consuming and does not readily permit easing of the pressure on your feet during the ski day. More important, many women skiers do not have the strength in their hands to lace the outer boot tight enough.

Speedlacing was developed to take care of the inner boot problem. Speedlacing is based on a system of special eyelets, which allow the lace to slide easily. All it requires is one pull from the top to tighten the laces, but one must be careful to keep the lace from loosening while the knot is being tied. A patented clip to prevent this is a feature of some boots.

BUCKLE CLOSURE

IN ANSWER to the frustrations of lacing, buckles were invented in 1955. In this system a series of four or five buckles not only closes the boot, but provides the necessary tension to hold the foot tight in the boot. With their tremendous leverage, buckles save a great deal of effort in tightening the boot.

65

THE EQUIPMENT

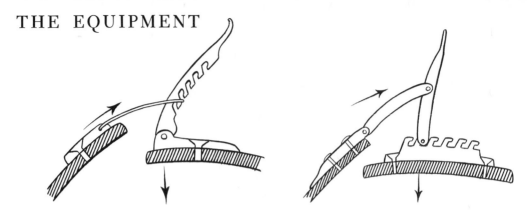

Two popular buckle systems, showing how pressure is applied to the foot as the buckle closes.

Ideal as this system might appear, it originally had several drawbacks and posed serious manufacturing headaches. Instead of distributing the tension over ten anchor points as in the lace system, it reduced these points by half. Thus it at least doubled the stresses on the leather, particularly in the vicinity of where the buckles are attached to the uppers. This required even stronger and stiffer leather since it was quickly found that after relatively short use the stresses exerted by the buckles stretched the leather beyond the point of snug fit.

Combined with this problem was the fact that the inventors oversold themselves on the convenience of buckling and abandoned the inner boot. Although great care was taken in forming the upper, the buckle boot was for most skiers quite uncomfortable. This discomfort was compounded by the extremely stiff leather required by buckle boots. These problems have now been overcome, in part by ingenious design changes, in part by a return to lacing on the inner boot.

There are now several buckle systems on the market. Boots using them should be judged by the quality and strength of the buckles; the ability of the two sections of the uppers to slide smoothly over each other when the buckle is snapped shut; and the alignment of the buckles, which assures that tension is applied as evenly as possible. Of course, other criteria of boot quality also apply.

66

FITTING

FITTING ski boots is no job for amateurs. It is best left to experienced ski boot fitters in a reputable retail shop. They have the know-how to ask the right questions and to judge when the fit is right.

Boots should fit snugly, yet comfortably. However, don't try to compare them to street shoes in this respect, especially when they are new. As one of the best known boot fitters in the business has said, "Ski boots are for skiing—not walking, standing or sitting in a chair."

Fit is not merely a function of size, it depends also on how the boot is built around the heel, ankle and over the instep. Therefore the last on which it is made is important. Americans as a group have narrower feet than Europeans, and while European bootmakers use lasts made for American feet, these lasts differ from one manufacturer to the other and occasionally from model to model. This is why it may be necessary to go to a size, brand, model or price bracket not originally anticipated.

When fitting a boot, wear a heavy wool sock over street socks, what you would wear in skiing.

Try both boots. Before lacing or buckling, make sure that there are no wrinkles in the socks, then tap the heel on the ground so that your heel slips fully into the heel pocket of the boot. Then start lacing. When lacing the inner boot, make sure that the two sections of the boot aren't brought too close together. Inner boots stretch more than outer boots, and if the opposing eyes are too close together to begin with (particularly around the ankle) it is virtually certain that they will soon stretch to the point where you will be unable to obtain a firm grip. Then lace the rest of the boot.

If the boot fits, it should feel snug and should grip the heel firmly. While this may not be comfortable by ordinary shoe standards, it is right for skiing provided that there are no painful pressure points anywhere. Pressure points are usually around the ankle, across the arch and the widest part of the foot at the point of the little toe. Make a few skiing motions to determine if any of these develop. If a change of size does not relieve these pressure points, try

67

a different brand or model. Resist the hope that pressure points will disappear with time, even if you've set your heart on a particular boot.

If you cannot find a boot that fits, either because of an unusual boot size or because of a persistent pressure point, the best, but unfortunately very expensive, solution is to have boots custom made. This will cost you at least $100. If this is beyond your means, settle for the best-fitting boots and let the shop try to modify them with a boot-stretching device. This alternative isn't 100 per cent satisfactory, but in the case of bunions, the most common cause of difficult fit, it is worth trying and should not detract from the boot's performance.

BREAKING IN

EVERY ski boot requires a certain amount of break-in time during which the boot loses its initial stiffness and adapts to the contours of the foot. A number of esoteric systems exist for this purpose, but they accomplish the job no better and no faster than simply wearing the boots around the house for a few days and doing kneebends (good exercise, too) with the boots on. If the boots are a little too snug, use looser lacing at first, or leave the top laces or buckles undone to relieve the severe pressure from the stiff uppers. A few hours on the slopes will do the rest of the job without too much discomfort.

The only boots which don't respond to such a break-in method are boots primarily intended for heavy professional use or for racing. These boots are extra stiff and require hard wear to make them adapt to the feet. They also require strong ankles.

TYPES OF BOOT

THERE are two basic types of boot: single boots and double boots, most of them made primarily of leather. Cost is determined mainly by the quality of the leather and the level of workmanship. If both are good, the price will be high.

68

A pair of double boots; note liner on boot at left.

Single lace boots are found mostly at the lower end of the price scale, although medium-priced buckle boots and a few rather esoteric high-priced boots also use single boot construction. Low-priced single boots are satisfactory for children and for light recreational skiing. With these exceptions, double boots dominate the field, from low-medium price boots to the toughest racing boots.

In the last five years, a number of boots have come on the market made of materials other than leather, not counting the leather boots with sealed soles. At the lowest end of the price scale are rubber boots made for children. Most of them offer virtually no support and are suitable for very small children only. Their major drawback is that rubber does not breathe, and therefore there is a danger of frostbite. More sturdy in construction is a variety of rubber boot for adults which is found particularly in rental departments, but is also available for purchase. These boots approach leather boots in rigidity and have a special lining which allows the boot to breathe. Relatively inexpensive, 69 they are in many respects superior to the leather boots in this price bracket, and have the added advantage of not requiring break-in.

The last three years have seen considerable experimentation with synthetic boots. They are extremely stiff and should be highly durable. Inside padding is supplied. One type allows for individual pieces of padding which can be snapped in place inside the boot, as needed.

THE QUESTION OF PRICE

EXPENSIVE as they may seem, ski boots offer good value for the money. They are difficult to make, and even with the aid of machines need a great deal of hand labor, which is constantly rising in cost, even in Europe. The kind of leather they require is difficult to come by and expensive to treat. In addition, since few boots of quality are made in the United States, the skier must pay a needlessly high tariff. Despite this unfortunate extra, boot prices have been remarkably steady, probably because the field is so competitive.

What can the skier expect for his money?

Over $100

BOOTS in this category are often made to measure. They offer the finest leathers and the ultimate in fine craftsmanship. Some racing boots also fall into this category. Even though these are "off the shelf," they are usually made by the leading boot craftsmen, who measure their output in terms of a few hundred boots a year.

$80–100

IN this category are most of the prestige brands of the handful of the world's leading boot manufacturers. Their boots are carried by specialized ski shops only, and for all practical purposes are handmade. Most racing boots are sold in this price range, so it should be approached with some caution by the recreational skier. The boots in this category may be of the buckle or lace variety. In either case they will be of high qualitiy.

70

$60–80

THIS is the top price range for most popular brands. Boots in this category are double boots, regardless of whether they are buckled or laced. There are many racing boots, most of them extremely stiff. Stay away from these if your technique and participation are only average.

$50–60

MANY single buckle boots fall into this category. Lace boots are all double and offer very good value at this price. Because it is one of the most popular price ranges, it has the greatest choice of sizes and widths and the greatest variety in design.

$30–50

MUCH the same as above, but beware of buckle boots far below top-of-the-bracket price. They tend to be of questionable quality. Double boots are a much better bet here and should give many years of good service.

Under $30

SOME children's boots are serviceable in this bracket and are useful for limited skiing. Occasional adult skiers can get by with these boots. But don't expect too much.

BOOT MAINTENANCE

GOOD ski boots have a life span of five years or longer, particularly if they are well maintained. Clean and rub them regularly with shoe polish or a boot preparation. Silicone waterproofing compounds can be used on soles and stitching. When not being used for skiing, boots should be kept in a metal boot press or boot tree, which can be purchased for less than five dollars; a press keeps the soles from curling. For summer storage, a plastic bag will keep off dust; check to ensure press is tight.

CHAPTER 9

On buying skis

A FACT too frequently forgotten is that skis are basically extensions of the feet. Their function is to distribute the weight of the skier over a larger surface. It is this change in weight distribution that enables the skier to travel over snow without breaking through. For instance, a 150-pound man with size ten feet exerts a pressure on the snow of about 1.5 pounds per square inch. With a pair of skis on his feet, the pressure is reduced to three-tenths of a pound per square inch.

But the modern ski has more complex functions than the mere reduction of the pounds per square-inch load on the snow. It must be able to turn, to track, and to perform these functions at various speeds. And although it appears to be simple, it actually is one of the most complex structures in engineering.

CAMBER AND FLEXIBILITY

WHEN the skier stands on the ski, he applies pressure to its middle. This pressure must be distributed over the ski in a certain pattern, depending on whether the ski is to be used for slalom, downhill, giant slalom, general recreation, or deep powder. To achieve this weight distribution the ski is cambered like the arch of a foot and is made thicker in the middle, tapering gradually to a thin tip and tail.

73

THE EQUIPMENT

Camber of ski is measured by elevation of the ski's center from horizontal plane. Ski tapers from thick center to thinly built tip and tail. Camber and taper help distribute skier's weight evenly over snow.

The high point of camber for most skis is in the middle of the ski, directly under the foot. It should be about three quarters of an inch deep, regardless of the type of ski. A great deal more or less camber would tend to indicate that the manufacturer has tried to compensate for too much or too little flexibility in the ski—an undesirable expedient.

It is important to recognize that flexibility is not a function of camber. A ski is no more and no less flexible because of its amount of camber. In this respect, camber serves the same function as that of springs and shock absorbers in automobiles. Their purpose is not only to provide a more comfortable ride, but also to keep the wheels on the ground, particularly when turning.

It is generally recognized that more flexible skis are easier to turn, particularly in deep snow, and that stiffer skis are more stable in straight running and hold better on ice. For this reason, most recreational ski designs are compromises. The more expensive skis are both flexible for easier turning and for skiing in soft snow, yet are able to hold on ice and in straight running.

SIDE CAMBER

BECAUSE the ski must turn, its sides are curved. This is side camber. The amount of side camber built into a ski again depends on what the ski is used for. Skis for slalom, where the emphasis is on turning, are more deeply side cambered than skis for downhill, where the emphasis is on straight running.

74 But regardless of type, skis are widest at the tip, slightly less wide at the

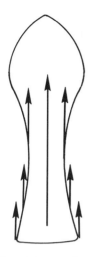

Side-cambered ski is widest near tip, narrowest at center, widens again at tail. As a result, edges skid when ski tracks in straight line.

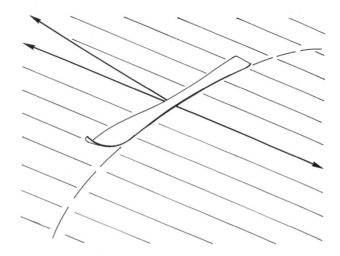

Side camber helps ski, when banked, to follow curved path.

tail, and narrowest at the waist. These dimensions are usually measured in millimeters.

The effect of the wider tip is to "multiply" the turning ability of the ski. When the ski is put on edge during a turn, the tip tends to bite more than the rest of the ski and with the aid of turning action by the skier will cause the ski to pivot around its tip.

While deeper side camber will build more turn into a ski, there are practical limits to what is possible. Beyond a certain point, depending on the flexibility and the torsional stiffness of the ski, the ski begins to "hook," that is, it will turn so sharply that it cannot be controlled.

TORSIONAL STIFFNESS

WHILE a ski should be flexible throughout its longitudinal axis, it should be quite rigid through its latitudinal axis. The ability to resist the twisting forces imposed on the ski is called torsional stiffness.

75

THE EQUIPMENT

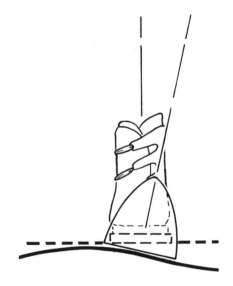

Torsion in ski enables tip to twist as it hits bump while the center of ski and boot are unaffected.

Due to the shape of the ski and, quite frequently, the nature of the terrain, the ski has a tendency to twist when put on edge. A complete lack of torsional stiffness would defeat the turning ability built into the ski, since the tip would flatten out and break away every time the ski is put on edge. At the other extreme, too much torsional stiffness would tend to deflect the ski from its true path every time it ran over the side of a bump. The ski should therefore have relatively high torsional stiffness, how high depending on its use. But a little bit of torsion must be present. The amount of torsion increases the more the ski is intended for high-speed, straight-downhill uses.

VIBRATION AND DAMPING

When the tip of a ski is deflected, it will vibrate. Vibration is desirable up to a point because it helps break the vacuum between the skis and the snow and therefore allows the ski to run faster. Excessive vibration, however, is highly undesirable, for it breaks the contact with the snow, making the ski chatter in a turn and difficult to control in straight running.

76   The amount of vibration a ski generates depends to a large extent on the

material used. There is relatively little difference in the behavior of the better skis since those materials in them which have a high vibration rate have been damped by various modifications of design.

In selecting skis, the skier has to rely on the reputation of the ski manufacturer or on his own judgment or that of his ski shop. Even among what are considered the top brands, there are slight differences in behavior which may be noticeable only to the experienced skier. Such differences need not be of concern to the average skier since they can only be applied to favor peculiarities of individual styles. Skis for purely recreational purposes allow for a wide latitude of material characteristics, and the average skier should not become preoccupied with fine details which mean little or nothing to his skiing.

EDGES

EXCEPT for skis meant for the smallest of tots, edges are an essential feature, both for control and for protection.

Edges are basically of two types: segmented and one-piece. Segmented edges are not a basic part of the ski's structure since they do not change the flexibility pattern of the ski. The segments are usually about six inches long and the joints between them can be butted, beveled or interlocking. Beveled or interlocking edges are preferred since the pressure of one piece of edge against the next is eliminated when the ski is flexed.

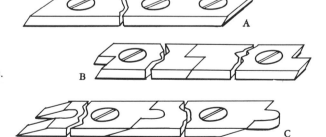

A—plain beveled edge;
B and C—interlocking edges.

77

THE EQUIPMENT

An advantage of segmented edges is that they can be readily replaced in the event they are damaged or worn out through filing. Slalom racing skis are required to be ultra-sharp, and are filed frequently.

Because steel is considerably slower than waxed wood, polyethylene, lacquer or any of the other running surfaces, the edges, whether segmented or one-piece, are frequently hidden, particularly in the more expensive skis. The advantage of a hidden edge is that it exposes only the necessary minimum of edge. The section by which it is fastened to the skis is hidden under or covered by the running surface (see illustration below). While edges of this type are faster, they are more difficult and costly to repair, and make for a more expensive ski.

While sound edge construction must be taken for granted in the more expensive skis as their edges are usually hidden, edges are a fair clue to the quality of skis in the lower price brackets. If the edges are put on correctly, they should feel smooth to the touch both from the side and from the bottom, without projections from imperfect segment joints. The screws should be flush, neither above nor below the surface of the edge, and without evidence of excessive grinding. The latter indicates that the screws have been put in at too great an angle, either because of sloppy workmanship or because the manufacturer has little faith in the quality of the wood and is afraid the screws will break out if they are too close to the side of the ski.

The one-piece edge is a much more sophisticated approach to the edge problem. It is usually fastened to the ski by means of extremely strong but flexible adhesives which allow the edges to move slightly. This is necessary in

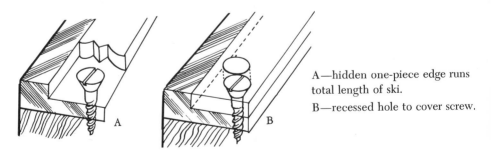

A—hidden one-piece edge runs total length of ski.

B—recessed hole to cover screw.

most designs because steel is much less elastic than wood, aluminum or plastic, the main materials used in skis.

The advantage of the one-piece edge is that the absence of joints reduces friction and enables the ski to slide faster. Because it is carefully bonded to the ski, it becomes a part of the ski's structure and influences the ski's characteristics. It makes the ski stronger and stiffer, a factor which must be compensated for in the flexibility of the ski.

Although the bond between the one-piece edge and the ski is exceedingly strong, when something does go wrong repair is difficult and expensive. Anything but a minor separation requires that the ski be returned to the factory for servicing. However, with rare exceptions, one-piece edges can be considered permanent and maintenance-free.

Edges for recreational skis are usually harder than those for racing models. The racer requires an extremely sharp edge and therefore needs edges he can file easily. For the recreational skier the edges can be harder, and while they will be more difficult to sharpen, they retain their sharpness for a longer period of time.

Edge maintenance is an important concern of both competition and pleasure skiers. Segmented edges should be checked regularly to make sure all screws are tight and that none are missing. The edges should also be checked from the side. What may appear to be a tight screw is tight only because the edge has buckled or lifted from the ski. This is particularly important when inspecting hidden edges.

Even the edges of the best recreational skis need occasional sharpening. Since the edges of the better skis are difficult to file, it is better to take the skis to a ski shop for grinding. If the job is done by the skier, care should be taken that the edge is not only sharp, but also smooth. Even the slightest burr can destroy the skiability of the ski.

When the skis are stored, the edges should be lightly coated with oil or vaseline to prevent rust. While rust quickly wears off, extensive exposure to rust will pit the edges. These pits have a tendency to pick up ice, and if extensive enough can cause slight changes in the characteristics of the skis. 79

THE EQUIPMENT

RUNNING SURFACES

No matter what the basic material of the ski—wood, metal or fiberglass—it requires a special running surface in order to slide easily on the snow.

In the days before plastic bases, skis were treated with hot pine tar and a variety of secret wax formulas, a highly aromatic adventure. Even today, cross-country and certain types of touring skis have to be treated with pine tar because of its unsurpassed ability to hold wax over hours of sliding.

However, most alpine skis have some sort of plastic base. At the bottom end of the price scale it may be a simple lacquer, which is painted on; but across the rest of the price range it is usually a plastic, occasionally of the phenolic type, but in recent years primarily polyethylene.

Polyethylene has the advantage of not sticking to anything, particularly snow. It is extremely slippery and can be readily mixed with additives such as paraffin, silicones, and dyes of various colors. This versatility makes it possible to increase its sliding qualities and to vary its hardness according to need.

The original polyethylene bases, introduced about ten years ago, were fast enough, but had the drawback of being soft, fast-wearing and easy to scratch. As a result, polyethylene bases, usually under the trade name of Kofix or P-tex, were used mostly on racing skis where speed was more important than durability. With the help of additives, polyethylene was gradually made harder and even faster.

An advantage of polyethylene is its ease of maintenance. Polyethylene melts readily under a soldering iron, and scratches and gouges can be easily fixed by melting polyethylene from a "candle" into the hole and then sanding it over. This can be done by the skier himself providing that the cloth by which the polyethylene is bonded to the ski is not damaged. Other plastic running surfaces lend themselves to similar treatment. Lacquer bases can be fixed by sanding the area of the damage, painting over it with the same material, then sanding smooth.

80   Even though polyethylene runs well under most snow conditions, there

are occasions when a layer or more of wax is desirable. When the snow is wet, the smoothness of polyethylene and other plastics tends to cause suction, which slows down the skis. The wax, which should be painted on in a series of steps, will break this suction.

Running surfaces should be inspected after each day of skiing. If a rock cuts through the bonding cloth, moisture can penetrate between the cloth and the ski. When this moisture freezes it can cause a separation between the running surface and the ski, an expensive repair.

THE GROOVE

ONE or more grooves in the bottom of the ski are essential to make the ski run in a straight line when it is flat on the snow.

The groove enables the ski to run straight because the pressure of the ski on the snow forms a small ridge, which keeps the ski in its track until some positive action is taken to change direction. The groove is particularly useful in straight running, but is also helpful in maintaining direction during the first preparatory motions for the turn when the ski is momentarily "light" and relatively free to slip off to the side.

While the extent of the groove's usefulness is often debated, there is no question that it is necessary. One of the reasons why it is so difficult to ski on ice is because the groove is not functioning in its tracking capacity.

On anything but ice the groove is undoubtedly effective. A ski whose groove is rounded at the edges is easier to turn than a ski whose groove has a sharp edge. However, the latter tracks better. Groove design usually is governed by the purpose for which the ski is intended.

From time to time manufacturers experiment not only with groove shape, but also with multiple grooves. The idea behind multiple grooves is that the ski will maintain directional integrity even though it is partially edged. This idea has considerable merit on hard-packed racing trails, but under average conditions it makes the skis harder to turn.

81

THE EQUIPMENT

PROTECTIVE FEATURES

In addition to edges and running surfaces, and beyond the standard coat of paint, all but the cheapest skis have other protective features. Most have some form of tip and tail protection to reduce the damage from the chopping action of the edges, which is almost unavoidable. Tail protectors have the additional job of keeping the skis out of their own puddle when they are stood up to dry off after a day of skiing.

To further reduce the damage of the chopping action of the edges, all except metal skis should have a top edge. In wood skis, these top edges are usually made of plastic and can be replaced. In the better synthetic skis, the top edge is usually made of metal or of a separate, replaceable plastic strip.

Virtually all but the lowest-price skis are covered with plastic sheeting. The major function of this sheeting, which is easily repaired, is to seal the main body of the ski against moisture.

Keeping the basic elements of design and function in mind, it is time to look at the basic types of skis and, subsequently, to talk about what you can expect for your money.

The ideal ski would be one that turns with a very minimum of effort, tracks perfectly under all conditions, and lasts forever. Unfortunately, skis are still a long way from this state of perfection. Thanks to technological advances, however, each year brings us closer to the ideal. To appreciate this fact, one has only to take a run on skis made ten years ago. The difference is startling.

The big difficulty the skier faces in selecting a ski is in pinning down his objectives. He may want to ski powder, but if in fact he lives in an area where he will encounter hard-packed snow nine times out of ten, he will be an unhappy man if he indulges his powder fantasy to the point of buying skis specifically made for this condition.

As a rule, the more inexperienced the skier, the shorter and more flexible his skis should be. A normal ski is one whose tip can be easily reached by the skier's outstretched arm with the hand cupped over the tip. A rank beginner is advised to buy skis a bit shorter. However, these are rough rules of thumb only. A heavier than normal skier should have stiffer skis, a tall, light skier should settle for shorter skis. Furthermore, the flexibility of the ski should be modified by the conditions the skier is most likely to encounter—the harder the snow, the stiffer the ski.

WOOD SKIS

UNTIL World War II, all skis were made of wood. Originally, they were made of one solid piece (still the case with the cheapest and many children's skis), but in the mid-thirties ski manufacturers found that a laminated structure of three or more pieces not only had more resistance to warpage and greater strength, but also gave them much greater control over the characteristics of the skis. The most advanced manufacturers mixed ash and hickory, the former for its unsurpassed liveliness, the latter for its great strength and resilience.

In its current state of development, the wood ski has the advantage of generally low initial cost; good to excellent performance on packed snow and

Cross sections of different types of wooden skis: top to bottom—solid wood construction; low-grade lamination; high-grade lamination.

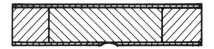

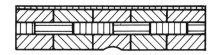

83

ice, due mainly to the excellent damping characteristics of wood; and relatively simple and easy maintenance. In many respects, the characteristics of wood skis are unsurpassed—international slaloms are run almost exclusively on wood skis—and many top skiers prefer them despite their disadvantages.

The main difficulty with wood skis is that they don't retain their favorable characteristics for long. Because of internal stresses, they lose their liveliness and camber rather quickly, and are more subject to breakage than either metal or fiberglass skis. Although they can be made quite flexible, usually they have to be rather thick throughout the profile to have sufficient strength. This thickness makes them difficult to turn in soft snow.

METAL SKIS

AFTER a long period of experimentation, metal skis became a reality in the late 1940's. The solution to the various difficulties encountered with metal skis up to that time was an aluminum alloy sandwich perfected in aircraft engineering during World War II. Many modifications of this sandwich were necessary before metal skis were on a par with wood skis.

The metal ski, although in many respects appearing to be simpler than a wood ski, is actually far more complicated. Although there are a number of design variations, the sandwich—consisting of two thin sheets of aluminum alloy separated by a wooden core—is basically an I-beam, a structure of great strength. When the ski bends, one metal skin stretches and the other compresses. This, combined with the tremendous springiness of the metal, causes the ski to return to its original shape immediately, accounting for the extreme liveliness of metal skis.

Because of the great strength of the aluminum alloy, the skis can be made thinner and more flexible than wood skis. And because of the great torsional rigidity of the I-beam principle, it is possible to make a ski which is very flexible along its longitudinal axis, yet extremely stiff along the latitudinal axis. This enables the ski to act as a unit throughout its length and relieves edge contact with the snow at the same time. It is this instantaneous reaction to

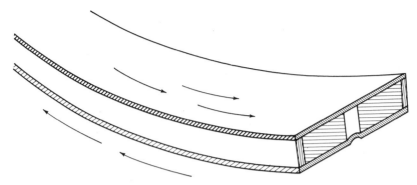

Springiness or flexing quality of metal sandwich ski is shown as top sheet of aluminum compresses, bottom stretches.

change in attitude, plus a thin profile, that makes the ski easy to turn, particularly in deep snow.

The metal ski is also extremely durable. Some of the first metal skis ever made are still in use. Because the four corners of the ski are metal, it resists the chopping action of the edges, and as long as it stays bonded together it will not warp, lose its camber or its original flexibility.

However, the very characteristics which make the metal ski so easy to use are also the source of some of its disadvantages. For the same reason that it turns easily, it is difficult to make it track. And the very strength of its structure makes it difficult to repair when something goes seriously wrong. Repair costs, like the initial purchase price, are on the high side.

At first, metal skis appealed mainly to recreational skiers. Racers and fast skiers criticized the metal ski for its shortcomings on hard snow and at high speed. They were also alarmed by the growing number of pleasure skiers who, improving rapidly on metal skis, started to invade slopes and trails once exclusively their domain. This was how metal skis came by their nickname of "cheaters."

Through a series of engineering changes, metal skis were made suitable for the experts. But it was not simply a matter of making the skis stiffer. 85

THE EQUIPMENT

Stiffer metal skis introduced a host of new problems, not the least of which were the critical tolerances. Minor variations, unnoticeable on the more flexible recreational skis, suddenly caused variations in performance from unpleasant to catastrophic.

It was at this point that most European ski makers parted company with their American counterparts. The Europeans either went into fiberglass skis or into wood skis covered with metal. The Americans refined and modified metal characteristics to achieve the "fast" ski.

One manufacturer (Head) came up with the sophisticated solution of sandwiching a thin film of rubber between two metal top sheets of different thicknesses. This damped the vibrations of the metal and allowed some torsion without loss of structural strength. It had the added advantage of introducing the "snake" effect, which allows the ski to shear and roll over an obstacle. This helps to maintain steady contact with the snow and improves tracking.

The refinements in metal skis enabled them to crack the racing ranks for good in the 1959–60 season. The first gold medal on metal skis was won in the 1960 Olympic downhill in Squaw Valley, and from that point on metal skis have been used almost exclusively in downhill. Metal, and later fiberglass skis, also made heavy inroads in giant slalom.

FIBERGLASS SKIS

EVEN as metal skis came to dominate the thinking of skiers, a few manufacturers were experimenting with the remarkable properties of fiberglass.

One of the charms of fiberglass, from the manufacturer's point of view, is its versatility. There are thousands of fiberglass variations, allowing for unusual freedom in fabrication. The only real limits to the manufacturer's imagination are material and tooling costs—and these are high.

One of the attractions of fiberglass skis is their promise of combining the most favorable aspects of both wood and metal skis. This promise has still to come true, but remarkable advances have been made in the last five years.

86 The basic material is fiberglass-reinforced laminated sheets of polyester

or epoxy resin. The fiberglass threads are woven into a loose sheet, which is dipped into a resin and then cured under heat and pressure into a hard, glass-like material. An important feature of this process is that by varying the pressure under which curing takes place the density and therefore the springiness of the material can be varied. Low pressure produces a sheet reacting much like hickory; a sheet produced from high pressure reacts like the aluminum alloy of the best metal skis.

It is possible to build a plastic ski along the lines of a metal ski—that is, with top and bottom sheets of fiberglass and a separator of wood, or by moulding it under pressure. Either way, a ski capable of easy turning and good tracking is possible.

The major drawback of fiberglass skis in view of their price has been, in many cases, their lack of durability. The reason for this lack of durability is the occasional breakup of the fiber structure, causing the ski to lose many of its favorable characteristics. The development of new resins and fiber structures may in time circumvent this problem.

PRICE

FINALLY, what can you get for your money? A surprising amount, if you are realistic and know what you are looking for.

Over $150

THIS is the Rolls Royce class of skis and includes highly specialized models in metal and particularly fiberglass, finished to the nth degree. There is little excuse for their price other than snob appeal, the high cost of promotion, and, in a few rare cases, the high cost of development for a product of limited appeal.

$120–150

THE very best metal and plastic skis with the most prestigious brand names can be found in this category. Included are most of the specialized racing

87

skis and the more demanding types of "combination" skis for advanced non-racers. A high level of finish and sophisticated structural design are common ingredients, and the skis are backed by solid guarantees.

$80–120

THIS price range encompasses most "standard" metal skis, the best European wood racing skis, and several fiberglass models, also of the "standard" type.

The wood skis in this price class carry the names of the most prestigious European ski manufacturers. These skis are most suitable for advanced skiers who like the special characteristics of wood, particularly for slalom racing. Their drawback is that they do not hold these special characteristics very long under heavy use.

Metal skis in this bracket have a reputation for easy skiing, and are considered the most suitable for average skiers. In addition, these skis have a solid reputation for long life and good, rapid service.

The fiberglass or fiberglass-reinforced wood skis in this category are also of the recreational type. They have pleasant skiing qualities, and guarantees against breakage are good. However, experience with these skis is limited and purchases should be made with caution.

$50–80

THIS group includes the best Japanese wood skis, the better European and American wood models, and some inexpensive metal and fiberglass-reinforced skis. The wooden skis in this category have hidden edges, usually over 20 laminations, and good to excellent materials and finish.

$25–50

AGAIN, most of the wood skis in this price range originate in Japan, although there are a few brands from Europe and the United States. The skis are made up of multiple laminations, with beveled or interlocking edges, polyethylene running surface and protective plastic top edges. Very soft flexes should be avoided in this price category since they will get softer with use. These skis have a limited life and they should be carefully stored—blocked to maintain their camber, and kept in a cool, dry place to prevent warpage.

Under $25

ALMOST all skis in this price bracket, including most of those bearing American brand names, come from Japan. They are made of low-quality wood and usually have only a few laminations. Steel edges are roughly screwed on and the finish, if bright, is nevertheless rudimentary. These skis are suitable for small children and barely adequate for adult novices. But they cannot be expected to last more than a season and will have almost no trade-in value.

SKI MAINTENANCE

WOOD skis, in particular, need careful maintenance and storage. In summer they should be stored under fairly dry conditions. Each wood ski should be fixed against a flat wall by clamps placed near the shovel and tail of the ski; insert a block of wood about two inches thick between the center of the ski and the wall. This procedure helps maintain the camber of the wood. Metal and fiberglass skis do not need such elaborate storage. Simple blocking of wood skis, using a block between the centers of the skis and straps at the ends, is sufficient for brief periods of storage during the winter.

Methods of waxing are described in Chapter 13.

CHAPTER 10

Bindings— the safety factor

BINDINGS ARE mechanical devices for fastening boots to skis. In the last decade or so, their function has become far more sophisticated. They are now also the gadgets that stand between the skier and a broken leg.

As noted in the chapter "The Turn is Born," the popularization of skiing coincided with the invention of toe irons by Fritz Huitfeldt. Replacing the ancient cane bindings, toe irons provided crucial lateral control over the skis. Although they held the boot toes tight and allowed no release in a fall, they were nevertheless reasonably safe; first because speeds were relatively slow, and second because the arrangement was flexible enough—a lower, more supple boot was held in the toe iron by straps—to allow for some twisting in a fall.

All this began to change in the decade before World War II. Speeds became higher, hence precise control over the skis became more critical. The problem was solved by downpull bindings, which held the whole boot on the ski. The device by which it was accomplished was the cable—at that time aircraft control cable—which passed over the heel of the boot, through side

91

A standard forward-releasing cable.

hitches, and to a clamp, which tightened the cable. This worked admirably, but as the popularity of these bindings increased, so did the injury rate.

The first attempts to make a release binding go back to the days before World War I. However, the first such binding which had any substantial success was not marketed until 1939. It was invented by Hjalmar Hvam, and while it was imperfect, it was just good enough to get skiers thinking about the advantages of coming out of their skis in a bad spill.

Popularization of Hvam's binding was delayed by World War II, but starting in 1950 a number of bindings appeared featuring release mechanisms. Initially, these bindings were shunned by racers and faster skiers, who maintained that the bindings couldn't discriminate between a hard turn and a dangerous fall. But by a process of continuous refinement these prejudices were overcome and today even the hottest Olympic racers use them. There is

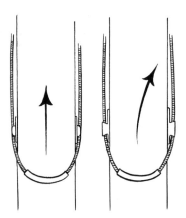

Cable tension forward and to side.

no longer an argument about their desirability, though controversy still continues over the merits of the various release mechanisms.

There are two basic parts to a binding—the toe unit, which can release in a twisting fall, and the heel unit, which is made to release in a severe forward fall.

TOE RELEASES

THE best way to look at the toe release principle is to view the toe piece and the boot as two opposing triangles. Each triangle must turn to release by pivoting on its apex. Clearly, the boot, pressed against the toe piece, cannot turn out and release unless either the heel of the boot (the apex) moves back slightly to enable the swivel and the boot toe to release; or, if the boot cannot move back, then the toe piece must be designed in such a way that it will allow the boot toe to come out.

The most widely used toe piece is the high impact type in which a spring-loaded ball in one-half of the binding sits in an indent in the other half. Given sufficient shock or pressure, the two halves pivot apart by pushing the ball down on its spring. The severity of fall required to release is determined by changing the spring pressure. Some toe pieces rely simply on a narrow

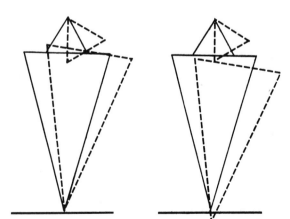

Triangulation effect: impossible (*left*);
release action (*right*).

93

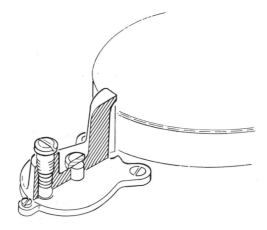

Single-point-of-contact toe release with ball and spring action.

point of contact with the boot to solve the problem of getting the boot to swivel out of the binding. Others use a larger area of contact with the boot and have a double pivot to give an eccentric cam effect. A few allow the two halves of the toe piece to split apart like a pair of scissors, both pivoting on a base plate fixed to the ski.

The advantage of the high impact type is its simplicity and compactness. It is a hard binding to ski out of in a turn, and its original drawback of releasing on chattery ice has been almost totally eliminated. Well designed, it is an excellent binding for intermediate to expert skiers. It has disadvantages, however, for most beginners. It is relatively difficult to adjust and gives little protection against slow, twisting falls—the type of fall which is most common among beginners.

There are three types of toe pieces designed to surmount just this difficulty. One type does not rely on a ball and spring to govern release, but uses the forward pressure of the heel cable to press the toe against the toe piece. The triangulation effect holds it in place, and the width of the abutting sections of boot and binding, together with the tension of the cable, determine the point of release. The advantages of this type are that the toe piece itself needs no adjustment and releases easily in a slow fall. Therefore it is a good

94

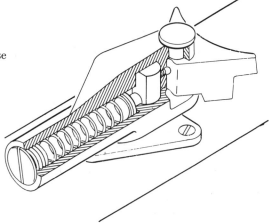

Spring-operated piston toe piece can release in slow fall.

novice binding. However, it is not a particularly good binding for the advanced skier, who has the power to ski out of it in a hard turn.

An important variation of this binding, which overcomes the problem of unwanted release, has the toe piece mounted on a sturdy pivot column on which it can slide up and down slightly. During turns, the action of the boot forces the toe piece up and engages two lugs firmly in two indents. Under these conditions it becomes a high impact binding. But as soon as boot pressure on the toe piece is lost, as in a slow twisting fall, the binding reverts to the triangulation type and releases quite easily.

The third toe piece which offers protection in a slow twisting fall is the most sophisticated. This is a double swivel, spring-operated toe piece working on the cam principle. It is able to absorb shocks without premature release, yet permits release in a slow fall.

HEEL RELEASES

WHILE toe pieces will release the boot from the ski in a twisting fall, they cannot effect a release in the event of a straight forward fall. This is the function of the heel release.

95

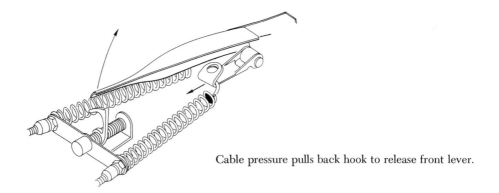

Cable pressure pulls back hook to release front lever.

The most common type of heel release is the front throw cable release. In its simplest form, a tension spring is coupled to a sliding hook which is hooked over the end of the closing lever. As the cable is pulled, the hook slides along the lever until it reaches the end. It then slides off and allows the lever to open. There are a number of simple variations on this design principle.

The main advantage of the front throw cable release is its simplicity and ease of adjustment. Unfortunately, in order to function the cable must be free to slide through several friction points, including the cable hitches on the sides of the skis. Since these are easily jammed, and because the cable is easily kinked, the release mechanism may be prevented from functioning.

A more recent innovation is the "step-in" heel unit that does away with the cable completely. This unit holds down the boot and presses it against the toe piece by means of a spring-loaded grip engaging the heel groove in the boot. The big advantage of the cableless heel release unit is that the point of release is immediately at the heel and that it does away with a lot of hardware, including the troublesome cable guides. On the other hand, extremely careful installation is required to make sure the step-in heel is securing the boot tightly to the ski.

TURNTABLES AND LONGTHONGS

ALTHOUGH there are a number of release turntables now on the market, the primary purpose of this type of heel binding is to allow the expert to use a

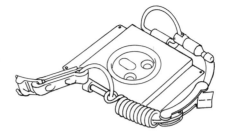

Longthong turntable. This type does not release.

longthong without depriving him of the protection offered by the toe release.

The racer or expert uses longthongs to tie his foot to the ski and to provide additional support to his ankle. They can be wrapped in such a way that when he leans forward in a turn the thong tightens up and removes the last bit of play between his foot, boot and ski. The thong is about four feet long and its use requires some patience, the ability to operate in the cold without gloves, and some appreciation of the risks involved.

The turntable is essentially a means of allowing the heel to pivot while still retaining the advantages of longthongs. It is a heel plate which pivots, and the thongs, instead of being fastened directly to the ski, are fastened to the pivoting section of the plate. While this allows the toe release to operate in case of a twisting fall, most brands until recently made no provision for release in a forward fall. This is a definite hazard.

BOOTLOCK

STILL another kind of binding works on the principle of gripping the boot by direct spring tension. The binding comes as a complete heel and toe combination. It is designed to be used with metal plates screwed onto the boots that engage the spring-operated "locks." The bootlock uses one or several springs against which the boot must press in order to release. Its main advantage is that it can be designed to release in every conceivable direction and can be adjusted for a wide range of conditions. Unfortunately, for reasons that have more to do with status than with function, these bindings are often shunned by top competitors. A practical disadvantage is that the metal boot plates 97

THE EQUIPMENT

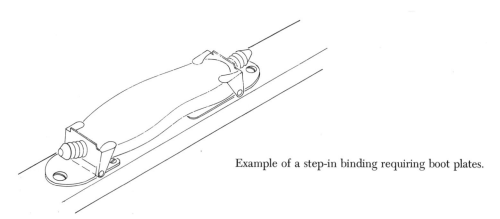

Example of a step-in binding requiring boot plates.

make it impossible for the skier to use skis which do not have the specific bootlock for which the plates were designed.

MOUNTING BINDINGS

THE mounting of bindings on skis is not a job for the occasional fix-it man. While the location of the bindings on the skis is not as hypercritical as some make it out to be, proper installation is a precision job which should be done with the tools and jigs especially designed for this work. This is particularly true in the case of metal and fiberglass skis, where mistakes are expensive and difficult to correct.

First-rate installation work is important because of recent evidence that improper mounting can negate the release mechanisms of even the best bindings. For instance, if a toe piece is not mounted correctly it can release with little provocation in one direction, but is unable to release at all in the other direction. This is but one of many possibilities of error, and it will pay in the interests of safety to make use of the checklist that follows.

There are a number of systems for binding placement, none of them perfect or inevitably best. Different types of skiing require different binding locations. For average use, the following formula works out just about right:

Divide the length of the ski (measured along the running surface from tail to tip) in half. The toe of the boot may be placed at or slightly behind this point, but *never* in front of this point.

According to more precise systems, particularly those used by the racers, this is the location best suited for hard-snow slalom and beginning skiers. Better skiers may want the binding about half an inch further back for general skiing, and as much as an inch back for powder skiing and downhill racing.

BINDINGS AND SAFETY

IT must be recognized that bindings have two completely irreconcilable functions. They must hold the boot firmly to the ski, and they must also release the boot in situations where the leverage exerted by the ski threatens to fracture a leg or ankle. This is far from simple since the release mechanism has no means of discriminating between a dangerous fall and the high torque generated by a hard turn. That bindings succeed to the extent they do is no mean tribute to the talents of their designers.

But the problem with binding safety is not so much a matter of design as it is the human factor. A continuing study by upstate New York inventor Gordon Lipe has produced evidence that the ski accident rate could be cut significantly if skiers would shop more carefully for their bindings, make sure that they are properly installed, and keep them adjusted and maintained. This study estimates that about two-thirds of all skiers are skiing with bindings that are not in good operating condition. More startling—and pleasing—was the conclusion that good bindings, properly installed and adjusted, can provide a very high margin of safety.

Lack of understanding of proper installation and adjustment has led to a lot of unjustified criticism of release bindings. Until 1960, there were no means to make a reliable check on the performance of these bindings. The Lipe Release Check was perfected in 1960, though it was not fully recognized for several more years. Now the device can be found in hundreds of ski shops 99 throughout the country, and a somewhat smaller version for use by individual skiers is also on the market and can be bought for about $15. The Release Check simply tests adjustment by measuring the force required to obtain lateral release. It was with this device that most of the causes for non-release were pinpointed.

Here are twelve steps to make sure that your bindings will release when you take a dangerous spill:

1. Check your boots to see that there isn't excessive curl in the soles. All boots should be kept in a boot tree. If your sole is warped, make sure that

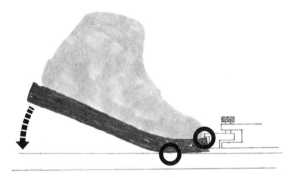

your foot is flat on the skis when you make the adjustment on your toe hold-down. The toe hold-down should barely touch the top of the sole at the toe. You may be able to slip your toe into the toe unit with your heel up, but when you step down you will build up excessive pressure under the ball of the foot and create friction that makes release more difficult. Even if the sole is flat, check the toe hold-down to make sure it is not pinching the toe of the boot to the ski. If the fit is too tight it will be impossible to obtain proper release.

2. If you use a toe unit that requires boot notching, check the notches at the toe of your boot. One notch may be cut deeper than the other. As a result, when the toe unit "bottoms" in the notches as forward pressure is applied through tightening of the cable, a release is caused more easily in one direction than the other. If you then tighten your bindings to pre-

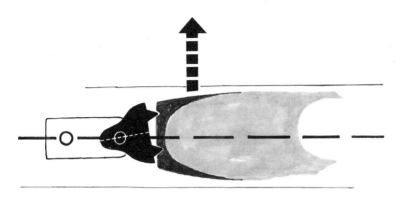

vent release on the easy side, you may lock yourself in on the other. If the toes of your boots have been chewed up by improper notching or placing of boot in binding, have metal plates installed at the toe.

3. Check to see that your bindings have been mounted straight. Sight an imaginary line down the center of your ski. If the toe unit angles off center, you will have a problem similar to that caused by improper boot notching: it will release more easily in one direction than the other.

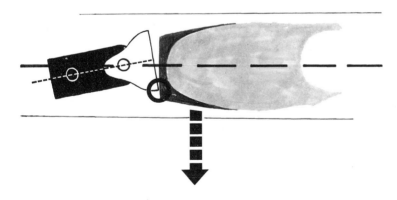

4. Mark your left and right skis so that you use the same boot on the same ski at all times. Few boots are exactly the same length. If you put the

101

wrong boot in the wrong ski (without binding readjustment) there can be a considerable difference in the forces required for release.

5. Make sure that there are no protruding screwheads on the binding and that no nails protrude from the boot soles. Protruding nails and screws frequently prevent release.

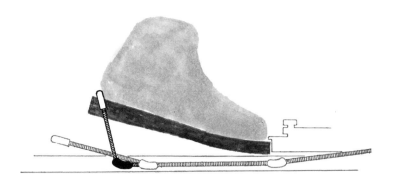

6. Check side hitches to make sure they are no more than two-thirds of the distance from toe to heel. Hitches placed too far back for purposes of holding the heel down often kink the cable and create a point of high friction. There is also the danger that the cable will hang up in the heel groove of the boot even after release has been obtained. Also check that the cables slide freely in the side hitches.

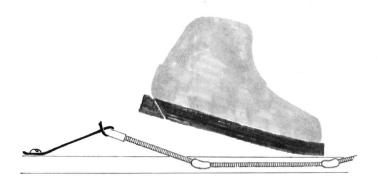

7. If you do use a cable binding other than the type that opens at the heel, consider putting a leather strap around the back of the cable, attaching it to the ski behind the heel. This will pull the cable out of the heel groove in the event of a forward fall.

8. Check your cables to make certain that the tension is adequate to holding the toe of your boot against the toe piece, *but no more.* Cable tension directly affects the functioning of the toe unit; by having the cables too tight, the force necessary for release will be too high for safe skiing.

9. Fasten the Arlberg straps to the cable *behind* the rear side hitches. If they are attached in front of the side hitches they can prevent the cable from sliding to the rear in the event of a forward fall.

10. If you use a longthong turntable, check to see that the turntable is centered on your ski when you step into it. If the table is not straight, the load of starting a release will be greater in one direction than the other.

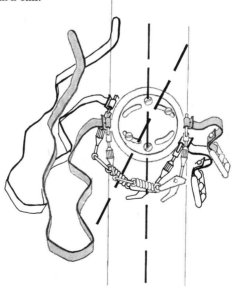

103

THE EQUIPMENT

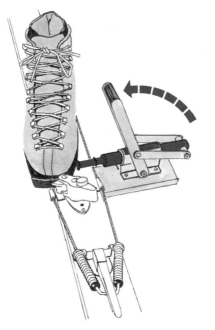

11. If your bindings pass all these checks, take your skis with boots in place to a shop and have the release settings checked mechanically. Or you may buy or borrow a checking device and do the job yourself.

12. To obtain consistent releases, check to see that all moving parts are lubricated. Silicone grease of the tube or spray variety is obtainable at your local hardware store and at some ski shops. Quite often bindings are "frozen" by corrosion from highway chemicals. (Bindings are seldom made inoperative by frozen snow and ice, as is commonly believed.) Also check for wear. Bindings do wear out if subjected to hard use.

BUYING BINDINGS

EXCEPT for a few simple children's bindings, any binding combination which costs less than $15 to $20 should be approached with extreme caution. Actually there is a very small price difference among the better bindings. It is relatively safe to say that a satisfactory binding system will cost about $25, give or take $5. There are few exceptions.

The important thing to remember is that bindings stand between you and a broken leg. There is nothing to be gained by skimping when the very best can be bought at relatively low cost.

CHAPTER 11

Poles and accessories

UNLIKE SKIS, boots and bindings, poles are very simple devices. What has made them important is modern ski technique.

When skiing was in its pre-lift stage of development, poles were primarily used for walking and climbing. As uphill transportation became widespread, they were relegated to a secondary position on the equipment list. In the period just before World War II, they reached their low point—literally. They had shrunk to the point where they were only waist high, and there was a school of thought that actually considered them a dangerous nuisance.

This trend was rapidly reversed immediately after the war with the popular acceptance of parallel techniques. Poles were found to be useful in establishing timing and rhythm in parallel turns and almost indispensable in aiding the beginning parallel skier in eliminating the stem from his turns.

Oddly enough, there was little development in ski pole design until 1959 when a lightweight aluminum alloy pole was marketed by Edward Scott of Sun Valley, Idaho. While 50 per cent more expensive than any pole then in existence, it had such obvious advantages of balance, weight and strength that it quickly revolutionized ski pole construction throughout the world. Now all but the cheapest poles incorporate the design features first popularized by Scott.

Although good pole design is relatively elementary, there are numerous **105**

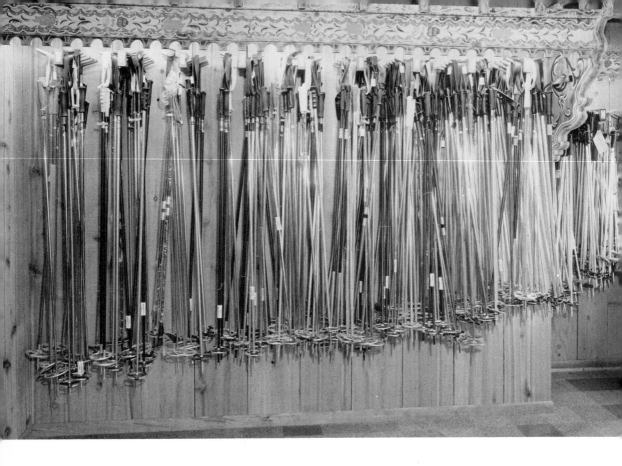

refinements which can improve on the basic product. And there is a very definite quality factor. Among the key items of ski equipment, poles are most subject to breakage.

Since the pole plant is considered the "trigger" to the sequence of events in many types of parallel turns, it is clearly important to be able to plant the pole as quickly as possible. To speed up the pole motion, the pole should therefore be as light as possible, yet without sacrificing necessary strength. For this reason, the best poles are made of highly tempered aluminum alloy or of high grade steel with very thin walls.

As important as mere weight is the "feel" of the pole or, actually, its "swing weight." In order to swing easily, the pole should be lighter at the tip. This is accomplished by tapering the pole toward the tip and moving the balance point as close to the grip as possible. A well-balanced pole has its balance point in the upper three-eighths of its length.

The other essential elements of a pole are grip, strap and basket. The grip is usually made of molded neoprene in the more expensive poles and of plastic in the cheaper models. Some grips are contoured to fit the hand and fingers and prevent the hand from slipping down the pole. Straps are usually made of leather and in the more expensive models are adjustable. The strap prevents the hand from slipping down the pole and bears some of the weight when the pole is planted. The rings or baskets are made of plastic, cane and leather, or, in the case of the best poles, of lightweight aluminum tubing and rubber. The function of the basket is to prevent the pole from plunging through the snow's surface.

Most aluminum poles have a separate steel tip pressed or bonded into the end of the shaft. This is necessary since even the hardest aluminum alloys wear rather rapidly.

Aluminum and steel are not the only materials out of which ski poles are made. Other materials include bamboo, tonkin and fiberglass. The first two were popular until the advent of lightweight, aluminum alloy poles. Although light, they had the disadvantage of being too flexible, of bending excessively when weight was applied. Fiberglass poles, while theoretically light and strong, have a history of breaking easily once they have been cut by the steel edge of the ski.

Features found in the more expensive poles include adjustable strap, contoured grip, and a basket made of lightweight aluminum tubing and rubber.

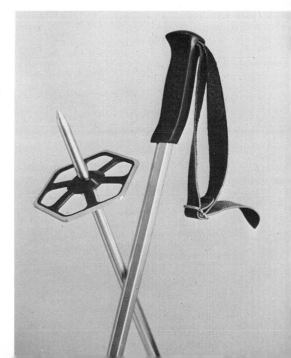

THE EQUIPMENT

For eye appeal and protection from edge wear and corrosion, poles are finished in an endless variety of methods and colors. Aluminum poles are usually anodized (any color, but usually gold) or hard-coated (black only). Steel shafts are usually chromed or plated. Plastic shafts can be finished in almost any color, and some have special coatings to protect them against edge cutting.

FITTING POLES

THE length of poles tends to vary slightly from year to year depending on the technique variation in vogue. As a fairly stable rule of thumb, the poles should pass easily under the arm pits. This is a sound standard for all but a few ultra technique-conscious skiers.

The effective length of poles does vary with snow conditions. A "normal" pole will seem a great deal shorter in deep, light powder and a little longer than usual on ice or hard pack. The latter condition is of no great importance, but deep snow may require either longer poles or larger baskets. Another possibility is to acquire a pair of adjustable poles.

Poles are usually made in lengths of two-inch intervals. If one size seems a little on the short side and the next size up a little long, choose the shorter pole.

BUYING POLES

EXCEPT for the metal in the shaft, most of the qualities of ski poles can be easily determined by sight and feel. Should there be any doubt, different brands and models can be readily compared.

Over $18

POLES in this price range are made of the best aluminum alloys and lightweight, thin-walled steel. Handles are form and contour fitted to the hand, straps are adjustable, and rings made of aluminum alloy and rubber carefully bonded together, are extremely light in weight. The tip is an integral part of the shaft in steel poles or of extra hard steel in aluminum poles.

$15–18

POLES in this category are basically stripped down versions of those in the $18-and-over price range. There are few lightweight steel poles in this category. Grips may be simpler and straps are not usually adjustable. Tips may not be as hard and the alloy may be of lower quality, particularly toward the lower end of this price range.

$10–$15

SOME of the rapier-like qualities of the best poles begin to disappear in this category. Poles are still adequate for average skiing, but are usually somewhat heavier, particularly in swing weight. Finish of shaft may be quite high, but quality of grips, straps and baskets is noticeably poorer.

$5–$10

POLES in this category are suitable only for the occasional skier. They are noticeably heavier than more expensive poles and are also apt to be weaker. Cheap leather and plastic takes the place of neoprene rubber in rings, grips and straps.

Below $5

LITTLE of value can be found in this group of poles except a few children's poles made of bamboo.

POLE MAINTENANCE

POLES need little maintenance. Most of what goes wrong with poles cannot be prevented or even repaired, although the difficulty can sometimes be anticipated.

With poles, corrosion is merely unsightly. If they have been exposed to **109** salted roads, corrosion can be prevented by washing the metal. In the off-season in humid climates, a light coat of oil on the shaft only (not on the rubber grips or webbing) will prevent corrosion. The life of the leather straps can be extended with an occasional treatment of saddle soap.

The loss of strap or grip can frequently be prevented by checking on the screw holding the grip and strap to the shaft. Occasionally, this loosens. If the assembly should come apart on a lift or in deep snow, it may be impossible to find it again, so it pays to check this point.

A more frequent source of trouble is the loss of a basket, usually in deep or heavy snow. This trouble can be anticipated by examining the cotter pin holding the basket to the shaft or the condition of the ring around the grommet. If the pin is loose or if there are cracks or tears where the ring is fastened to the grommet, a lost basket is not too many runs away.

Even the best poles can be broken, either by falling on them or by cutting them with the edges of the skis. The latter is far more frequently the case, particularly with aluminum poles. When the edge of the ski rubs against an aluminum pole, it leaves a small nick. If this happens often enough, the pole is weakened at that point and eventually snaps. One way to reduce edge damage on poles is to wrap two or three layers of cellophane tape around the pole for about six inches up from the basket. The tape doesn't last long and won't prevent the heavier cuts from penetrating to the metal, but it avoids a great deal of the wear and tear.

Poles will occasionally bend. It is possible to straighten a pole out, although there will always be evidence of the bend. If the bend is not too severe it is best to leave it since straightening the pole only helps weaken it. The life of a straightened shaft is limited and it is a good idea to have a replacement close at hand.

ACCESSORIES

In addition to skis, boots, bindings and poles, the well-equipped skier needs a number of accessories in his equipment kit. Some of these items are essential for safety, others add greatly to the skier's convenience.

In the safety category are Arlberg straps, sometimes called runaway straps. They are fastened to the binding cables or the heel releases and are wrapped around the boot and pulled tight by means of a buckle. When the binding releases, the strap prevents the ski from running away. A runaway ski is extremely dangerous to other skiers on the hill and an embarrasing nuisance to its owner. If the snow is deep enough or the mountain big enough, it is entirely possible that the ski will be lost permanently. Therefore, the $2 or $3 spent for Arlberg straps are a good investment.

Sunglasses and goggles with interchangeable green and yellow lenses are also essential to safe skiing. The glare on a sunny day is abnormally brilliant and the eyes should be protected by dark lenses. When the sky is overcast, however, the light is flat, making it difficult to see bumps and to judge the steepness of the slope. Yellow lenses will improve the contrast somewhat and make it possible to distinguish variable terrain. The choice between goggles and sunglasses is a matter of individual choice. Those whose eyes tend to water when exposed to wind should use goggles, which offer more protection. However, it should be understood that goggles are more awkward and fog easier. If you wear contact lenses, the type that covers the entire eye is preferable. These lenses are expensive and difficult to fit (some people can't wear them at all), but they are more practical than the iris type of contact lens, which not only offers less protection but also can be jarred loose easily in a fall with virtually no hope of recovery.

No skier should be without a small wax kit. Although most skis will glide easily under average conditions, waxing not only improves the skis' performance under all conditions, but also makes them track better, and offers a certain amount of protection against wear and minor scratches. The three-pack, consisting of silver (for wet snow), red (for corn snow), and green (for cold, dry snow) waxes is adequate for most ski conditions and costs about $1. For a full discussion of waxing, see Chapter 13.

For carrying wax and other small items, a belt bag is a useful accessory. These come in a variety of sizes, some with their own belt, others merely with loops. Included in the contents of a belt bag should be suntan lotion, waterproof matches, a few bandaids, a small screwdriver, and a pair of pliers, with suf- **111** ficient padding to prevent damage to yourself and the contents if you fall.

A $3 to $5 ski boot tree is a modest investment for the protection of expensive boots. Even in the best boots there is a tendency for the sole to curl. This curling should be avoided since, in its advanced state, it tends to pinch the toes in the vicinity of the ball of the foot.

A ski boot tree will prevent this condition from becoming permanent. The newer boot trees allow the boot to dry inside and outside at an even rate. This uniformity in drying while the boot is clamped flat keeps the sole from curling when released from the tree.

Ski boot trees come in a variety of designs and prices. Most use a rigid

A boot tree is a must.

A boot carrying case, with extra room for accessories.

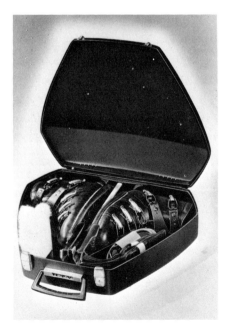

center post made of box metal. Adjustable clamps are used to fasten the boots to the wide sides of the post, and a handle allows for easy carrying.

When using public transportation, it is a good idea to protect the skis from the smashes they are likely to encounter en route. A ski bag, which holds both skis and poles, costs about $7.50 and is particularly useful when the skis are carried on buses with outside racks and where salt is used to melt snow and ice on the highways.

When carrying the skis between the hill and the car or lodge, a pair of rubber ski straps (about 75 cents) is helpful. They hold the skis together for easier carrying and prevent the edges from rubbing against each other.

Other useful accessories are an edge sharpener (there are several on the market which allow touching up of edges without worry about squareness); a small base repair kit consisting of a polyethylene candle and a small soldering iron; and a few hand tools—hammer, Phillips head and regular screw drivers, pliers, file—and some epoxi glue.

All of these accessories will not materially improve your skiing, but they will make it more convenient and give you the confidence that you are fully prepared for most eventualities on or near the slopes.

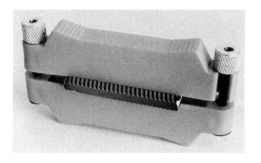

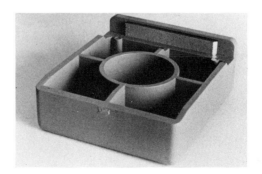

Two types of compact edge sharpener.

CHAPTER 12

Equipment for cross-country and jumping

TOURING EQUIPMENT

TOURING is skiing without the aid of a lift. It can range from a simple walk in the woods to a week-long adventure in the high mountains. In terms of equipment required, it is well to make a distinction between alpine touring and Scandinavian, or nordic, touring. The former involves steep mountainous terrain; the latter is a form of hiking on skis over rolling country. Equipment differs for the two forms of touring.

For the alpine tourer, equipment is essentially the same as for the downhill-only skier. Usually he uses the same skis and poles, though he may decide for uphill walking comfort to change to a softer pair of boots. Alpine touring boots are a compromise between climbing boots and regular ski boots. It is in con- **115** verting his bindings for touring that the alpine skier must make a change. In the days when toe irons were universally used, this posed no difficulty. The skier simply unhitched the cable from the rear side hitches. This gave him sufficient heel play for walking long distances. But since the advent of release bindings, this is no longer possible. There are two solutions: a touring attachment made for release bindings, or a toe iron with a release feature. The former is a plate with lips that fit on the ski just behind the toe unit. It prevents the boot from slipping off the ski and can be removed for the downhill run. It works reasonably well on relatively easy tours, but under stress it sometimes allows the toe piece to pivot due to insufficient cable tension. As for toe irons, there are one or two on the market now with a release feature. They are heavy and not the most reliable of release bindings, but for touring, where safety is of even greater concern than on the lift-served slope or trail, they are the most satisfactory solution to meet the needs of both uphill convenience and downhill safety.

Since the best climbing wax will not prevent backslip on the steeper slopes commonly encountered in alpine touring, and since the plastic bottoms of alpine skis don't hold wax well anyway, alpine tourers use "skins" for climbing. These used to be made of sealskin, but now various substitutes are used. Skins are fastened to the bottoms of the skis. The hair flattens out on the forward motion, allowing the skis to glide, and stands up if the ski tries to slip back. There are a number of other devices on the market for preventing backslip, but most of them have the disadvantage of being inoperative in soft or loose snow.

In contrast, the Scandinavian tourer, who is essentially out for a hike, is much more lightly equipped. There is an adage that "a pound on your feet is like five pounds on your back," and touring equipment more or less reflects this saying.

Nordic equipment for non-competitive uses is at most half as heavy as equipment used for alpine skiing, and it is a good deal less expensive. For the price of a good pair of alpine boots (about $50), it is possible to buy a complete nordic outfit.

Equipment for Cross-Country and Jumping

Nordic skis are made exclusively of wood, usually of multiple laminations incorporating various types. Spruce is almost universally used for the midsections, while birch, beech, hickory and ash are used for sides and tops. Both birch and hickory are used for the running surfaces; birch holds wax better and is lighter than hickory, but it isn't as durable. Metal and fiberglass have made no impact on nordic skis since neither has been found to hold wax as well as treated wood.

Except for the so-called mountain touring ski, nordic skis do not have steel edges, since these do not hold wax and would only slow the ski down. To protect the corners of the skis, hickory and "lignostone"—beechwood compressed by a special process to one seventh of its original volume—are laminated into the base during construction.

Nordic skis have a slightly different profile than alpine skis. Relatively narrow, they have a thin tip, a midsection quite thick, and a tail thicker than the tip. They also have a high camber. This profile results in a soft, springy tip and a stiff tail, and gives the ski a "forward-spring" characteristic.

Nordic skis come mainly in three categories—light touring, general touring and mountain—progressively stronger and heavier as the demands made on them increase.

Complex cross-section structure of three types of nordic skis: general-touring, light-touring and racing models.

BIRCH	
HICKORY	
SPRUCE	
BEECH	
COMPRESSED BIRCH	
ASH	

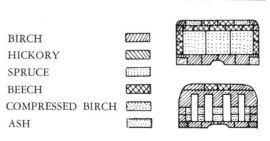

THE EQUIPMENT

There are several different models of touring bindings, but all are designed to attach the boot to the ski only at the toe so that the heel can be lifted for walking. So-called cross-country and light-touring bindings should be used only on skis so designated; they are not strong enough to be used for the heavier skis. Bindings should be mounted slightly behind the ski's balance point so that when the ski is picked up by the binding's "ears," the tip will drop at an angle of 20 to 30 degrees. This enables the tip to follow the snow even when the back of the ski is lifted.

Light touring bindings are simply toe irons with small pegs near the toe. The pegs mate with holes in the boot and prevent the boot from slipping out of the binding. The boot is secured by means of a U-shaped clamp which fits over the welt of the boot toe. Bindings for general and mountain touring usually use a cable to hold the boot in the binding. The cable can be a front-throw arrangement similar to that used in alpine bindings, or it can be attached directly to the toe iron and tightened by means of a heel clamp.

Boots for all but mountain touring are light and flexible, very similar to hiking or climbing boots. Quite frequently, one can find low-cost single alpine boots that are almost ideal for touring purposes.

Nordic poles are generally made of bamboo since that material has the

Top binding is for general or mountain touring; middle two are cross-country touring models; bottom is a fast touring or cross-country racing model.

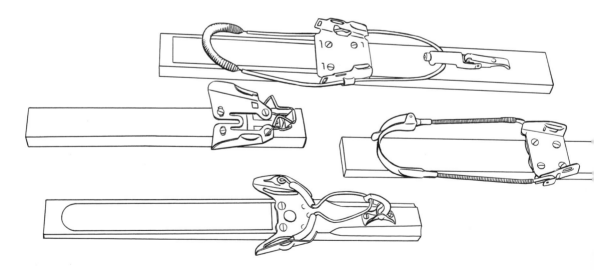

desired combination of low weight, strength and liveliness. Good nordic poles have a slight whip to help push the skier forward. Baskets are made of light-weight rattan, and wrist straps should be adjustable to swing the poles easily without pulling off when the poles are withdrawn from the snow. The metal tips should be set into the shaft at an angle or formed in a curve so that they do not snag in the snow. Touring poles are a little longer than those used for downhill skiing.

Among the tourer's equipment should be a rather complete waxing kit, containing a cork for spreading the wax evenly on the skis, and preferably also a waxing iron so that the wax can be melted on. A small rucksack to carry food and extra clothing is also considered essential.

CROSS-COUNTRY RACING EQUIPMENT

CROSS-COUNTRY racing equipment is distinctively different from any other kind of equipment. The cross-country racer will sacrifice almost everything, including a great deal of strength, for the lightest possible ski boots, bindings and poles. Every extra ounce is just so much excess baggage.

Compare construction and weight of cross-country and light-touring boots and typical alpine boot (*bottom right*).

THE EQUIPMENT

Compared with alpine skis, cross-country racing skis are feather-light slats. The best are made of a large number of laminations and incorporate a variety of woods to achieve desirable characteristics. The most advanced models even use balsa or simply leave sections of the ski hollow in order to cut the weight of a pair to four pounds or less. To make up for the loss of strength, thin, synthetic-fiber sheets are laminated into tips, mid-section and tail. Like most cross-country racing skis, however, they are extremely fragile and should be used only in prepared racing tracks.

Cross-country racing skis are very narrow, between a little over 2 to 2½ inches wide (as compared with 3½ inches for alpine skis). Their tips have relatively low torsional rigidity to allow them to follow terrain bumps without upsetting the balance at the center of the ski. This is an important factor as the racer must have his ski flat on the snow in order to get maximum push from his "kick."

The tips are turned up more than on any other type of ski, for a racer in full stride may lift the back of his ski so high that the tip meets the snow at an angle as great as 45 degrees.

Cross-country racing skis come in a narrow range of lengths. Most racers, almost regardless of height, use the 210 centimeter (6′11″) length. Far more important than length is the amount of camber and flexibility for the weight of the racer. A ski too stiff for a given weight will not make full contact with the snow, and will thus lose the benefit of the wax. A ski too soft will turn up at the tip and tail when it is weighted, thereby losing tracking stability.

Boots for racing are actually low-cut shoes, quite similar to track shoes. The boot is made of soft, pliable leather, often goat skin, and the sole consists of laminated leathers constructed in such a way that the boot flexes easily under the ball of the foot. The boot is made as narrow as possible so that the sides will not drag on the edges of the track. It fits into a binding quite similar to a light touring binding, except that it has a more precise limit of adjustment and is somewhat lighter. Poles are very similar to those used in general touring.

Waxing aids are vital in the cross-country racer's equipment kit. He will need a blow torch for burning the pine tar or base wax into the running surface of the ski, a waxing iron usually heated by heat tablets or pellets, and a waxing cork and a scraper to take off old wax. A small tool kit for changing bindings and making minor repairs is also essential.

The racer's clothing is light and loose. He usually wears a knicker outfit consisting of light flannel and knee sox. This is warm enough during the race; to keep warm before the race, he usually uses a long parka or lift coat.

One of the charms of cross-country racing is the low cost of participation. The very best equipment comes to less than $75 for the complete outfit —$30 to $35 for skis, $20 to $25 for boots, $4 to $7 for bindings and $5 to $8 for poles. The weight is about a third of that of similar alpine gear.

COMPARISON OF CHARACTERISTICS AND WEIGHTS OF NORDIC AND ALPINE EQUIPMENT

205 CM. SKIS				MEN'S SIZE 9 BOOTS		BINDINGS		TOTAL WEIGHT OF SKIS, BINDINGS AND BOOTS
TYPE	EDGES	MAX. WIDTH	PAIR WEIGHT	FEATURES	PAIR WEIGHT	TYPE	PAIR WEIGHT	
Special Cross-Country Racing	hardwood	2 1/16″	3 lb., 9 oz.	light, flexible, cut below ankle	1 lb., 10 oz.	cross-country toe-clamp	8 oz.	5 lb., 11 oz.
Cross-Country	hardwood or compressed hardwood	2 5/16″	4 lb., 14 oz.					6 lb.
Touring	compressed hardwood	2 9/16″	5 lb., 9 oz.	similar to cross-country, cut above ankle	2 lb.			8 lb., 2 oz.
General-Touring	compressed hardwood	2 7/8″	6 lb., 3 oz.	resembles hiking boot or single alpine ski boot	3 lb., 9 oz.	toe-iron, heel-cable	2 lb., 2 oz.	11 lb., 14 oz.
Mountain	compressed hardwood or steel	3 1/8″	8 lb., 7 oz. (steel edges)					14 lb., 18 oz.
Jumping (wood)	steel	3 7/16″	9 lb., 13 oz.	double boot with steel shank in sole	7 lb., 4 oz.	toe-release, heel-release	2 lb., 13 oz.	19 lb., 14 oz.
Jumping (metal)	steel	3 11/32″	9 lb., 8 oz.					19 lb., 9 oz.

THE EQUIPMENT

JUMPING EQUIPMENT

IN jumping, equipment is designed to provide greater speed on the in-run and stability in the air. Jumping skis are longer and heavier than alpine skis. To enable them to track in a straight line on both the in-run and the out-run they are made with three grooves on the running surface.

Youngsters learning to jump can use their downhill skis and boots. Most children's boots are flexible enough for jumping, and if the top eyes are left unlaced they should have no trouble leaning forward from the ankles. The binding is an old-fashioned toe iron and a front throw release cable. A jumping binding uses only two side hitches and these are located roughly under the ball of the foot. When the cable is tightened, it should allow enough freedom of heel motion so that the jumper can touch his knee to his ski. This arrangement also provides for enough freedom to release the skis in the event of a spill.

The proper length of a jumping ski, according to an old Norwegian saying, is "as high as you reach and a little higher." With most adults this will call for a ski from 8 to 8½ feet long. A pair of skis will weigh between 12 and 16 pounds. Until the technique of "riding the air" became prevalent, jumping skis were heavier than that, but the extra weight was found to be unnecessary with the new technique. However, the skis should not be too light, or they will be unstable in the air on longer jumps.

Although jumping skis are sometimes called "planks" in the jargon of jumpers, they are far from that. Jumping skis must have camber and flexibility to absorb the shock of landing. They are usually made of multiple laminations of hickory and other woods, and a few models are available built on the principle of metal alpine skis. The better models feature plastic edges (metal edges are dangerous and slow down the skis) and polyethylene running surfaces. The cost of jumping skis runs between $60 to $200 (for metal jumpers); cost is in part determined by the length of the skis.

Boots and bindings designed specifically for jumping are available at a few highly specialized ski shops. Bindings of the type described above cost from $7 to $15, the boots about $25.

CHAPTER 13

How to wax

Waxing was once the black magic of skiing. Virtually every skier, but particularly racers and ski instructors, had special wax mixtures which were supposed to guarantee perfect sliding under all conditions. "Vexing," a subject of violent argument, was almost as important as skiing itself. It was not at all unusual for a skier to carry a dozen or more sticks of wax, which he would then blend with all the artfulness of an alchemist. In the days before plastic bases became the rule, no one had to tell a visitor to a ski lodge where the ski room was. He could smell it. No matter what the time of day, there was always somebody in the ski room melting his waxes together.

This aspect of skiing disappeared not only because of the sliding capabilities of the plastic bases, but also because scientific research established the basis for proper wax manufacture. Even the most meticulous skier will now carry no more than three or four waxes, the average skier probably none.

How waxing can meet the contradictory requirements of both better tracking and easier turning is really not too difficult to explain. If the wax is correct for the conditions, friction is minimized and the skis will slide easily through the snow. When the skis are flat on the snow, running straight, the small grooves built up by brushing or rubbing on the wax will help the ski to maintain its track.

123

Waxing is essentially a matter of matching the running surface of the ski with the texture of the snow. This is determined by the air temperature, the amount of moisture in the snow, and the character of the snow (new, old, coarse or fine). A good rule of thumb for selecting a wax is "the harder the snow, the harder the wax; the softer the snow, the softer the wax." This is satisfactory for the majority of conditions the skier is likely to encounter. However, in the spring or on large mountains, conditions are likely to fluctuate, and some sort of compromise will have to be made, usually by adding some paraffin to the running wax dictated by the temperature. Most waxes today are compounded for temperatures below freezing (usually green), around freezing (blue or violet) and above freezing (red). To these is usually added silver (a combination of graphite and paraffin), depending on the moisture. The degree of moisture is determined by squeezing the snow in the hand. Dry snow will fall apart when the hand is opened; moist snow will ball up and wet snow will show a distinctly wet surface. The wetter the snow, the more paraffin should be added.

Wax should be applied to dry skis only. It comes in stick, paste and spray form. It can be applied directly (paste and sprays are convenient but wear quickly) by rubbing it on the ski. More lasting and satisfactory, however, is to melt sticks or cakes of wax together and to paint it on. If two or more waxes have to be blended, melting them together will assure that neither wax will predominate. Brushing should be done in short strokes so that the wax is applied in a series of steps. Too slick and hard a finish will cause suction between the skis and the snow, and will slow the skis.

The racer, of course, has to be much more precise in his selection of waxes. He will start off with a basic mixture of about 80 per cent medium temperature wax and 20 per cent high temperature wax and start experimenting from there. He must try to predict the temperature at the time of the race. If ski conditions are extremely variable, he must wax in very thin layers so that the wax wears off by the time he encounters the changed condition.

Cross-country wax provides both gliding and gripping properties. If the ski is weighted, the wax will grip the snow sufficiently to prevent it from slip- **125**

THE EQUIPMENT

ping back. Once the ski is in motion, the wax permits it to glide easily over the snow. Strange as it may seem, the wax that glides best for a given set of snow conditions will also be the best wax to prevent backslip. Wax that is too soft will pick up snow, wax that is too hard will cause backslip.

Complicated as this sounds, waxing for touring is not particularly difficult. Touring and cross-country racing skis use wooden running surfaces treated with a special tar base, which enables the running surface to hold wax

WAXING GUIDE TO SNOW CONDITIONS

Numbers refer to the waxes listed in numerical guide to waxes. The temperatures given are approximately those corresponding to the still-air temperature immediately above the snow surface.

RANGE	USUAL TEMP. (F.)	NEW SNOW	SETTLED SNOW	METAMORPHISIZED SNOW: HEAVIER CORN, PACK, ICE
Very dry	below 18	powder: blows easily from hand 1	small crystals will blow 6	pack—cut with sharp instrument 11
Dry	18–27		small crystals will form snow-balls 7	corn or crust varying from hard to damp—will clump in hand 12
Transition	27–31	barely clumps in hand 2		
Transition	32	clumps in hand 3	large clumps 8	
Mushy	32–36	rolling snow-balls "dig in" 4	hand wet after squeezing 9	
Wet	up to 41	soaking wet 5	slush 10	slushy corn 13

NUMERICAL GUIDE TO WAXES

Wax List—(h) denotes a hard, solid wax in a tin, (s) denotes a soft, solid wax in a tin, and (f) denotes a fluid wax in a tube. The listing of the different brands of wax opposite each other does not necessarily mean that they are equal.

NUMBER IN TABLE	BRATLIE	ØSTBYE	REX	RODE	SWIX
1	"Silk" (h)	"Mix" (h)	Green (h)	Green (h)	Green (h)
2	"Blend" (h)	"Medium" (h)	Blue (h)	Blue (h)	Blue (h)
3	"Blend" (h)	"Medium" (h)	Violet (h)	Violet (h)	Blue-Red (h)
4	"Klister-voks" (s)	"Klister-voks" (s)	Yellow (s)	Yellow (s)	Klister (s)
5	"Wet Snow Klister" (f)	"Klister" (f)	Red (f)	Red (f)	Red (f)
6	"Silk" (h)	"Skare" (f)	Green (h)	Green (h)	Green (h)
7	"Skare-voks" (h)	"Skare-voks" (h)	Blue (h)	Blue (h)	Blue (h)
8	"Wet Klister" (f)	"Klister" (f)	Violet (h)	Violet (h)	Violet (h)
9	"	"	Red (s)	Red (s)	Red (s)
10	"	"	Violet (f)	Violet (f)	Violet (f)
11	"Green Klister" (f)	"Skare" (f)	Blue (f)	Blue (f)	Blue (f)
12	"Skare-Klister" (f)	"Mixoln" (f)	Violet (f)	Violet (f)	Violet (f)
13			Silver (f)	Silver (f)	
Wax binder for Cross-country			Orange for all waxes (h)	Basewax for dry (h) "Chola" for wet (f)	Basewax for dry (h)

far better than any of the plastic bases in use for downhill-only skis. Cross-country waxes are classified in the same way as downhill waxes (green, blue, red), but instead of paraffin, klister is used. Klister is a semi-liquid, sticky wax that sets in the open air.

When waxing for longer tours, several thin layers are better than one heavy layer. When touring in variable conditions, the conditions to be encountered first should be waxed for last. Thus, a spring tour starting early in the morning would call first for a layer of soft wax, next a medium layer and then a hard layer for early in the morning when below freezing conditions will be encountered.

Whether waxing downhill or touring skis, the waxing should be done at room temperatures. Waxes go on best under these conditions if applied without first melting them. A blowtorch or a special wax heating iron can be used for touring skis, but not for skis with plastic bases.

The revival of touring in the United States has increased interest in waxing among all skiers. It is black magic no more. But regardless of the type of skiing you do, it can still help make your skiing more pleasurable and interesting.

CHAPTER 14

Clothing for style and warmth

ONLY A decade ago ski clothing amounted to little more than a glorified lumberman's outfit. Considering its bulk, it wasn't very warm. Nostalgia may run rampant over the departure of the baggy pants and parkas of the thirties and forties, but the ski clothing of those earlier eras left much to be desired, both in quality and variety.

Modern ski clothing is at once warm and fashionable, and to a large extent the product of modern textile technology. The slim, clean, streamlined look which characterizes the modern skier—the smooth stretch pants, the racy sweaters and the sleek, flat parkas—is the product of our most perceptive designers working with materials no one even conceived of a few years ago.

If there is a drawback, it is due to skiers having become fashion pacesetters. Clothing manufacturers with no interest in skiers as such have nevertheless looked toward authentic skiwear for inspiration. As a result, there is a lot of clothing that resembles ski clothing, but isn't suitable or warm enough for skiing; a lot that is more fashionable than functional.

129

THE EQUIPMENT

Despite the revolution in skiwear styles, the skier need not be a fashion plate before he ventures on the hill. Whatever the yearly changes in design, color, pattern and material, there are always available models of pants, sweaters and parkas which make up what might be called the skier's basic uniform—classics which refuse to date. An outfit of good quality along these lines can last a skier for years.

As a matter of fact, it makes all the sense in the world to start with just such an outfit. Add fashionable trimmings later. Such an oufit is good not only for skiing, but for all kinds of other outdoor activities, including the more chilly spectator sports. The basic requirements are: that the outfit be warm, that it allow great freedom of movement, that it be sturdy, and that it shed snow readily. Simple as these requirements may seem, they are likely to be available only from reputable manufacturers of authentic ski wear, who have experience in the skier's needs and who know the strains and stresses put on the clothing.

KEEPING WARM

WHILE fashion has become an important consideration, the skier basically looks to his clothing to keep him warm. With today's sleek-fitting pants and parkas, warmth is built more than ever from the skin out: the tighter clothing rules out the old six-sweater approach.

Fortunately, the skier starts off with a good heat generator: his own body. Active skiing produces warmth. The trick is to trap that warmth somewhere between the skin and the outermost layer of clothing, and thereby enable the skier to stay warm while standing in the lift line or while riding the lift.

Starting from the skin out, the first article of clothing should be made from natural fibres. Wool (the warmest) and cotton possess the porosity which is not only comfortable next to the skin, but also necessary. It is characteristic of natural fibres to absorb perspiration while allowing warmed air to pass through the fabric. Soft wool T-shirts, mesh cotton vests and turtlenecks all "breathe."

The combination of absorbency and porosity in this "second skin" is essential.

Over the natural-fibre underwear should go clothing made of a tightly woven or knit fabric. For most skiers this would be a hard-finish sweater or a closely woven shirt. The purpose of the second layer is to trap the body heat. The natural fibre next to the skin permits warmed air to pass through it. The warm air is then trapped between the undergarment and the second layer in an air pocket. The function of the air pocket is simply insulation. Next to the pure vacuum of, say, a thermos bottle, air is still the best insulator.

Over this air-trapping chamber goes the parka. As the item of clothing in direct contact with the elements, it must be highly water repellent and wind resistant. Water, if retained by a fabric, quickly turns icy cold. Nylon and tightly woven poplin are two good water shedders that are also wind resistant. With the top layer of ski apparel keeping out the wind and the sweater closing the air chamber next to the body, a comfortable body temperature can be maintained. Parkas may be further insulated with down, various synthetic fibre-fills or be a simple water-shedding shell. The choice depends on the temperatures and the susceptibility to cold of the individual skier. Down is by far the warmest.

In extreme cold, you can wear both a mesh vest and a turtleneck as a first layer. If a sweater is to be the outermost layer of clothing, a nylon or milium insulator cardigan worn between the underwear and sweater will create an air chamber in the same porous to non-porous arrangement.

Legs offer a slightly different problem. Pants are snugger than wear above the waist, which means that whatever layers there are must be thinner. Fortunately, perspiration is not a prime concern on legs, and the first layer can be either porous or non-porous as long as it fits snugly against the skin and creates some sort of air chamber. Long underwear having a wool content is perhaps the warmest.

Special attention should be given to the extremities since these are the most vulnerable to cold. Warm blood begins to draw away from the hands and feet as soon as the body temperature drops. In order to maintain circulation in hands and feet, you must keep moving. If you are on the lift or wait- **131**

Four stages of ski dress: first a suit of thermal underwear, then a cotton turtleneck, next a flat-knit sweater, and finally a ski parka. The latter two would be worn together only in cold weather.

ing in line you can swing your arms and stamp or swing your feet. While the "Lean Look" is the fashion these days, clothing should not be so tight that it restricts circulation. Wristlets on parkas and gloves and the fit under the arm-pits and in the crotch are major trouble spots in restricting circulation and should be inspected carefully when buying clothing. It's a good idea to wear the undergarments you will use on the hill when you shop for outerwear.

The rule of the air pocket applies to hands and feet. Silk mitt, or glove liners worn under regular ski gloves or mitts, serve the same function as under-wear, as do silk socks under the heavy wool socks usually worn by skiers. Hats or headbands are essential to protect the ears.

In skiing, it is especially important that you not become over-warm. The excessive perspiration of a run down can be the cause of a chill on the way up. Your clothing should permit you to ventilate, and to dress in such a way that you can take off one or more layers without difficulty.

SELECTING CLOTHES

FASHIONS change from year to year, but it is safe to say that the streamlined look of the last few years will continue to maintain its popularity. After all, skiers have been trying to reduce their bulk for a long time. The very nature of skiing dictates that fashion follow function, and not the other way around as is the case with so much other clothing.

A kaleidoscope of styles, patterns, colors, fabrics and prices await you when you set out to buy your skiing wardrobe. Because skiwear is in the fore-front of the sportswear world, you will encounter a lot of sales talk concern-ing the merits of an almost bewildering variety of new fabrics, most of which you've never heard of, and of strange chemical-sounding terms and esoteric brand names. If you feel uneasy, it is best to fall back on established brands, those with a reputation of having served skiers well for many years.

Pants

THE basic look of ski pants has become fairly uniform. Style differences occur in zipper placement, waist band and foot construction.

133

THE EQUIPMENT

The front zipper, standard for men, is also becoming standard for women. Waistband variations are numerous, but regardless of which style you select, make sure that there is a strip of rubber or elastic material at the pant top to anchor your tucked-in turtleneck shirt. Failure of the pants to hold in the shirt can result in a chilled back when you are closing your bindings or when you go through the contortions of a spill.

The most common foot constructions for ski pants are the elastic strap, the stretch fabric strap and the wrap-around heel. The latter two are the smoothest inside the boot. In any foot construction, watch out for bulky seams which could cause chafing. The foot should slide easily over the sock, yet fit snugly.

Width of the ski pant leg should not be so narrow as to resemble a leotard. Such pants are best left to the racers who count time in hundredths of a second. The recreational skier looks and feels better in a slightly wider pant that can accommodate insulated underwear without binding and is properly proportioned from waist to ankles. Waist size should allow room for both turtleneck and underwear. From the hips down, the pants should flow smoothly into the legs and there should be a straight, unbroken line from the buttocks down the back of the legs. Try several brands and sizes to make sure that you get the right fit. One manufacturer's model may have a slightly different cut that could make a substantial difference in your particular case.

Testing for proper length of ski pants; no more than two inches should be slack. Note fabric strap, most common foot construction.

Prices of ski pants range from about $20 to $65. Low-priced stretch pants generally have a high percentage of nylon and sometimes rayon. These fabrics are often not warm enough and their recovery properties may not be good. They will also have a tendency to pill. If you do a lot of skiing and use only one pair, you will be better off going to models costing $30 and more. They will be made of better material, the workmanship will be greatly improved, their stretchability will be better, and they'll be warmer and more water repellant. Pants intended for heavy use should have a stretchability factor of between 50 and 75 per cent, the higher the better; unfortunately it is also true that the higher the more expensive. Ski pants selling for $35 and up will probably make use of Spandex, a super-stretch material which provides easier fitting, more comfort and excellent recovery.

With the new super-stretch materials it is no longer necessary to cut a pant in five lengths—just two. However, it should be remembered that stretch is not an alternative to fit, it merely assists its perfection. On stepping into a pair of pants (with your regular ski socks on), the pants should reach to the hip bone without strain. Pull them up to the waist and fasten the band. Now scrutinize yourself in the mirror—bend, sit, walk, twist. If they don't seem just right, try another pair.

Parkas

THE familiar square or diamond quilted parka is still something of a fixture, but it has slowly given way to parkas with slimmer, more tailored lines. This is the result of new forms of insulation which allow warmth without bulk through the use of interior quilting, foam laminations, pile lining or fiberfill batting, or a combination of these. For absolute assurance of warmth, natural down insulation cannot be beaten. And even though the down may add bulk to the parka, the square, rugged look of the down-filled parka is not without its own fashion appeal.

Nylon in a startling variety of patterns, colors, textures and finishes is the most popular material for the outer shell of the parka. Take your pick according to your own taste, but make sure that the parka has been treated to resist water and oil, a process that adds greatly to the durability of the garment. **135**

THE EQUIPMENT

Parka lengths, like women's skirts, rise and fall for no particular reason. However, a parka covering the seat will never be far out of style. It is attractive and may be worn belted or unbelted. If you plan to wear the parka unbelted, look for an inner construction which creates a close fit to keep out upward breezes. Also look for such windstoppers as knit inserts at the wrists and collar. A hood, hidden in the collar or stowed away flat inside the back, is useful on snowy and extra cold days as an extra hat. Also make sure that all pockets have secure closures, either zippers or sturdy buttons.

When fitting a parka, always try it on over a sweater. Swing your arms to make sure there is enough room across the shoulder and under the armpits.

Left. A lift coat is adjustable to two lengths: long for warmth while riding a ski lift, and short for skiing. *Right.* A one-piece ski suit of stretch material.

Clothing for Style and Warmth

Ski Suits

SKI suits are available in several basic styles: the one-piece suit with long sleeves; the one-piece sleeveless suit to be worn with a sweater or parka or its own matching jacket; and the two-piece jacket suit. All but the last are items for women only.

With new super-stretch materials, suits should present no great fitting problem, but fitting should nevertheless be done with great care. Ski suits are expensive ($80 and up).

Knickers

KNICKERS, once the trademark of the hot skier, no longer enjoy overwhelming favor, but they are ideal for skiers who don't have stretch-pants figures, for spring skiing, and for those who enjoy wearing colorful socks. Knickers are made of stretch material as well as the traditional wide wale corduroy. What's more, they are reasonable: from $12 up.

Sweaters

IN addition to providing extra warmth under a parka, sweaters come into their own as an outer garment for warmer spring skiing. Colorful designs range from the slim, clean and uncluttered to the dramatic and bulky, including many native handicraft patterns. Shoulder and sleeve styling should be comfortable, particularly throughout the shoulders and around the armpits. There should be no extra bulk in sweaters used under parkas.

Turtleneck Shirts

THE once drab turtleneck shirt is now a fashion item: the choice in colors, fabrics, patterns and styles is almost unlimited. For between $4 and $8 you can get almost any type you want.

In buying turtlenecks, make sure that the collar isn't too tight, that both torso and sleeve length are adequate, and that the fabric is not too flimsy. At small extra cost, it is possible to get turtlenecks with zippers, a desirable feature that permits you to ventilate.

137

THE EQUIPMENT

Gloves, Hats, and Socks

THESE seemingly secondary items are more important than most skiers realize. They protect the most vulnerable parts of the human anatomy—the extremeties —and if only for this reason deserve special attention.

Mitts are warmer than gloves, but many skiers will put up with some cold for the improved grip gloves allow them. However, when temperatures plummet to below zero, even the glove-wearing skier will change to mitts. The well-equipped skier will have both.

Use a wool or silk liner under a pair of lined gloves or mitts. Even the best gloves or mitts won't keep your hands warm in cold weather unless you keep your arms moving, but they can, if they are good, store the heat that the hands generate. This isn't much. For this reason gloves and mitts should be made of the best wind and water repellant materials available: lined leather properly treated. They should also be long enough at the wrist to fit snugly under the cuffs of the parka.

In addition to keeping your hands warm, ski gloves also serve a protective function. A good ski glove is padded across the knuckles to protect them in a fall on hard snow, ice or breakable crust.

When buying gloves make sure that they fit easily over the liners, keeping in mind that leather will stretch a little in use. The leather should be pliant and of high quality, and the stitching should be especially sturdy in the area between the thumb and forefinger, where many gloves break down. Another desirable feature in gloves is snaplinks, which make it possible to hook the gloves together and to a beltloop when they are not in use. And if you ride ropetows frequently, look for gloves which are reinforced across the palm.

A ski glove with snaplink and reinforced palm for rope tows.

Somewhat less critical are the socks the skier wears. Ski boots are his best insulation from the cold. Even under extreme conditions, a light sock under a ski sock—a so-called rag sock—should be more than enough to keep his feet warm. Wearing two heavy pairs of socks—as is the habit with some skiers—does nothing for keeping the feet warm, and moreover is likely to reduce control of the skis. Sometimes, persistently cold feet can be caused by something wrong with the boots.

Extreme cold will affect the feet. In that event, if exercise does not warm them up, the best thing to do is return to the lodge, take the boots off and warm the feet in front of a fire—gently. Then, before putting the boots back on, warm the insides of the boots by placing or holding them upside down over a radiator. This is also recommended if the boots are cold first thing in the morning. Incidentally, laughable though it seems, the best device for warming and drying boots is a lady's electric hair dryer.

There are a few hardies who can do without a hat, but for most it is an essential clothing item. Ears are quite vulnerable to the cold, particularly the lobes and edges. A headband provides some protection, a hat does a better job.

A hat should be so designed that it will stay on under all but extreme circumstances. There are hats available which do this job without the use of tie strings, and are still comfortable. Hats also come in a great variety of styles, from the conservative to the zany.

The skier's clothing should be of such quality and character that he should rarely have to give it a second thought. Although ski clothes have become part of the world of fashion, they remain a functional aspect of the sport.

After-ski boots are a popular
extra item of clothing.

CHAPTER 15

The skier's car

IF YOU are like most skiers, a great deal of your traveling will be done by automobile. To assure a safe and comfortable journey, both you and your car should be fully prepared for the worst.

PREPARING YOUR CAR

YOUR car should be routinely winterized by your local garage with special attention to four areas: the battery and the electrical system, the oil, anti-freeze, and the tires.

The battery is the most vulnerable part of your car. Cold weather cuts sharply into its efficiency. Of course, it should have all the routine maintenance —water and clean terminals—but it should also be checked for signs of aging. An old battery might still give you months, even years of good service in milder climates, but in the temperatures to be met in the heart of ski country, it may die a very sudden death. Don't take a chance on it. A tow charge in the country can come high—up to 50 per cent of the cost of a new, heavy-duty battery. At the time your battery is checked, make sure that the electrical system is functioning perfectly. Old spark plug cables, points, plugs and loose connections may keep your car from starting even if it has a first-rate battery.

Oil is another item which reacts sharply to cold weather. Absolutely essential is a light oil—either a combination 30–10 weight oil, or a straight 10 weight. Anti-freeze should be sufficient to protect your radiator down to 40 below zero. You should also add anti-freeze to your windshield washers, making sure that it is the kind especially designed for this use.

The choice of winter tires is growing. You can get various varieties of snow tires, including some which have great traction but wear rapidly. The most suitable tire for the skier's car is a recent innovation, the studded tire. First introduced in the Scandinavian countries, it not only assures good traction in snow, but also on ice. And it has the cardinal virtue of sharply reducing the possibility of a skid. The studs are made of special carbide steel or ceramics and are fastened into specially prepared tires. In the better tires they are almost impossible to pull out. Studs are available in both regular and snow tires. Unfortunately, they are not yet legal in all states. Be sure to check on this point, both for your own state and states in which you expect to drive.

SKI RACKS

REGARDLESS of the type of car you have, it should be equipped with a ski rack. Ski racks can be purchased at prices ranging from about $10 to $30, with most in the $15 to $20 bracket.

Skis carried inside the car not only can damage the interior, they can be dangerous in the event of a hard stop, even hurtling through the windshield.

There are two basic types of racks: those that fasten to the roof and those that attach to the trunk. The roof type is more convenient, if the design of your car allows it. Trunk racks have the drawback of limiting access to the trunk or engine. Most of them require that the skis be removed to make access possible, and some require that the whole rack be removed.

When putting the skis in the rack, be sure to secure all straps and cables. If these are allowed to flutter in the wind they will scratch and even dent the **141**

The two basic types of ski rack: roof rack (four-pair capacity) and trunk rack.

car. The most important requirements of a rack are that it be sturdy and capable of secure fastening. These points should be carefully checked before purchase.

MISCELLANEOUS EQUIPMENT

To be prepared for the worst, your car should also carry the following items: spray cans of anti-mist and de-icer to treat windshield and other windows; headlights and tail lights; pieces of carpet or wire mesh as traction aids; flares and flashlights (the stand-up type that can act as a blinker is particularly helpful); a bag of sand or cinders; a tow chain (heavy duty); tire chains with chain tighteners (the latter are frequently forgotten); a sheet of plastic for lying or kneeling on when you work around the car; a strong windshield scraper with a brush on the other end; and jumper cables.

CHOOSING A CAR FOR SKIING

IF you buy a car with skiing specifically in mind, you should consider, in addition to other factors, the car's drive system. A front-engine, rear-wheel-drive —used in most station wagons—is not ideal for the skier. If you have a large family, however, you may have no other alternative, for a station wagon is your roomiest possibility. With up to four people to consider, a rear-engined car may be a better solution. However, rear-engined cars are usually small, they have something of a reputation for tricky handling, and since most of them are air-cooled their heating systems are comparatively weak. But they are fine for economy and traction, two virtues most skiers prize highly. Even better is the front-wheel-drive car, which has the advantage of pulling instead of pushing the car through the turn. It not only handles better in snow, but also has greater resistance to skids.

143

THE EQUIPMENT

WINTER DRIVING

THE two important points to remember in driving on ice and snow are (1) conserve what little friction is available to you and (2) if you lose it, don't panic.

Control of your car depends for all practical purposes on *rolling* wheels. If your wheels are not rolling in the direction of your car's principal momentum, the result will be a skid—loss of friction between tires and road surface. While harsh and sudden braking will lock wheels, control of the car is lost until the wheels start to roll again. It is therefore always advisable to apply brakes gently in a series of pumping motions. This dissipates the momentum of the car slowly, keeps the wheels rolling, and thereby prevents loss of control.

The commonly-stated rule about skids is, "Turn in the direction of the skid." This means that if the car's back end skids to the right, you turn to the right. If it skids to the left, you turn to the left. What you are doing is keeping the front end of the car in line with the back end. Your action should be a smooth, gentle steer in the direction of the skid accompanied by a gradual easing of pressure on the gas pedal.

If you find yourself unable to stop short of an obstacle, remember that you must retain your maneuverability at all costs. Slow the car down, either by gentle braking and/or shifting to a lower gear, but avoid locking your wheels. If your car remains steerable, you may be able to dodge the trouble, or at least reduce the seriousness of the impending accident. If you cannot avoid a collision, yet still have some sort of steering option, it is better to hit something soft than something hard, better to hit something going your way than something stationary, and better to hit something stationary than something coming toward you. The point is to keep thinking and working, not to give up. Control is usually not so much lost as it is surrendered.

144

Part Three

WHERE TO SKI

CHAPTER 16

Planning a Trip

THERE IS a well-to-do Chicago skier so enamoured of Rocky Mountain snow that every Friday night he jets to Denver, drives to the ski area with the greatest promise of powder, skis until Sunday afternoon, drives back to Denver, takes a plane as far as Omaha, where he picks up a sleeper train which gets him to Chicago well rested just in time for his regular office hours on Monday morning.

There are few skiers so fanatically dedicated, but many go to almost as much trouble to ski at their favorite areas. On any Friday evening following a good snowfall, the New York Thruway is almost bumper to bumper with ski-laden cars making the six to eight-hour haul from New York City to the various upstate and New England resorts.

Similar scenes are to be found in every major metropolitan area north of the Mason-Dixon line, for skiers will go to almost any lengths to get to their kind of skiing. The attraction may be Rocky Mountain powder, a big mountain, a particular kind of atmosphere, or simply because friends go there. Whatever they are looking for, they have over one thousand ski areas in the United States and Canada in which to find it.

The ideal ski area would be hard to define. Naturally, mountains should be big, have a variety of terrain, and be adequately supplied with lifts and **147** other base facilities. But size, either of ski terrain or facilities, is not always decisive. In the Midwest, for instance, Boyne Mountain, which has less than 500 vertical feet, consistently draws thousands from six-hour distant Detroit. And amid some of the grandest peaks in the Canadian Rockies, Sunshine Village had an enthusiastic group of followers when it could offer only two relatively modest T-bars.

Of course, some skiers are limited to what is closest at hand. For most, however, a choice is possible, particularly when it comes to ski vacations of a week's duration or longer. To decide on where you want to go, you may want to take into account the general characteristics of several ski regions, their principal sub-regions and what some of their major resorts have to offer. For more details on individual areas within a given region or state, consult Appendix A.

Any ski trip is worth planning well, whether it is for one day at a nearby slope, for a long weekend at a famous ski area, or for a three-week vacation in Europe. Planning is, essentially, getting information. This may involve simply asking questions of a skiing friend or, at the other extreme, writing for folders, reservations for all manner of things, a study of timetables, and painstaking pencil work to make sure that the itinerary not only works, but also that you can afford it. Of course, one can draw heavily on summer experiences in planning trips, but it should be remembered that winter imposes some special conditions. Lack of a properly confirmed reservation may not be a serious matter in summer, but it can be close to a catastrophe in winter, particularly if children are involved.

As ski resorts continue to boom, it is more important then ever not only to get information, but also to make sure it is up-to-date. Your skiing friend may indeed have skied in Austria for less than $5 a day, but that may have been four or five years ago, before the Austrians themselves caught up with the economic times. Similarly, the area you thought two years ago was "not much" may in the meantime have developed into a full-fledged resort with all conveniences.

There is a well-established skiers' grapevine that will relay the message

Boyne Mountain Lodge at Boyne Falls, Michigan.

that a particular area is the place to go—sometimes sight unseen. You soon learn to recognize grapevine reports and they should be treated with caution, particularly if the resort is a new one.

Particularly helpful in providing you with a starting point for planning are the ski publications, state and national tourist offices (see Appendix A), and commercial airlines.

The ski publications have buying and travel guides, which contain listings of resorts and areas, their skiing facilities, the available number of beds, addresses and telephone numbers. While limited in detail on any one area—close to a thousand areas are listed for the United States and Canada—they do provide a basis for comparing resorts throughout North America and in any particular region. Guides put out by state and national tourist offices make generous use of pictures and quite frequently contain the names and addresses of lodges, motels and hotels. More specific still are the brochures of the resorts themselves or, if the resort is a large one, the local Chamber of Commerce. 149

WHERE TO SKI

Depending on whether your plans are for a weekend or a ski vacation, here are some basic factors to keep in mind: Does the resort offer enough variety and challenge for the length of the stay? If novices are in your party, does it have adequate beginner terrain? Are the ski facilities easily accessible from the lodges in the event you use public transportation to get to the resort? Is evening entertainment available? Does it have such services as a ski school, baby sitting, equipment rentals, medical facilities beyond first aid, and anything else you may particularly require? And, above all, what does all this cost?

The answers to these questions are reasonably easy to determine from brochures and with a letter of inquiry. Somewhat more difficult to find out is whether the resort's character will be to your liking. Strangely enough, brochures, although they are designed to show the resort's best face, often provide true clues to the resort's character. If the brochure is cluttered, fussy and dwells

A children's ski class at Mt. Snow, Vermont. Ski resorts are catering increasingly to family needs, and such children's facilities are now to be found at most large, popular ski areas.

excessively on the beginners' slope, you can be reasonably sure you will find an area that is cluttered, fussy and with only limited expert terrain. Conversely, if the brochure stresses the challenges, its immense lifts and the depth of the snow, the chances are good that the area will appeal to the better skier. Unconsciously brochures give the show away. If you find the brochure appealing you will probably enjoy yourself.

Equally instructive is the resort's program of events. If the area is promoting a large number of costume races, this will give an idea of the social life of the resort. If there is a strong schedule of *bona fide* races, including regional and national championships, you can be sure that a large portion of the terrain will appeal exclusively to the better skier. Only a small number of resorts are so large and diverse that they can encompass the full range of desirable terrain, snow conditions, accommodations, after-ski diversions and atmosphere.

BASIC COSTS

THERE is a wide range of prices for lifts, lodging and food, a slightly smaller range for equipment rentals, ski lessons and other services. Lift tickets run from $2 a day at a small rope tow area to $8 a day at major resorts with chairlifts, gondolas and aerial tramways. Many areas charge less on weekdays than on weekends. Others have multiple-day ticket plans with reductions of 25 per cent or more. There are a number of other ticket plans, including coupon books which require the skier to surrender a certain number of coupons per lift ride, the number depending on the size of the lift; half-day tickets, usually obtainable in the afternoon only; interchangeable tickets good at any one of a number of areas in a given vicinity; and season tickets.

If you ski a lot at one area, a season ticket may be your most economical way to ski. The cost rarely exceeds $160 and there are usually discounts for additional members of the family. The more you ski, the lower the per-day cost of skiing. However, it should be kept in mind that you are risking paying for snowless days and that the cost precludes your trying other areas. **151**

A racing scene at Stratton Mountain in Vermont.

Lesson costs do not vary much from area to area. A two-hour group lesson will cost about $3.50, give or take a dollar. The cost of lessons can be substantially reduced sometimes by buying a block of lessons over a span of two or more days. Private lessons are given on an hourly basis and cost $10 to $15 an hour, sometimes a little more if a famous instructor is involved. There is usually a $5 charge for each additional person up to three or four.

Unless you are on a day trip and pack a lunch, there is the cost of food. Expect to pay at least 15 per cent more at a ski area than you would at a local restaurant or cafeteria. If you are on an overnight trip, budget $7 per person, per day for meals, unless you plan to stay at an American-plan lodge. Several of the larger resorts have outstanding restaurants. You'll probably want to try at least one of these, and in that event should add a little more to the food budget.

Lodging runs from $2 dormitory bunks to highly expensive suites, apartments and cottages. Cost is partly determined by the plan under which the lodge operates: the European plan (breakfast only), the American (all meals), or modified American (breakfast and supper only).

An average double room at most major ski areas will cost between $10 and $15 per day for a couple plus $3 or $4 for each additional person in the room. Rates at the leading resorts run about $5 a day higher, and modified American plan will usually add another $5 to the daily cost. (For a more detailed discussion of accommodations see Chapter 18.)

DAY, WEEKEND AND VACATION SKIING

GENERALLY speaking, the American skier does most of his skiing on weekends, particularly on long holiday weekends. This creates a pattern with some unfortunate effects: it results in long weekend lift lines, and makes skiing more expensive than it needs to be. Without going deeply into the economics of ski areas, it should be obvious that if only two out of seven days bring in substantial revenue, the per day, per skier cost for using lifts and other area facilities is going to be substantially higher than if attendance were to be distributed equally over the entire seven days. As long as lifts and lodges costing hundreds of thousands of dollars have to be built to accommodate weekend crowds only, the charges are going to be relatively high.

A more economical way to ski on weekends is to make day trips to nearby areas. Those fortunate enough to live in such cities as Seattle, Denver, Portland, Salt Lake City, or Montreal have the advantage of finding major ski areas within one to two hours drive. Those in other cities in the northern half of the country, however, are not as deprived as they might think they are. Due in part to skiing's tremendous expansion over the last decade, in part to the spread of   153 superhighways, and in part to developments in snow-making, most metropolitan areas have skiing within easy driving distance. These ski areas are rarely spectacular, but they are usually more than adequate.

The most economical plan is to ski during the week. In many cases, weekday lift rates are lower, and since the areas are less crowded one can get in a great deal more skiing. Many metropolitan ski areas also have night skiing, making it possible to get in a few runs in the evening after a day at the office.

A ski vacation is usually the most satisfactory way to go skiing. The choice of where to ski is larger, there is greater flexibility in cost, and the frantic aspects of weekending are avoided. You are certain to get more skiing and other kinds of recreation on a vacation than you will on weekends or on day trips.

But the very fact that a ski vacation affords a great deal of skiing should give pause to some. Of course you don't have to ski every day, but you'll want to. Are you in shape to do so? Two weeks in Aspen may sound idyllic, but it may be more than you are up to. This is an important consideration for those just learning to ski. A moderate amount of preconditioning is essential if you want to take maximum advantage of a ski vacation.

Regardless of the type of resort, your vacation will be cheaper if you avoid the high season. High season is when the resorts are busiest because of holidays or school vacations or both. This includes the two-week period starting the Sunday before Christmas; the period from mid-February to mid-March; and Easter, if it comes before April 7. As far as the quality of the skiing is concerned, these high-season periods have no particular advantage. The snow cover may be a little thin before the Christmas period, but with today's groomed slopes this means little. January has the reputation for being cold, but particularly in the Rocky Mountain resorts it is also the month with the lightest, dryest snow. Strangely enough, skiing after mid-March is often the best. The snow at lower elevations may get a little mushy toward mid-afternoon, but the days are longer and the chances of getting sun are much better.

One of the disadvantages of high-season ski vacations is that they limit the choice of accommodations. Those lodges offering the best value are sometimes booked years ahead, and if they do have a vacancy, they may require

1. Ski races at Heavenly Valley, California.

2, 3. In the Cariboo Range, Canada, near Mt. Hostility.

5. Whitefish, Montana.

4. *Left*. Late afternoon skiing on spring snow at Belleayre, New York.

6. High altitude skiing at Arapahoe Basin, near Loveland Pass in Colorado.

7, 8. *Left and above*. Two sides of the Big Mountain, Montana.

9. *Next page*. The timberline vastness of Mt. Shasta, California.

a stay of two weeks over Christmas-New Year and at least a week during other high-season periods. One solution to the problem of a high-season vacation is to visit a number of smaller, non-lodge resorts within reasonable driving radius of home and use accommodations to be found in towns along the way.

TYPES OF TRIP

HAVING decided where you will go, and when, you must next decide how you will get there. Most skiers prefer to travel in company.

The company may be pre-determined—your family. In that case you must make all arrangements, from lodge reservations to transportation. If you are taking young children, allow enough time for rounding them up, tracing lost mittens, and similar chores.

Many skiers band together in small groups to share the expenses of a trip. Such groups work out well if all members have about the same skiing ability,

The Springfield Ski Club hill in Massachusetts, typical of "exurbia" skiing around many American cities.

are reasonably punctual, and are generally agreeable. Unless exempt by special invitation, members are expected to share equally in the costs, male and female alike.

Particularly in the larger cities, there are ski clubs that sponsor trips to ski areas one or more times a season. Clubs have great advantages of economy and convenience. The trip chairman is usually the one responsible for making all arrangements, including bargaining with area managers and lodge owners for reductions in rates. Clubs generally travel by charter bus, which further reduces the cost of a trip. Some clubs also have at least one member qualified to give lessons, or occasionally will hire a certified instructor as an incentive to join.

Package trips can be arranged through ski shops, travel agents (some of whom specialize in skiing), railroads, airlines and bus companies. Some of them, specifically tailored for the beginner, offer everything—rentals, bus fare, lift tickets, meals, instruction, and lodging—but most are not that inclusive.

Another type of money-saving arrangement is a "learn-to-ski week," which can be enjoyed by beginner and expert alike. Most of the larger areas have such programs. They may offer only a simple lift ticket-ski lesson combination, but frequently also include meals and lodging. Many of these learn-to-ski weeks are actually less than a week, running only from Sunday night to Friday afternoon, but they are available at very reasonable prices. During certain parts of the season the cost is so low as to make living cheaper than it would be at home. For most learn-to-ski weeks you must make your own transportation arrangements.

WHAT TO TAKE ALONG

THERE is nothing quite so annoying or needlessly expensive as to arrive at a ski area only to find that you have forgotten some essential item of equipment or clothing. And while of less consequence, it can also be embarrassing to find yourself unprepared for certain if infrequent social occasions calling for something more formal than stretch pants and sweater.

156   It may seem too obvious a point to stress, but boots, skis, bindings and

poles are essential for a day of skiing; a good portion of a rental shop's business is with people who have forgotten one or more of these essentials.

A vacation requires a good deal of clothing, not so much for skiing as for after-skiing. While informality is acceptable at even the largest resorts, there are some hotels and restaurants, particularly in Europe, which require suits and ties for men and dresses for women. And there are some social occasions calling for formal dress. You may also want to take along a bathing suit if the lodge you are going to has a heated swimming pool. The rule to apply is: when in doubt, take it with you. Everything is invariably more expensive at a ski resort than at home.

SKIER'S TRIP LIST

To help you make sure that you have all the equipment and clothing for a ski trip—whether short or long—check the following list. If you are driving to the slopes and have an unlimited amount of space you may want to take the maximum number of clothing and equipment items suggested here. When flying, check special baggage regulations in effect for ski equipment.

SKI EQUIPMENT FOR ALL TRIPS

Skis with release bindings	Boot tree
Poles	Wax
Boots	Ski ties or carrier

DAY TRIP

Parka	Car coat
Sweater	Hat/Headband
Turtleneck shirt	Mittens/Gloves
Stretch pants	Goggles/Glasses
Long johns	Après ski boots
Light socks	Lip and sun cream
Heavy socks	Driving gloves

RESORT WEAR

To any of these lists, add:

WOMEN	MEN
Dressy blouse	Flannel slacks
Festive slacks or skirt	Blazer or sport jacket
Dressy flat shoes	Colored shirts
Nylon stockings	Tie or ascot

WEEKEND TRIP

Items listed for day trip, plus:

Second sweater	Slacks
Second turtleneck shirt	Shoes
Second stretch pants	Socks
Second pair light socks	Underwear
Second hat/Headband	Pajamas
Light sweater	Slippers
Shirt/Blouse	Toilet kit

SKI WEEK

Same as weekend list, plus:

Light parka	Sport jacket/Dressy
More turtleneck shirts	sweater
Additional sweaters	Two or three shirts/
More stretch pants	Blouses
Second set long johns	Second pair of slacks
Extra light socks	Additional underwear
More hats/Headbands	Camera

Charter buses at Sun Valley, Idaho.

CHAPTER 17

How to get there

ALTHOUGH THE skiier travels a great deal, he is somewhat different from the usual tourist. His principal concern is to get to the slopes; scenery along the way, while it may be pleasant, is secondary. One problem he finds is that few ski areas are on the main lines of railroads, airlines or even buses.

The automobile, despite its limitations, is undoubtedly the skier's best means of transportation. It gives him the largest leeway in choice of route and time of departure. Although day and weekend bus and railroad trips are available and probably somewhat cheaper (at least for the owner of the automobile), going by car costs less in terms of direct cash outlay and avoids the inconvenience of lugging equipment and suitcases to the station and from the depot to the lodge. A car also has the advantage of being a portable locker. Its limitations are its relatively low speed over longer distances, its vulnerability to weather conditions, and its lack of comfort on long trips.

The next choice is between bus, train or plane, and sometimes it takes all three to get there. With the general decline of railway passenger service in North America, the opportunity for train travel to most ski areas has become limited, particularly to eastern U.S. and Midwest areas. But for, say, the Midwestern skier planning a leisurely trip to Colorado, New Mexico or Montana, the train offers a good alternative, sometimes with attractive excursion rates. **159**

WHERE TO SKI

Packaged bus tours operated by ski clubs, travel services and ski shops are one of the best ways of introducing new skiers to weekend skiing. The "package" usually includes the round trip bus ticket, lodge accommodation, equipment rental, and ski lessons given by an instructor accompanying the tour. Some packages also include lift tickets or a special ticket discount. While economical and frequently convivial, these bus tours can be disappointing if you are not in good hands. Try to check on the reputation of the people operating the tour. When renting equipment through a tour operator, do not settle for simply giving your foot size and weight by telephone; have your boots and bindings fitted and adjusted personally. This will also give you a chance to examine the quality of the skis and equipment being offered. Condition of equipment can tell you much about the operation of a tour. It is also advisable to obtain specific information from the tour director on lodge and hotel reservations; you may want to check out the reservations yourself. And you might ask about that "instructor" on the bus, whether he is actually certified.

Older ski hands who have become weary of driving long distances to ski areas in their own cars, and who wish to avoid the bunny-oriented bus tours, now make increasing use of special bus services. This kind of arrangement charges only for the bus. You board the bus on your own. Once you reach the area (frequently non-stop), you are free to stay where you want, eat what you want and get to the mountain when you want. New York, San Francisco and Detroit are among the cities which have such "super ski bus" services.

In traveling other than by car, the skier's major problem is the baggage and equipment he has to carry. Every baggage transfer is an unpleasant chore, particularly with a party. Furthermore, each transfer runs the risk of loss or misplacement, and there is the additional strain of making connections. Thus an overnight sleeper that takes you close to the resort may be more satisfactory than a plane, which will get you to the nearest major city in the fastest time, but may require several additional transfers to limousines, buses and/or trains before you finally arrive in your remote mountain valley. It is therefore a good idea to study all the schedules—rail, bus and airlines—before settling your plans.

In making travel plans, one of the more important considerations is the size of the party. A group of ten or more traveling to the same destination may be eligible for discounts up to 30 per cent on most domestic airlines and on a number of overseas carriers. This has been standard for several years. An airlines sales representative (not a reservations clerk) or a knowledgeable travel agent should be consulted when such a group trip is being considered. Eligibility requirements change periodically and group fares may not be available at certain peak travel periods, such as Christmas and Washington's Birthday.

From a purely economical point of view, there is no better way to go than by charter, whether by bus, train (seldom available), or plane. To give an example, regular winter jet, roundtrip, economy fare from New York to Munich is over $400. For a charter plane, this fare is reduced to $250. Airline charters operate under the Civil Aeronautics Board (CAB) and the International Air Transport Association (IATA), both of which have been known to crack down on illegitimate charters.

To be eligible for an airline charter you must be a member of the sponsoring organization for at least six months prior to the date of departure. The sponsoring organization itself must be a local group organized for purposes other than cut-rate travel. Almost any ski club, employee group, alumni association or lodge can run a winter charter. If your membership has lapsed, you can still qualify by paying back dues. If you sign up for an illegitimate charter, you run the risk that it will be exposed and cancelled. It is best to stay with airlines with established reputations and groups that have run successful charter flights in the past.

Although charter groups work with travel agents who make up special packages, you have to remember that charters only fly you there and back; once there you are on your own. Usually you have to make your own arrangements for accommodations and ground transportation.

Charters have other drawbacks. You must leave and return when the group does, possibly on dates not to your liking. The object of your trip may be a tour of the French resorts. If the plane lands in Munich, the trip's economy and convenience will be reduced. A more drastic problem is the possibility of a **161**

Winding through Haute Savoie, Switzerland. Much of the transportation between Europe's ski areas is by mountain railway.

shortage of passengers. If the price for the trip is based on 100 passengers and fewer actually sign up, you may well be asked to make up the difference on a pro-rated basis. And even legitimate charters have been cancelled at the last minute. In such a case you would either have to pay the full fare to protect the deposits you have made or stay home. You can protect yourself against this eventuality by buying insurance that covers the regular fare in both directions. This insurance also protects you in the event injury prevents you from returning with the group.

Strange as it may seem, domestic charter flights are much more difficult to arrange than overseas charters. Transatlantic airlines have more planes than they can use on scheduled runs during the winter. Also domestic airlines are in a better position to shift their equipment to routes busier in winter than in summer. And domestic charter flights are likely to end up with propeller driven planes instead of jets. However, this situation has been improving with the growth of American resorts.

Travel between ski areas can be a chore, and is often more complicated than getting to a resort from your hometown. With a few notable exceptions, most major American resorts are situated discouragingly far apart. European resorts, while closer to each other, require more traveling time. For instance, it is about 350 miles from Aspen to Salt Lake City, a seven-hour drive. That is about the same length of time it takes to go from Chamonix to Zermatt by train, although the two are only 45 miles apart.

If you are going to Europe and plan to drive, you should get an International Driver's License before leaving. The AAA can handle this for you if you show them your domestic license and give them two passport photos and $3. If you happen to be in the market for a new foreign car, buying one in Europe is appreciably cheaper than buying it in the U.S. Your own foreign car dealer can provide you with details.

Transportation is likely to be the largest item in the total vacation budget, and it may determine how many days you will actually have on the slopes. Every $25 you save on transportation means an extra day of skiing.

A heated outdoor swimming pool at Mt. Snow, Vermont.

CHAPTER 18

A roof over your head

LODGING AT ski areas can range from primitive to luxurious, with prices to match. A good lodge can more than make up for an area's shortcomings or bad weather. Conversely, a poor lodge can make being at an otherwise ideal resort a miserable experience. Lodges, over a period of time, get reputations for offering certain types of atmosphere and attracting certain types of clientele. While price is a fair indication, some detective work is needed to determine exactly what you'll be getting into. If a choice is available, make telephone calls to the managers. And by all means, consult friends and acquaintances who have stayed there in the past, making sure that the management hasn't changed since they've been there (or perhaps that it has).

There are basic differences between European and American accommodation, and it is unreasonable to compare the two. After all, the service and atmosphere of the *gasthof* or *auberge* are unique. Remember that European ski resorts were resorts long before they catered to skiers. Their facilities and service reflect a tradition going back centuries. European hotels usually come complete with liveried porters, chambermaids, *et al.* They are proper hotels in contrast to American or Canadian ski lodges—although lodges can themselves be quite luxurious. Most lodges came into being after the ski lifts were built and were specifically designed to cater to skiers. Because their summer business **165** is inconsequential, they are usually run by owners (themselves skiers) and are not very large. A lodge that can accommodate one hundred is big by American standards. However, it will offer the features favored by American skiers—a lounge with a large fireplace, and private baths with every room.

The larger the resort, the greater its variety of accommodations. In an American resort—Aspen, for instance—accommodations can range from simple dormitories to luxury condominium apartments. In Europe, say Kitzbuehel, they range from low-priced pensions to elaborate multi-room suites.

Although the range of accommodations may be narrower at smaller resorts, this does not mean that they offer a lot less in every respect. Luxury features may be missing, but many hosts go out of their way to make up in organized entertainment and hospitality whatever their resort or lodge may lack in swimming pools and precipitous slopes. If lodges in the smaller resorts can be faulted at all, it is in their tendency to be oversolicitous.

TYPES OF ACCOMMODATION

IF you are young, single, not overly concerned about privacy and determined to get the maximum skiing mileage out of your dollar, a dormitory bed or a pension is the answer. Dormitories can be almost anything—extra attic space (bring your own sleeping bag), bunk rooms holding ten to fifteen members of the same sex, or even an entire lodge. Some dormitory lodges are remarkably elaborate, offering a two-to-a-room bunk arrangement with semi-private bath. Prices range from $2 to $5 per person, the one disadvantage being that you have no choice of roommate unless you are in a group large enough to take over completely whatever dormitory space is available.

In any event, expect to find a young crowd almost totally dedicated to skiing. Families with older children may actually find it an advantage to put their youngsters in dormitories. Not only will this save money, it will throw children together with others their own age, something they are bound to enjoy.

166 With separate rooms you have the widest latitude, both in conveniences

Squaw Valley Lodge in High Sierras near Lake Tahoe.

and in cost. Rooms run from $6 a day up to $30 a day, the cost depending on a number of factors which should be taken into account before making a selection. It makes little sense to pick the lowest priced lodge only to find that you have to spend money for cab fares to the slope or for a night on the town. Similarly, if a daily sauna is your heart's desire, it is better to pay a dollar a day more for a lodge with this facility than to spend an extra two dollars at another lodge for the same service.

European hotels increase their rates in high season, while American resorts offer reductions during the low season. Thus, in the U.S., expect to pay the published daily rate during high season, and a lower daily rate in low season, with a further reduction if you stay a week or longer.

Should you be single, you'll have difficulty finding single rooms in American areas. If you cannot find someone to share a room with you (you have to provide your own roommate) or insist on being alone, you'll be expected to pay the double rate, at least in high season.

American plan is certainly the cheapest way to eat at a resort, but it doesn't give you much choice of food. Many lodges offer food family style with very limited choice, others have three or four items on a menu from which you must choose your dinner before leaving the lodge in the morning. Only a few offer a complete menu at the time of the meal. The wider the choice of food, the more costly the room.

For room only, in the United States and Canada, expect to pay no less than $10 per day for two at an average resort, $14 to $20 a day for two at a prestige resort. In Europe, where quality and price are regulated by law, pensions, guest houses and third-class hotels range from $5 to $12; second-class hotels from $6 to $18; first-class hotels from $9 to $22; and de luxe hotels from $10 to $27. These prices include room for one person, bath, three meals, tips and surcharges of various kinds.

Multiple room suites are the top accommodation available in Europe, but in the United States there are several types of kitchen units and apartments. The prices on these are on the steep side, usually starting at $25, but when you realize that two times $14 is $28, they seem good solutions for larger parties. The better ones are laid out in such a way that two or more couples can still have a reasonable amount of privacy.

For stays longer than two weeks, you may want to consider renting a house or an apartment from a private party. The per-day cost will be less—though not a great deal less—than at a lodge, but the responsibilities are somewhat greater. Minor breakages have to be paid for, the walks shoveled, there is no manager to provide little services, and you have to seek your own entertainment. A private arrangement can have advantages, but it is not recommended for your first trip to a resort. You may find that the resort has been oversold to you and you want to move. This is easier done in a commercial establishment where, at most, it will cost you your deposit.

RESERVATIONS AND DEPOSITS

IT is the height of folly not to make reservations, particularly during high season. Make your reservations early, starting in mid-summer for Christmas, in late fall for February and early March. At the more popular resorts, it may take quite a few letters to get what you want. Many skiers who go to the same resort year after year make their reservations for the next year prior to leaving.

Once you have made a reservation, nail it down with a deposit. Deposit policies vary from resort to resort, but anticipate paying about 30 per cent of the total cost of the stay if it is for a week or more, or the equivalent of two days if the stay is for less than a week. Deposits are usually refunded in full upon thirty days notice (this also varies). Increasing percentages are deducted as the cancellation approaches the reservation date. This may seem like an unreasonable policy, but it has to be recognized that the lodge owner has only a limited time in which to realize his income. Because of your reservation, he may have turned down dozens of others (who have then gone somewhere else), and it may no longer be possible to fill the space at that late date.

OWNING YOUR OWN SKI HOME

THERE may come a time—particularly if you are in the process of raising a family—when you add up the season's lodge receipts, the cost of telephone calls for reservations and all the headaches, and you conclude that you are spending enough money to buy your own ski home.

A ski house, under certain circumstances, not only can convert receipt stubs into equity, it can also be a source of cash profit. At the most popular resorts you can finance your entire ski budget by renting your ski house in high season and using it yourself during low season and the summer. A fee of $200 a week during the high season is not unusual if both the area and the house are right.

The advantages and economics of a ski house depend largely on the size of your group, how often you ski, the type of accommodations you are accustomed to, the size of the mortgage payments, taxes and other costs.

Providing you have chosen the site and the building wisely, and have maintained them properly, the chances are much better than even that the 169 property will increase in value. Even though there has been a lusty boom in ski area development for the last five years, it is nowhere near its peak yet. Every time a lift is built in the vicinity, your ski home becomes a little bit more valuable.

A great many ski areas are in the real estate business, or rather are in the ski area business in order to be in the real estate business. As an incentive to buying real estate, some will offer reduced-cost skiing privileges with each sale.

The ski house itself has many economic advantages. Depreciation and the amounts paid out for interest, taxes, and improvements are legitimate tax deductions. Under certain conditions, a ski house can qualify as a business venture and as such any losses can be written off for taxes.

Most important of all, there are the conveniences. You never have to worry about the availability or quality of accommodations. You can eat and drink when you please. You are free to choose your fellow guests. And you'll have as much storage space as you'll ever need.

But, as any homeowner knows, ownership does have its drawbacks. And the drawbacks in a vacation home are the same as in your primary home, plus a few extra.

Problems are reduced to a minimum if you use the house only for yourself and your own family. You can expect to find it as you left it, and you can leave it as you wish. But if you expect to rent it, you will have to keep it neat and tidy, or pay to have this done. And while it is possible to do the renting yourself, it usually requires the services of an agent, who charges 10 to 25 per cent of the rental fee.

Maintenance costs are going to be high. That long driveway connecting the house to the main road will have to be shoveled clear. Heat and electric bills will be higher. And that costly water well could run dry.

If you rely on rental income to pay for part of the mortgage, a bad snow year could be disastrous. And even if you don't depend on rental income, the house may be useless to you during such a year. There is nothing quite so dreary as a ski house during a snowless winter.

170   Unless you are unusually wealthy, the very ownership of a ski house

A typical A-frame ski house.

Many ski clubs build their own
A-frame lodge in the mountains.

tends to commit you to one ski area, or at best a limited selection. It is silly to own a house in one area and then drive many miles to another area. Better to find a site equidistant from several areas, both as a hedge on snow conditions and to assure skiing variety.

And finally, there are the problems of construction. What may be an ideal site from a ski point of view may have major drawbacks in terms of labor availability, access, utility hook-ups and other services. And, of course, this holds true for maintenance after the house has been built. A plumber or furnace repairman is difficult enough to get in the city. In the country, he may be virtually non-existent.

If you still want to build your own ski house, your first step will be to pick a site. A half-acre lot within easy driving distance of a first-class ski area can cost anywhere from $1500 to $10,000, depending on the availability of utilities, roads, location, view, and the prestige of the area. This may seem unreasonable in view of the fact that the acreage may have been purchased originally for as little as $100 an acre, but running water, gas and power lines are expensive propositions in the country. The more you get in this respect, the more you will have to pay for the lot.

Unimproved acreage is still available in ski sections of the country and at rock bottom prices, but as a site for a ski house it is a highly speculative proposition. Unless the acreage adjoins a maintained road, you will have to build your own and maintain it too. Electric power lines will have to be brought into the property at your own expense, and you will have to drill your own well at between $6 and $10 a foot.

Having decided on a lot, your next task will be to select a house plan and find a builder, unless the party that sold you the lot is himself in the building business. In that case, if you like his designs, it is merely a matter of making a down payment—about 30 per cent—and arranging for a mortgage. On a $20,000 property this works out to roughly $600 down and payments of about $100 a month for fifteen years. Add to these figures local taxes, heat, electricity, water (if you are on a system), maintenance and insurance.

172

If you do not like to bother with such items as maintenance, taxes, etc., you may prefer a cooperative or condominium arrangement. This usually involves a management contract of some kind which not only takes care of these details, but also makes provisions for renting the property, if you so desire.

If you build yourself, you have the choice of working from commercially prepared blueprints; from pre-cut house kits; buying a package home; or retaining your own architect or builder.

What you will build depends, of course, on what you are prepared to spend, but even if initial cost is not an overwhelming consideration, eventual resale should be. Ski houses worth around $15,000 with emphasis on sleeping and comfort facilities prove to be the most liquid, while lavish structures tend to become white elephants. Similarly, elaborately renovated older houses are difficult to sell because of the expense of heating and maintenance, and because they don't usually appeal to outdoor oriented skiers.

Pre-cut and packaged homes come in a wide range of prices. Depending on the size of the home, the convenience features built in, and how much you are willing to do yourself, you can get a house from $3500 to over $20,000. At the lower end of the scale you will get a sturdy cabin at best or a poor house at worst.

About $2000 to $3000 in extras can greatly enhance the value of your property and make it easier to rent. A dishwasher—no one wants to wash dishes on vacation—is almost a must and is a bargain at $250. A big stone fireplace, traditional with skiing, may cost as much as $1000, sometimes even more. A large, sturdy, wind-sheltered sundeck ($250 to $500) makes the house more desirable in spring and summer; a small sauna ($500 and up) adds a touch of luxury which will be greatly appreciated by tired skiers; and an extra bathroom (about $500 if planned for at the time of construction) will make the house more rentable to groups consisting of more than one family.

173

CHAPTER 19

Land of varied snows: the east

"EASTERN SKIING" can range from Cataloochee Ski Slopes in North Carolina's Smokies in the South to Enchanted Mountain, Jackman, Maine, in the North and to Valley High at Bellefontaine, Ohio, in the Midwest. Not surprisingly, considering this geographical spread, skiing in the East offers enormous variety.

What the Eastern areas do have in common are low base elevations and the unstable weather patterns prevailing over the Northeastern portion of the United States and Canada. As a result snow conditions are relatively unpredictable, from day to day as well as year to year. Periods of extreme cold alternate with devastating thaws, and a major snow drought can be reasonably expected every five years or so.

Despite these drawbacks, Eastern areas offer some of the most interesting and stimulating skiing in the United States, jokes about "Eastern powder" (wet, heavy snow) notwithstanding. Particularly in the New England states—

Cannon Mountain in New Hampshire, showing (*left to right*) Lower Cannon Trail, Lower Ravine Trail, and Turnpike Trail.

175

From a trail at Jay Peak, Vermont, a vista to the north and Canada.

Vermont, New Hampshire and Maine—skiing can be excellent, especially in the latter part of February, throughout March and early April. Late in this period skiing can be at its best and delightful by any standard. The very ice which occasionally plagues skiers earlier in the season is responsible for the pleasures of corn-snow skiing in the spring. What makes this corn-snow skiing superior is that the previously formed ice melts more slowly and provides a firm base for the corn above. This prevents the snow from turning into deep, heavy mush.

To insure against poor snow conditions many of the areas, particularly those in the vicinity of major cities, have installed snow-making machinery. Except in unusual warm spells, this enables most of them to continue operating even though the surrounding ground is bare. Unfortunately, the cost and water demands of snow-making are such that it is only suitable for small areas or for small sections of large areas.

The highest ski terrain in the East is along the spine of Vermont, parallel to the state's Route 100. It is on or within a few miles of this highway that most of the East's most famous ski areas are to be found—reading from south to north: Mt. Snow, Stratton, Bromley, Magic Mountain, Killington, Sugarbush, Glen Ellen, Mad River Glen, Stowe, and Jay Peak with its aerial tramway. These are by no means the only ski areas in the state, but they are the ones that draw the largest number of skiers and set the tenor for skiing in much of the rest of the East.

The atmosphere along the Route 100 resorts is highly varied, ranging from the carnival spirit at Mt. Snow, through the jet-set image at Sugarbush, to the charm and serious-skier appeal at Stowe, which is to the East what Aspen is to the West, the most prestigious of the resorts. These areas have impressive terrain, plenty of lifts and a wide variety of lodges. Because so many skiers who go to Vermont are sophisticated New Yorkers and Connecticut exurbanites, there is a lively after-ski life and a number of first-rate restaurants.

In contrast, New Hampshire and Maine skiing attracts mostly Bostonians and this is reflected in the accommodations and after-ski life. These are more straightforward, more geared to the outdoorsman who happens to need lodging for a night, and less expensive. The entertainment inclines toward the homemade, the menus are not as extensive and the atmosphere from resort to resort less varied. In the excitement over Vermont, a number of first-rate

The base building and chair lift at Mad River, Vermont. Mad River is often called "the skier's ski area" because of its demanding trails.

areas in New Hampshire are frequently overlooked, specifically Cannon Mountain and Wildcat, two of the more challenging spots in the East. It is significant that these areas were not skiable until relatively recently. Fortunately some of the more rugged aspects of Eastern skiing "like it used to be" are still to be found at these areas. Also overlooked in the past, but rapidly coming into prominence because it has so often had snow when others had none at all, is Sugarloaf in Maine. Not only does this area offer an impressive number of lifts, but it also sports a distinctive Down East flavor, which it refuses to surrender despite its growing regional and national fame.

New York State offers only one "big mountain" area—Whiteface near Lake Placid—but there are over seventy smaller ski areas scattered throughout the state all the way to the Pennsylvania border, some as close to New York City as an hour's drive. These areas until recent years had no particular distinction, but lately they have tried to make up in atmosphere, accommodations and service for what they lack in terrain. As a result skiers are beginning to flock to them, preferring to take their big-mountain skiing in the West or in Europe. Not all these areas are small. Some, like Hunter, Windham and Gore have verticals in the 1500-foot range and can provide a full weekend of first-rate sport.

A somewhat similar situation prevails in the Pennsylvania areas. Blue Knob, Elk Mountain and Laurel Mountain are sizeable installations within easy driving distance of most mid-Atlantic cities. Almost all Pennsylvania areas feature snow-making, for snow is an unpredictable commodity in the state. There are plenty of steep mountains, but few really suitable for skiing. Still, thanks to the new prevalence of snow-making, facilities at Pennsylvania ski areas have been greatly upgraded in recent years and many of them merit the attention of other than just local skiers.

One of the serious problems of Eastern ski areas is that they are afflicted by weekend skiers—they are overcrowded on weekends and undercrowded during the week. Liftline waits of a half-hour or longer are not unusual, partic-

178 Steel towers built into the mountainside support the double chair lift at Whiteface Mountain. The ski center, operated by N.Y. state, is at Wilmington not far from Lake Placid.

ularly at the more popular resorts. The ski areas are not unaware of this problem. One of the features of Eastern skiing is that you can get a bargain-rate
Sunday afternoon to Friday afternoon vacation. What's more, ski school
classes are small during the week. There are more good schools in the East
than anywhere else, so it is a good place to learn. If you can ski well in the
East, Easterners claim, you can ski well anywhere else.

Although not technically the first ski section of the United States, New
England has had more to do with introducing skiing into this country than any
other section. A little bit north of Wildcat is the city of Berlin whose Nansen
Ski Club was the first modern ski club in the United States. The club also
owns a ski jump, which is the site of one or more important annual jumping
tourneys.

A little further to the south, near Franconia, you will find at Cannon
Mountain the first aerial tramway in the United States. Slightly to the south-

One of the southernmost ski slopes: Gatlinburg, Tennessee. Southern skiing depends on
mechanical snow-making and whims of the weather.

east, on the Connecticut River, is Dartmouth College, whose Outing Club once pioneered the sport. Only about two miles from the campus is Oak Hill, the site of the first overhead cable lift in the United States. It's still being used, and is fundamentally unchanged from its original rough-riding state. About twenty miles east of Hanover is the site of the first U.S. rope tow, at Suicide Six near Woodstock, Vermont. The contraption has long since breathed its last, and Suicide Six is less suicidal than it used to be (but still a good challenge). Still further to the east is Lake Placid, New York. Without the fanfare provided by the 1932 Winter Olympics at Placid, it might have been another decade before skiing in the United States got off the ground. There isn't much downhill type of skiing at Lake Placid proper (the big mountain is nearby Whiteface), but there is a jump, some good touring trails and all kinds of memorabilia from the 1932 Games.

One of the real charms of Eastern skiing is its almost unlimited variety. There is a resort for every taste, and one not too far from any population center. If the weather is fit for neither beast nor skier, it is part of the spice of the Eastern sport to try to outwit it, and if not outwit it, outwait it.

Skiing on snow fields at Sugarloaf Mountain in northern Maine, reached by gondola lift. Small trees become encrusted with snow as much as six inches thick.

CHAPTER 20

The flatlands rear up: the midwest

THE MIDWEST is something of a skiing anomaly. It has a longer continuous tradition of skiing than any other section of the United States, yet it came to Alpine skiing relatively late. In terms of enthusiasm, there are few groups who can match the Midwestern passion for skiing, yet its ski areas are something less than impressive; one wonders how the small hills could generate any enthusiasm for the sport.

Midwestern skiers and skiing are the butts of numerous ski jokes. When an Eastern skier complains about his lot, he is apt to be reminded how much worse it could be in the Midwest. One of the few sure ways ski cinematographers can get laughs is to devote a section of their reel to the struggles of a Midwesterner stumbling his way down a suburban hillock. Quite a few Midwesterners themselves admit that their skiing is a good excuse to go somewhere else in winter.

Lookout Mountain's 1900-foot chair lift (Virginia, Minnesota) stretches over lower slopes. **183**

Yet strange as it may seem, Midwesterners are as a whole remarkably proficient skiers and are totally unawed by the mountains they encounter elsewhere. They acquire this proficiency on those much maligned hills of Michigan, Wisconsin, Minnesota, Illinois, Indiana and Ohio.

Midwestern ski areas compensate for their deficiencies first by featuring strong ski schools; second, by lifts and tows by the dozens; and, third, by the gusto of their after-ski activities. Nor are most Midwest ski area owners bashful about lack of vertical drop.

Boyne Mountain, near Boyne Falls in northern Michigan, features at least half a dozen chairlifts, one of them a quadruple chair. The area's owner, Everett Kircher, claims "even on a packed weekend it is possible to take twenty-five to thirty rides a day for more than 15,000 vertical feet of skiing" —above average for even the largest areas of the Rocky Mountain West or Europe.

Although its base facilities are fancier than most, Boyne is by no means unusual in the number of lifts and tows it offers. Mount Telemark near Hayward, Wisconsin, has a chairlift, three T-bars and ten rope tows; Sugar Hills at Grand Rapids, Minnesota, is similarly equipped; and Caberfae near Cadillac, Michigan, holds the record with six T-bars and sixteen rope tows on 270 vertical feet.

The hills as such may offer little real challenge to the expert skier, but for learners, they can be ideal. For one thing, neither the skier's friends nor his own foolishness will tempt him to slopes and trails beyond his capabilities; for another, having yo-yoed a given slope a number of times, he is likely to find practicing on one slope more appealing than simply shooting up on one of the high-speed lifts and schussing down again.

Midwesterners have been aided in their passion for practice by growing clusters of ski areas in the suburbs of Detroit, Chicago, Milwaukee and Minneapolis-St. Paul. Thanks to snow-making and the bone-chilling cold to be found throughout much of the Midwest in December, January and early February, these areas offer reliable skiing if not massive mountains.

The base lodge at Mt. Telemark, Wisconsin. This area has one of the largest snow-making installations in the world.

The ultimate in this type of development is Pine Knob, a mere thirty minutes drive from downtown Detroit. With two chairlifts and seven rope tows, it offers not only skiing, but base facilities fit for a motor magnate, which is exactly what one of its base lodges used to be—a Detroit tycoon's home.

185

The Flatlands Rear Up: the Midwest

After-ski life at most Midwestern areas tends toward the Germanic and Scandinavian. There is a lot of jolly beer drinking and group singing and the accompaniment is more likely to be the accordion than the guitar. But sophistication isn't passing the Midwest by. At the larger resorts, the frug can be found as easily as the polka, and bartenders whose customers used to be straight-shot lumbermen have adapted remarkably well to mixed drinks and scotch ordered by name brand.

Until the end of World War II, lift skiing was a distinct oddity in the Midwest. Skiing meant jumping. Then, in a little less than a decade, downhill skiing became the Midwestern rage to such an extent that it threatened to totally overshadow jumping. Only the formation of strong junior programs prevented jumping from disappearing in the Midwest.

The lift skier who wants to mix downhill skiing with jump spectating finds plenty of opportunity in the Midwest. There are jumping hills almost everywhere and major jumps at Iron Mountain, Ironwood and Ishpeming in Michigan; at Westby, Eau Claire and Racine, Wisconsin; at St. Paul and Duluth, Minnesota; and at Fox River Grove, outside of Chicago. Most of these jumps have ski areas nearby. Ishpeming has an additional attraction: the Ski Hall of Fame. Leading skiers have been honored with plaques, and there is an interesting ski museum with emphasis on the development of the American sport.

Nor is the Midwest lacking in alpine competition. Downhills often have to be run in two parts, but the Midwest is well up with more generously endowed regions in producing competitors for American teams. As is so characteristic of all aspects of Midwestern skiing, what is lacking in impressive geography is more than made up for by enthusiasm and dedication to the sport.

Fox River Grove, near Chicago, is the scene of many jumping competitions in the Midwest. **187**

CHAPTER 21

Powder empire: The rockies

FROM CHICAGO west to the Rockies the land is almost flat. It rises gently for a distance of about one thousand miles until it reaches an altitude of about 5000 feet above sea level. At that point, the earth thrusts up sharply into the Rocky Mountain West.

The Rocky Mountains run in a long chain of ranges from New Mexico into Canada, traversing in the process New Mexico, Colorado, Utah, Wyoming, Idaho, Montana and the Canadian provinces of Alberta and British Columbia. These mountains divide a largely arid plain and are the major source of water for thousands of square miles of land and millions of people. They are the only barrier to intercept the vast storms generated in the north and prevent them from sweeping to the east and south. As a result the Rocky Mountains not only get vast quantities of snow, but due to the general aridity of that part of the continent, the snow has a particular quality which makes it ideal for skiing.

Alta, Utah: "The powder snow capital of the world."

WHERE TO SKI

The dry powder of the Rocky Mountains is not uniformly dry. The southern Rocky Mountain States—Utah, Colorado and New Mexico—are more arid than the northern states, and as a consequence their powder is drier. On the other hand, snow depths are greater in the northern Rockies. Such differences between sub-regions are not substantial, however, and matter only to dyed-in-the-wool powder enthusiasts.

The quality of this snow is legendary. Not even Europe can match its consistency. Even when packed, it rarely packs into hard snow or ice. It enhances the skier's sensation of flying, and actually makes skiing easier. Oddly enough, the region has produced relatively few champions, despite the excellent terrain it has to offer. The reason: snow conditions are simply too favorable. The stone-hard *pistes* which are the lot of the international racer have no real counterpart in the Rocky Mountain West. There are plenty of tough trails, but most of the time snow conditions are such that they present few problems to challenge the best skiers.

Part of the Rocky Mountain ski legend has it that it only snows at night and that the sun shines every day. Were it only so. It is true that overall the region has more sunny winter days than other ski regions in the United States, but this is no guarantee that the weather will always be bright. With a lot of skiing done on relatively open slopes at high altitude there are occasional whiteouts, when skiers find themselves actually skiing in the clouds. So-called "flat light" is not uncommon in other ski regions, but it is more of a problem for the skier in the Rockies because of the absence of reference points on the open slope. This makes it difficult to judge the steepness of the slope and the character of the terrain.

These drawbacks aside, Rocky Mountain skiing is American skiing at its best. It is not surprising that the region contains the country's most prestigious resorts and that even its smaller resorts match the largest resorts of other regions in size, if not necessarily in facilities.

Paralleling a "moat" at the base of Mt. Woodrow Wilson in the Wasatch Range, Utah.

Skiers above Aspen, Colorado.

Of all the Rocky Mountain resorts, the one that comes closest to the ideal is Aspen. It consists of four ski areas—Aspen Mountain, Aspen Highlands, Buttermilk and Snowmass—each with its own distinct characteristics; it has twenty-five lifts, a lodging capacity for over five thousand in a picturesque town, and a rich and diversified night life reputed to be the best between Chicago and San Francisco. What makes Aspen unique is that while skiing is its primary winter preoccupation, it is also a year-around intellectual and cultural center. Thus a day of skiing can be followed by a gourmet dinner, a lecture at the Aspen Institute, and late-night attendance at a jazz session.

Close to rivalling Aspen are Vail, a brilliant new resort, and Sun Valley, a lively shrine whose pioneering thirty years ago in what was then a new sport did much to establish the eminence of skiing today.

192   Vail, a mere one hundred miles drive from Aspen, wasn't as much as a

gas station as recently as the winter of 1961–62. But the daring of its concept —it came into existence almost overnight—has excited thousands of skiers. Built close to the slopes, it provides an intimate atmosphere amid highly modern architecture and decor. Its skiing glory are the south bowls, which, in good season, provide superb powder skiing with virtually no impediment.

Sun Valley is so steeped in American ski history, one can forget that it is also one of the finest American resorts. When it opened in 1936, it was so far ahead of its time that only now are American and European resorts recognizing the merit of what was done in the big sheep pasture in Ketchum, Idaho. The inspiration of W. Averell Harriman, then president of the Union Pacific, Sun Valley is a replica of a small Tyrolian village *sans* cuckoo-clock decorations. Everything a skier could want is found there. Beginners are nursed along at gentle Half-Dollar and Dollar Mountains. Intermediates take the runs

Powder skiing at Jackson Hole, Wyoming.

on Baldy. Hard-skiing experts find satisfaction on Rock Garden and Exhibition. And there are a number of bowls for the powder enthusiasts. The resort is currently undergoing expansion and should be even more exciting in the future.

Just below the Aspen-Vail-Sun Valley quality are a series of resorts of more specialized appeal. At Jackson Hole, Wyoming, a massive complex is taking shape offering the longest vertical drop in the United States—4,135 vertical feet. It is too early to tell what role Jackson will play in the Rocky Mountain scheme of things, but it is bound to loom large. Alta in Utah has rather spartan facilities (there is also a prohibition on bar sales in Utah, so bring your own bottle) but it more than deserves its reputation as the powder snow capital of the world. The powder comes in great depths, it is feather light, and instructors there will teach you how to ski it. Nearby Park City isn't as generously blessed with powder, but neither is it quite as avalanche-prone. Its particular merit is the variety of its facilities in a mining town setting (the mining is still going on). Taos, New Mexico, is expanding, but it has built its appeal mostly on the basis of its uncompromising expert terrain, largely as an expression of the skiing flair of its owner, Ernie Blake. There is no resort so closely identified with the character of one man. Of the large resorts, Big Mountain, Montana, is probably the most folksy and, in some ways, the most dramatic. The remnants of a forest fire on some of its slopes many years ago give it an out-of-this-world appearance to be found nowhere else.

This by no means exhausts the list, but it more than indicates the scope of what is available in the Rocky Mountain West. There are other areas in this region, perhaps not as richly blessed with facilities for longer vacations, but with more than adequate slopes and lifts for several days of interesting and challenging skiing. Winter Park, Arapahoe Basin, Loveland Basin, Purgatory and Breckenridge in Colorado; Red River, Sierra Blanca and Santa Fe

Vail, Colorado, scene of many of the country's most important alpine races.

WHERE TO SKI

Ski Basin in New Mexico; Solitude, Brighton and Brianhead in Utah; Bogus Basin, Brundage Mountain and Schweitzer Basin in Idaho; and Red Lodge and the Missoula Snow Bowl in Montana are all areas which would be more prominent were not the reputations of Aspen, Sun Valley, and Vail so dominant.

For those interested in competition, the chances are excellent in this

Skiing at Taos, New Mexico, is among the most demanding to be found in the U.S. Nestled in an alpine setting, the 180-bed Hondo Lodge and Chalet Alpina dormitory are a short distance from the Taos main lift.

region for one race a week in which the nation's top racers will participate. Prominent racing fixtures are the Roch Cup at Aspen, the Harriman Cup at Sun Valley, the Vail Cup at Vail, and the Snow Cup at Alta. In addition, the American International Team Races, which draw the top European racers, and one or more national championships are usually held in the Rocky Mountain region.

Grotesque snow shapes are to be found in the areas near Big Mountain, Montana.

CHAPTER 22

Sun and high sierras: the far west

THE FAR WEST means mostly California, with oases of skiing in Nevada and Arizona. Were it not for the tempting offerings in the Rocky Mountain West, several of the California resorts would loom much larger in the national ski scene than they do. As it stands, Far West skiing needs no apologies. There are several areas built to true California scale.

Skiing in California is concentrated in two relatively small sections of the state. Within a hundred miles of Los Angeles, there is a cluster of about a dozen areas catering mostly to residents of that city. The other cluster is to be found in the Donner Pass-Lake Tahoe region in the center of the High Sierra. About halfway between these widely separated complexes, like a balance point on a scale, is Mammoth Mountain, California's most famous resort and a hotbed of racing talent, both local and imported.

Skiing at Mammoth Mountain, California, lasts into July.

Squaw Valley, only a few hours' drive from San Francisco, was the scene of the 1960 Winter Olympics.

Although they seldom figure in the ski travel plans of any but Los Angelenos, the southern areas are not insubstantial. Several feature vertical descents of over 1200 feet with highly varied terrain. When there is snow, these areas are good. But this is precisely their problem. In the south of the state snow is a highly unpredictable commodity. It may not come at all. It may come at unexpected moments. It may disappear just as quickly as it came. Furthermore, temperatures can be such that snow-making becomes almost impossible, although several areas have the equipment. The skier who relies on Southern California snow must be both tolerant and patient.

More specifically geared to the vacationing skier is the Donner Pass-Lake Tahoe group of areas. As a result of massive improvements in highway 40 from San Francisco, these areas are rapidly developing into one of the most densely developed ski complexes in the United States. Most of them are large, capable of accommodating the vast crowds pouring out of the Bay Area, and accommodations for the skier are not hard to find. The Lake Tahoe region is a popular summer resort, and on the Nevada side there is the year-around attraction of legalized gambling. There is a choice of motel, hotel or lodge for every taste.

200 The most famous resort in this group is Squaw Valley, site of the 1960

Olympic Winter Games. The '60 Games focused attention on this region and things have never been the same since. It is a rare year that doesn't see the construction of one or more lifts. Squaw Valley once was a relatively exclusive resort for transplanted Eastern socialites. As a result of the Games, it is that no longer. Its peaks are studded with lifts, and the valley floor is filling up with lodges, shops and private houses. Where there was nothing in 1950, there is now a completely self-sustaining village with a lively nightlife. Although night-club entertainment is available at nearby Reno and Stateline, the crowd that stays in the Valley evenings is an active one. It likes to dance, to limbo and play group games.

On the back side of Squaw Valley is Alpine Meadows, not quite as large and more geared to the family skier. The atmosphere is somewhat less frenetic, more suited to the skier who is interested in skiing with a minimum of fripperies.

At the south end of Lake Tahoe, just on the California side of the state

A typical base lodge in the Tahoe ski region of the mid-Sierras in California.

line, is Heavenly Valley, one of the largest ski areas in the country, but one that has been coming into its own only slowly. The reason: Heavenly Valley is a great deal more difficult to ski on its bottom slopes than on the top. This discouraged beginners and intermediates until in 1963 an aerial tramway was built to the beginner terrain. Now the area is booming and is scheduled for major expansion. Not the least of its attractions is the fact that it is within a short distance of the nightclubs and gambling casinos of Stateline. Those who like to mix their skiing with sybaritic entertainment will find Heavenly Valley the ideal spot.

In rather severe contrast, Sugar Bowl, in Donner Pass, doesn't even hint at such pleasures, even though it is less than an hour's drive from Stateline. The oldest area in the region, it makes its own entertainment, much of it in the private homes located in the area. The Sugar Bowl is the semi-private preserve of San Francisco society; its atmosphere is on the conservative side, its skiing on the demanding side. It has softened this image in some respects over the last few years, but it still does not readily identify with the more uninhibited goings-on nearer the Lake.

Skiing on a somewhat smaller scale can be found at a handful of areas sandwiched between these giants of the region. They are ideal for the more timid who wish to become better acquainted with skiing before trying the imposing runs of Squaw, Heavenly Valley, Alpine Meadows and Sugar Bowl.

For those intensively dedicated to skiing, and for those who find the Lake Tahoe region a little too garish, Mammoth Mountain, about 150 miles to the south, may be more appealing. There is no lack of first-rate accommodations, but they are there solely for skiing. Mammoth started out as one of skiing's little acorns and gradually worked its way up into one of the sport's massive oaks. Mammoth is large, and it will be larger. Its season almost invariably lasts from November through June, one of its major attractions for promising young racers. Another is its owner, Dave McCoy, who has a special soft spot

Skiing over a cornice at Sugar Bowl, a popular area for San Francisco society.

The base lodge at Mt. Shasta in northern California.

for competitors. There are few outstanding American racers who haven't received part of their training from McCoy. All this is reflected in the atmosphere of the area.

Snow conditions in the High Sierra region of California are unusually reliable, so reliable in fact that there is more apt to be too much snow than too little. At least once a year, the Sierra resorts are overwhelmed by a massive snowfall which may drop as much as two feet an hour for days at a time. So there is always a certain risk that you will get snowed in. There is also a good likelihood that the snow will be on the wet side. Warmed by the brilliant Sierra sun, it can make for sticky going, particularly in the latter part of the season.

Sun and High Sierras: the Far West

Standing alone in the northern part of California, Mt. Shasta looks down from every direction like a massive white city. Until the 1850's Shasta was an active volcano, and the Indians believed that the great spirit had made the mountain his wigwam and built a fire in its center. The area has managed to maintain an atmosphere of solitude and beauty despite the network of lifts and facilities which are still being added. High above timberline, Shasta offers open bowl skiing with many different routes of descent and a season which runs from late November to the beginning of June. Panoramic skiing, friendly people and informal living all help make Shasta a prime ski area.

If there is a distinctive characteristic to California skiing, it is the tempo of its development. Skiing in the state came very much into its own with the 1960 Winter Olympics. It hasn't stopped growing since. Like other things in California, it is rapidly becoming somewhat larger than life size. Midway between Los Angles and San Francisco, at the Sierra town of Porterville, Walt Disney announced in 1965 plans to build a multi-million dollar ski resort, Mineral King. Such are the dimensions of the California ski boom.

CHAPTER 23

The deepest and longest-lasting snow: northwest and alaska

IF THERE is a central condition to skiing in the Pacific Northwest, it is that its two largest cities, Portland and Seattle, are within an hour's drive of the snow-rich Cascade Mountains. The two cities are well known for their damp climate. Next to Midwestern skiers, the Pacific Northwest specie is one of the most joked about and one of the hardiest of the breed. Most of the jokes originate in the Northwest, and one suspects that skiers of the region take a certain masochistic delight in describing their suffering.

Actually, they don't suffer too much. The snow may occasionally be on the damp side, but like the skiers it is of a hardy variety, perfectly capable of resisting an occasional downpour. Moreover it comes early, stays late and is

The chair lift at Snoqualmie Summit, just 46 miles from Seattle.

deep. Thousands of skiers may scrape away at it, but because it is wet and packs well, it resists these abrasions admirably.

Northwest skiing has the advantage of being eminently available. The Seattle or Portland skier merely has to throw his skis in the car and drive for an hour or so to get all the skiing he wants—a choice of three areas on the flanks of Mount Hood if he lives in Portland; a choice of three areas in Snoqualmie Pass if he lives in Seattle.

It is really just that simple. The only difficulty the skier is likely to encounter is finding a parking space. There will be thousands of others who had exactly the same idea. It is estimated that one out of ten residents of these two cities skis.

If there is a drawback to this convenience, it is that it has left facilities on the skimpy side. Although there are signs of change, you are expected to go and return on the same day. Apres-ski consists mostly of what Portland and Seattle have to offer in the way of night life. Furthermore, the areas closest to these cities tend to be of the pipe rack variety. The rope tow is still the staple of uphill transportation, although chairlifts are available at all areas.

An exception to this state of affairs is Timberline Lodge on Mount Hood, one of the most massive mountain hostelries ever built. It has survived long years of mismanagement, but is now efficiently run, if slightly awesome. If summer skiing is your wish, you are most likely to find it there. The slopes from the lodge on up are rarely without snow. The lodge is also headquarters of a summer racing school. A similar school and excellent late season skiing also exist at Mt. Baker, Crystal Mt., and other areas.

Signaling a major shift in Pacific Northwest ski offerings is Crystal Mountain in the shadow of Mount Rainier, about eighty miles from Seattle. Not only is Crystal elegantly equipped with lifts, but in its relatively short life it has sprouted good restaurants and a wide range of accomodations.

Somewhat senior to Crystal is White Pass, a popular resort with skiers from the eastern part of the state. White Pass had more primitive beginnings than Crystal, but it now features half-million-dollar White Pass Village, which is beginning to take care of the area's accommodations problem.

Timberline Lodge at Mt. Hood, Oregon.

Mt. Baker, Washington, is a summer skiing mecca.

Crystal Mountain, Washington; late lingering snows permit the holding of a summer race camp.

Perhaps the most competition-minded area in the Pacific Northwest is Mt. Bachelor, near Bend, Oregon. Bachelor owes much of its reputation to its close identification with racing. It is the site of the annual summer training camp held for the American ski team. It is also one of the larger areas in the Northwest, with a wide variety of terrain, much of it geared to more advanced skiers.

While vacation-type offerings are becoming more diverse in the Pacific Northwest, Northwesterners still make up the majority of guests at Sun Valley. In one of those curious trends, they have taken to breaking up the 750-mile trip with skiing stops at Spout Springs, between Walla Walla, Washington, and Pendleton, Oregon, or at Anthony Lakes near Baker, Oregon, two small but charming areas with considerable appeal. (Another such possible stop is Bogus Basin, near Boise, Idaho.)

The Deepest and Longest-Lasting Snow: Northwest and Alaska

Although it has a reputation as the land of snow and ice, Alaska was late in its ski arrival. Rapid strides have been made since snowshoes were the favored mode of winter transportation. Alyeska, not far from Anchorage, is a major area by any measure and has lots of snow, a long season and surprisingly mild temperatures. The site of the 1963 National Championships, Alyeska has many open slopes and dramatic vistas. The sourdough atmosphere is prevalent, but there is also a considerable international flavor since Anchorage is a major stop of the trans-polar airlines.

The sparsity of the population has prevented other major developments in Alaska (although there are five areas in addition to Alyeska), but the incredible mountains of the state are receiving more and more recognition as targets for ski adventures. There are magnificent glaciers covered with snow the year around, and many peaks still unclimbed. As skiers look for new horizons, they are bound to seek out the mountains of Alaska.

Alyeska, Alaska, offers skiing by the ocean (note inlet at top left).

CHAPTER 24

Canada

THE AVERAGE American skier thinks of Canadian skiing as merely a northerly extension of skiing in certain American regions. Thus the Eastern skier who goes to the Laurentians in Quebec still considers himself skiing in the East. He finds it hard to realize that he is skiing in a foreign country.

Skiers are inveterate border crossers, and Canadians are no exception to this rule. While thousands head north to the Laurentians, an equal number will head for Stowe, Jay Peak and the more northern American resorts.

However, there are differences. The Canadians are polite by instinct, but, depending on where you ski, there is no mistaking the French or British heritage of the country. This subtle altering of atmosphere can often be more delightful than a sharp switch, say from Midwestern skiing to Austrian skiing.

For the Canada-bound skier, a handy if rather glib rule of thumb is: the Canadian Rockies for adventure; Quebec for romance; Ontario if you have friends in Toronto; and Vancouver for a short drive to the lift.

The truth of the matter is that the state of Canadian skiing is changing rapidly. Canadian racers are moving into the front ranks after years of obscurity. Canadian ski instructors teach their own excellent technique (which also

Skiing on Mt. Temple near Lake Louise in the Canadian Rockies.

213

The Mt. Norquay Lodge and Ski Shop at Banff.

has followers among American instructors). The country has more skiers per capita than the United States. And, if skiing can be described as booming in the United States, it is exploding north of the border. If there is a hill near a town, it is bound to have a ski lift.

Skiing may seem less concentrated in Canada, but this is only an illusion. Canada is larger than the United States geographically, but its population is only one tenth of ours. With the exception of the prairie provinces, you'll find skiing wherever you go.

Of the few major ski resorts in the Canadian Rockies, Banff is the best known. Promoted as the site of the 1976 Winter Olympics, it is on the Canadian Pacific transcontinental railroad and a 90-minute drive from Calgary. The skiing is concentrated on rugged Mt. Norquay. Lodging is plentiful, except on weekends, and is varied. Keep in mind that the huge Banff Springs Hotel you see featured on all those Canadian travel ads is shut tight in winter. Alberta liquor laws somewhat restrict the night life, but there are exotic hot mineral baths. For the week or two-week vacationer, Sunshine Village is something special. A bus takes you up the rugged road from Banff to Sunshine and deposits you in beautiful scenery and deep powder. The skiing is easy, the setting exhilarating. The lodge is a little gem, intimate, musical and bring-your-own-bottle.

214

The main lodge, Sunshine Village.

About forty miles northwest of Banff on the main rail and highway route is the Lake Louise ski region. There are a number of excellent lodges with accent on the informal. A gondola lift takes you up Mt. Whitehorn for morning skiing. As the sun shifts, skiers move to the slopes of Temple, a ski circuit reminiscent of those in the Alps.

On the British Columbia side of the Rockies, there is fine powder skiing at Tod Mountain, an hour's drive from Kamloops. Here is North America's longest chairlift (9,413 feet) and a vertical drop greater than at Sun Valley. Lodge life is pleasantly informal and personal, lift lines are short.

Scattered along the border all the way to Vancouver are numerous smaller areas, of which Red Mountain near Rossland is the largest. This area is a community venture and has recently undergone refinement and expansion. The racing fever is at a high pitch here.

Vancouver has skiing in its back yard, literally. The areas—Mt. Seymour and Grouse Mountain—can be reached with ease by means of the city's bus system. When the weather is right—Vancouver suffers from the Pacific Northwest syndrome—you get a magnificent view of the city and the harbor area. The ski areas are well equipped to handle the large crowds they attract. Snow is plentiful, if occasionally wet.

Only sixty miles from downtown Vancouver is Garibaldi Park and **215**

WHERE TO SKI

Diamond Head Chalet, highly recommended for ski mountaineering types. A recent addition to this vicinity is Whistler Mountain.

At the opposite end of the country, the province of Quebec has acquired so many lifts it gets more difficult every year to count them—plus snow-making machinery, limited-access highways and motor inns. Despite these changes, skiing in the province seems to have lost none of its foreign allure to Eastern American skiers. They are nostalgically determined that somehow

Banff Springs mineral baths.

Heavy traffic on Mt. Seymour near Vancouver, British Columbia.

Garibaldi Provincial Park in British Columbia offers varied terrain for every type of touring and downhill skiing. Mt. Garibaldi in the background was once an active volcano.

they will still be met at the station by horse-drawn sleigh complete with pipe-smoking old *habitant* who will fill them with home-brewed pea soup on arrival at the simple rustic lodge heated by glowing cast-iron stove. That little of this still exists in the Laurentians seems to deter no one. After all, an exotic French continues to be spoken, the food is great, and the tables still are flecked with the foam of overflowing steins of Molson's ale. And it is still necessary to make reservations two years ahead if you want Christmas accommodations at Mt. Tremblant Lodge or Gray Rocks Inn. Nor have the resort names lost their allure: Chalet Cochand, Val David, St. Gabriel de Branden, Chantecler.

If somewhat less romantic than pictured, skiing in Quebec has become more exciting, particularly in the fast-expanding Eastern Townships region. A cluster of areas has sprung up just north of the Vermont line, in the vicinity of Sherbrooke, of a more than respectable size and with the old romantic appeal. For the ultimate in old-world charm, there is a small group of areas around Quebec City, including Mont Ste. Anne which is served by an aerial tramway.

Ontario is a gigantic regional complex, much along the lines of the Midwest. There are more than one hundred areas in the province, mostly served by ropetows and T-bars. The denizens of this region have strong tendencies to spend their ski vacations at areas other than those in Ontario. Nevertheless, or because of it, Ontario areas have in recent years acquired luxury touches, such as chairlifts, swimming pools, airstrips, first-class accommodations and a thriving after-ski life. The areas featuring such amenities are Collingwood, Blue Mountain, Georgian Peaks, Talisman, Mansfield Skiway, Rainbow Ridge and Sir Sam's Inn.

Overall, Canadian skiing offers dependable snow at the occasional risk of very cold weather. Take an extra sweater, also your driver's license for border identification. Otherwise you'll need nothing extra to enjoy Canadian skiing.

Gray Rocks Inn in the Laurentians. Mt. Tremblant stands in the background.

A Swiss mountain guide instructs a party before crossing the "Eismeer" in the Jungfrau district of Switzerland.

CHAPTER 25

Land of ski and apres-ski: europe's alps

ALPINE EUROPE is the beau ideal of the ski world—and with good reason. It is here that skiing as we know it today started. Here is the original; no copy can ever quite match it.

There is a picture of skiing in Europe: vast mountains with giant lifts; skiing from romantic village to romantic village and from country to country; long, long runs with stops halfway to indulge in incredibly delicious pastries at a picturesque mountain hut; handsome ski instructors with bevies of the famous and exotic in tow; five-course lunches while basking in the sun at an exhilarating altitude of 10,000 feet; and all of this at two-thirds the price at what you would pay in the United States.

The remarkable thing about this picture is that a good portion of it is true. Still, for the skier who plans to spend three weeks or longer in Europe, **221** a few realistic strokes should be added. There are flaws in the picture, and no one should spend a thousand dollars without being aware of them.

First there is the matter of prices. They are no longer as low as they once were. In fact, they are not much lower than prices for certain services in the United States. The mistake that many make is to view a European trip as an economy vacation. It isn't and shouldn't be. A European trip is something special, and the fun can be easily spoiled if one skimps for the sake of a few dollars.

Snow and weather are not always ideal. While the snow is more dependable than in the Eastern U.S., the weather is much the same. Resorts can be fogged in for a week or more at a time. When this happens the higher slopes particularly are not very skiable.

In high season especially, the lift lines can be horrifying, both in their length and in the behavior of the people. For reasons not entirely clear, the otherwise polite Europeans have never taken to orderly queuing. Be prepared to defend yourself by any means.

Those long, long runs are wonderful, but they are likely to include long

Davos, with 10,000 inhabitants, is one of the largest of Europe's ski resorts.

flats, one reason they are so long. They wouldn't be tolerated without sneering comment at any American or Canadian resort. Unless there is a specific purpose for taking such a run, avoid them. As for those village to village tours, they are fine if you want to go sightseeing. But the trip back may be time consuming unless there are lift connections. You may end up with less daily vertical footage than you would have in a small area at home.

Because powder snow in the Western sense is scarce, European skiing takes relatively little advantage of those wide-open slopes. Usually they are crossed by way of marked tracks, which are icy on occasion. Off these trails, the snow may be crusty or soggy. Unless you know how to handle conditions of this kind stay on the *piste*, or else hire a guide or ski instructor.

While Alpine Europe turns out the world's best racers, its recreational skiers are below the level of the average American skier—and a good deal more stubborn in the matter of taking lessons. Don't count on the skier in front of you knowing what he is doing, even if the trail is for experts.

Unless you are an old hand at European skiing, stay with the established resorts—the ones everyone talks about. In the first place, they are more likely to fit the picture painted at the beginning of this section; in the second place, those little unknown gems are likely to be unknown for good reason. They are probably no better than what you would find at home and may have no one who speaks English.

With these illusions out of the way, you are prepared to fully enjoy Alpine Europe. As we said at the beginning, the remarkable thing about the popular picture is that so much of it is true.

Barring an unlucky turn in the weather, you can count on the skiing at the major resorts to be superb. And if you get to the lift when it opens in the morning, you'll avoid a great portion of the crowds even in high season. By the time the Europeans get out to ski, you can be up and away in the high country, skiing to your heart's content. Those European networks of lifts can be marvelous. Considering the cost, a guide is a good investment. He will jockey you around from place to place so that you always have the best combination of sun and snow, regardless of the time of day.

Ski terrain in the Dolomites. Note stand-up baskets used for lifts.

Val d'Isere, France, has one of the longest ski seasons in Europe.

Land of Ski and Apres-Ski: Europe's Alps

If European skiing has an advantage over North American skiing, it lies not so much in the vastness of its slopes or the variety of its terrain as in the multitude of its exposures. With few exceptions, weather conditions in the United States are such that ski areas must have northern exposures to guarantee snow. This is not the case at the major European resorts. Following the very best snow through the day can be a rewarding and fascinating experience.

By all means reserve a day or two for a glacier tour. Climbing on skis may not be your forte, but if a long run (without disconcerting flats) is your desire, your effort will be well repaid. Besides, an overnight stay at a European mountain hut, preferably one manned by a farm family, is a wonderful experience unique to Europe. You will get more of the atmosphere of grass roots European skiing there than at a first-class hotel.

It is off the slopes that Europe comes into its own. The development of American type ski resorts has reduced somewhat the glamour of the European ski village, but it hasn't changed its service. It is not so much what is done as how it's done that accounts for European flair. From the chef and *maitre d'hotel*

Breaking a trail up the Mt. Collon Glacier on the way to Zermatt.

down, the employees are professionals, dedicated by tradition and training to serving you. Dinner under these circumstances is not a meal, but an occasion. One experiences a sense of luxury, even at an ordinary hotel.

Europeans, especially Europeans who go to ski resorts, are a sophisticated people. This sophistication is reflected in their after-ski life. Quite possibly because Europeans are not as leisure-oriented as Americans and look to their vacation as a chance to splurge for the season, they expect more from their resorts in the way of after-ski entertainment. Music and entertainers will be first-rate, and the evening meal, as already noted, will be superb. The night club you go to for a finishing liqueur will be sparkling and gay. You will leave an Alpine resort feeling that you have lived.

Alpine Europe, a geographical region no larger than Colorado, offers every conceivable atmosphere. The Austrians are the gayest (if in a slightly compulsive way); the Swiss the most conservative; the French the most elegant; and the Italians the most energetic. Their resorts reflect these characteristics. Gstaad may cater to the jet set and St. Moritz to the wealthy and aristocratic (titled and otherwise), but underlying both of these Swiss resorts is Swiss solidity and competence. In Austria, Kitzbuehel may mean new money and St. Anton may mean tradition, but both are Austrian to the core;

a little ragged at the edges, not quite as neat and tidy as Switzerland, but *wie gemütlich*. Chamonix may be gloomy, Val d'Isere very fashionable, and Courchevel the closest thing to an American ski area in Europe, but one can never get away from Gallic style either in architecture, your ski instructor's wit or on the lift (some go around corners). Sestriere's silo hotels may seem grotesque and Cortina almost frigidly elegant, but the Italians insist on living with explosive force, as though every day were their last. There are shadings within these distinctions, but never expect a European resort to present any other nationality than its own. There is no "Little Bit of Switzerland" in Austria.

You will find European skiing different. Americans are used to hard sport, they ski from morning until the lifts close. Europeans prefer not to exert themselves that much. By all means ski to your heart's content, but try to do it the European way, too. Have breakfast in bed (unless you want to beat the crowds to the lifts), take maybe one leisurely run, have a big lunch, work it off skiing, come down when the sun gets low (but not too low), have afternoon coffee and pastries, attend the tea dance, have a long, leisurely dinner, dance, and stay up until the wee hours sipping liqueur. It's not a bad life at all, and it's easy to get used to.

Silo hotels at Sestriere, Italy.

Far left:
Megève in France is ski home of Brigitte Bardot, French jet set.

Left:
Liechtenstein, where European royalty skis.

CHAPTER 26

Exotic mountains of other lands

IF SKIING is your excuse for traveling, you need not confine yourself to Alpine Europe. Your opportunities are global.

Aside from the Bavarian corner of Germany, which is truly Alpine, there are many German mountains suitable for skiing. They are not as spectacular as the Alps, their facilities are less glamorous, but they have a degree of native flavor no longer present in the tourist-conscious Alps. Further to the east, Czechoslovakia, Yugoslavia and Poland have sizable Alpine installations of which Zakopane in Poland, the site of the 1939 FIS World Alpine Championships and the 1962 FIS World Nordic Championships, is the most famous. After you get through the forbidding paperwork, you will find that resorts in these countries have native, if not sophisticated charm, and that you are genuinely welcome there. If anything, the welcome will be almost too effusive.

Stein Eriksen skiing in New Zealand's Alps.

229

WHERE TO SKI

Many people will want to know if you are acquainted with their American relatives.

There are alpine resorts in Norway and Sweden developing along Alpine European lines, but the real charm of the Scandinavian countries is in the thousands of miles of touring trails. Scandinavian touring should not be confused with the Alpine variety. Most of it is over easy, rolling terrain for which the narrow lightweight skis are ideal. While touring, you'll find lots of company. It's the national sport in these countries. The natives think nothing of going 30 to 40 miles on a day's outing. This may seem incredible until you get the hang of the art. Not nearly as much effort is involved as the distances imply. If refreshments are needed, they come out of your own rucksack, and there are lots of warming huts along the trail. Language in the Scandinavian countries is no problem as most Scandinavians speak English.

The mountains of Yugoslavia photographed at a ski meet at Planica near Kranjska Gora.

The aerial tram station at Kuznice,
near Zakopane, Poland.

Cross-country touring from
hut to hut in Norway.

WHERE TO SKI

There is skiing in some surprising corners of Europe. The Pyrenees are well endowed, both on the French and the Spanish sides. There is skiing in Scotland, although it is of a rather rugged nature, combining some of the worst elements of the East, Midwest and Pacific Northwest. Nevertheless the Scots claim to enjoy it. Such postage stamp countries as Liechtenstein and Monaco also have skiing. It is virtually impossible to go anywhere in Europe without finding skiing somewhere within easy driving or train distance.

There is skiing even in the Middle East. Moroccans ski on surprisingly reliable snow in the Atlas Mountains, and there are beautiful open slopes in the shadows of the Cedars of Lebanon. And in Iran, the Shah is a great patron of skiing and there are two big areas. There is an oriental atmosphere to all of these ski areas, and seasoned travelers recommend them providing you know what you are doing, have a sense of humor and are prepared for the unexpected.

At the other end of Asia, the Japanese are fanatic skiers. After their American-trained Chick Igaya won a silver medal in the 1956 Olympics and a bronze medal at the 1958 FIS World Championships in Badgastein, they sought to establish skiing on a large scale—but without the necessary preparation. As a result, Japanese ski areas are overcrowded, highly hazardous unless you are used to the Japanese way of doing things, and amusing (if you are a spectator). But there is evidence of order evolving out of this chaos. In recent years, the Japanese have been sending highly disciplined ski teams to major world events in both alpine and nordic competition, and the teams have done remarkably well. Although the vast cost of the trip rules out going to Japan for a ski vacation, the country can provide interesting skiing if you happen to be there on business or courtesy of Uncle Sam. Accommodations are Japanese style—novel, picturesque and somewhat chilly.

If you want to reverse your season, in other words have a real ski vacation during the North American summer, South America, Australia and New Zealand offer the answer.

Portillo, Chile, is without question the most sophisticated resort in the Southern hemisphere. Although isolated in the Andes, accommodations, instruction and slopes are first-rate; you will find the atmosphere more

232

There are more than three million skiers in Japan.

St. Moritz than Santiago. More representative of the country is Farellones-La Parva, but the facilities are of the clubby variety. There is also limited skiing in Argentina, Colombia and Bolivia. These countries have no lack of mountains with snow, but there are few lifts and fewer facilities.

Both New Zealand and Australia are rich in ski terrain, and as everywhere else the sport is booming Down Under. There are more than a dozen highly

WHERE TO SKI

developed resorts with complete facilities, much along the lines of American resorts. Skiing in these two countries has a history quite similar to skiing in the United States, although their boom did not start until after World War II. The skiing in New Zealand is more alpine in nature than it is in Australia. The leading resort is Mt. Ruapehu on the North Island. The South Island is less developed, but has some spectacular glacier runs. In contrast, the so-called Australian Alps are more like our New England mountains, with about the same elevation. Resorts are developing rapidly, but public facilities are often

Sun Deck Chalet, an alpine resort in the Perisher Valley, on the slopes of Mt. Kosciusko in the Australian Alps.

The Gran Hotel Portillo in Chile, scene of the 1966 FIS alpine races.

The essence of Australia's ski terrain: a lot of overhangs, due to many blizzards, and dead trees, because of bush fires in summer.

in short supply. The atmosphere is quite British in New Zealand, highly individualistic in Australia. Americans usually find themselves more at ease with the Australians, who are quite American in outlook and at least as enthusiastic about the sport.

This survey of skiing on this continent and around the world is of necessity sketchy. You will find more details on each resort in Appendix A, along with the names of state and national tourist offices which can provide colorful and informative travel folders.

Part Four

LEARNING TO SKI

CHAPTER 27

The best way to learn

SKIING IS surprisingly easy to learn. Reasonable competence can be reached with about a dozen lessons from a good instructor. Expert skiing—meaning parallel skiing with speed on all types of terrain and snow conditions— can take several months or several years to learn, depending on how much you ski and how dedicated you are. Fortunately, the pleasures of skiing are open to anyone, whether he winds his way down the mountain with simple snowplows or covers the same terrain with exquisite wedeln turns.

What prevents many people from even giving skiing a try—though they'd like to—is the attitude expressed in the frequently uttered phrase, "I can't do that," *that* meaning a graceful run down a steep, exciting expert trail. Naturally *that* can't be done right away, nor can a half gainer off the diving board or driving a golf ball 250 yards.

For some unexplained reason, non-skiers seem to feel that expert skiers were born with skis already on their feet. Actually, there is a logical, relatively simple progression of steps which can make anyone an expert—in time and at almost any age. Naturally, it is easier to learn when you are young, but there are expert skiers at almost every age, including the late seventies.

Skiing, it should be remembered, is a highly individualized sport. There is no score. The satisfaction comes from doing, and only the skier himself can

239

measure this satisfaction. While speed is certainly a factor, it is too frequently overstressed. Mere speed doesn't make an expert; the ability to handle yourself well, whatever may come your way, does. Not long ago, someone suggested the classification called "the capable skier," that is, a skier who lacks certain refinements, but who knows how to hold his own. There are a lot of impressive skiers who do not know how to do the latest wiggles. There is no point to relegating them forever to the ranks of the intermediates.

Perhaps the most important single piece of advice for any skier or would-be skier is to *relax*. It is a constant theme, not only during the learning process, but also when skiing on your own. If as a finished skier you have one of those days when nothing seems to go right, the chances are that you have become tense and are not allowing your muscles to do what comes naturally.

Most of us have had some fear of height and high places since babyhood. In skiing, one of the major reasons for muscle-knotting tension is fear, a perfectly reasonable emotion if you've never been on skis before or are about to take a steep trail for the first time. The only way to overcome it is to discover what is scaring you and divide it into a series of maneuvers that you can learn to handle. This is essential in any learning process, but particularly in skiing. Only with practice is it possible to link the parts together and to recognize the difficulties of the slope below you. What seems awesome at first quickly becomes more acceptable. Learning to ski, particularly in the initial stages, is about 30 per cent getting to know the technical aspects and 70 per cent building your confidence.

In learning, be particularly wary of well-intentioned friends who would like to teach you how to ski. They are probably excellent skiers, but they have long forgotten what it was like to be a beginner; they don't know any of the hundreds of tricks instructors use to get people to ski correctly; and, although they don't say so, they are actually very anxious themselves to be off and skiing on steep trails and slopes.

Ski school, of course, is the answer. But before you report to the ski school meeting place, do yourself, your fellow students and your instructor a big favor by arriving prepared. One of the best ways to get prepared is to

A school for novice skiers at Hunter Mountain, New York.

attend a dryland ski school. These schools are staged by some ski areas, by ski clubs and by ski shops. Their programs include familiarization with equipment and how to use it, some of the beginning maneuvers, a few light exercises and a movie on skiing. The dryland ski school is not a substitute for snow ski school, but it will help you progress faster once you are on snow because you will be familiar with the language of the instructor and what he is trying to accomplish.

It should be stressed that ski school is not only for the learning skier. If you find yourself in unfamiliar terrain and snow conditions, a lesson is the easiest way of becoming familiar with the area. The social enjoyment and competitive goal of learning in a group should also not be overlooked.

Ski school procedure is simple and practical, and more or less standard at most resorts. You register for a lesson at a desk in the base lodge. Depending on how many lessons you buy, you either get a ticket or a book of tickets. **241**

LEARNING TO SKI

Most group lessons run for two hours. At the designated time, students assemble at the ski school meeting place where they are classified by the type of turns they can make. If you haven't taken a lesson in this particular school before, it is a good idea to have a relatively modest opinion of your abilities. If your stem is on the ragged side, say so because it will soon be discovered, by which time you may have spoiled the lesson for others in the class.

Private lessons—that is, lessons where you have the instructor to yourself, or at most share him with one or two others of your own choosing—have much to be said for them, particularly if you are easily embarrassed. Aside from the additional expense, however, the beginning skier is not really in a position to get full benefit from such a lesson. He will probably find that too much physical effort is required. Even in a class of half a dozen or so, he usually finds himself getting more work than he can handle.

Experienced skiers are in a better position to benefit from a private lesson. If you want to work on certain phases of technique or to shed an undesirable skiing habit, a private lesson may be a quick answer to your problem.

In the beginning stages, the instructor will first line up his class, demonstrate a maneuver and then ask each of his students to do the same. There will be some repetition, then a change to another exercise. Gradually the pieces will be put together, and the lessons reach higher levels of proficiency. At the point where the class can negotiate a good portion of the hill with reasonable dexterity, instruction will change—there will be less lecturing and more skiing. The instructor will lead his class down the hill, making corrections and criticisms during the brief rest periods. This may, at times, not seem much of a lesson, but what the good instructor is doing is to steadily push the learning skier to higher and higher levels of performance by either skiing faster or by going over more difficult terrain.

While ski schools have a great record for making skiers out of people who allegedly were miserable failures in their high school physical education classes, there is a limit to what a ski school can do for you, no matter how good its instructors.

CHAPTER 28

Conditioning and warm-up

ONE OF the best ways to speed up the learning process and, at the same time, to enjoy the sport is to be in adequate physical condition. Not only is the sport more enjoyable when you are in shape, but your chance of injury is substantially reduced. There is a considerable body of evidence to support this statement. For instance, a Westchester, N.Y., ski club averaged five thousand skiing days a year for eleven years with no fractures and only two mild sprains. During this time, pre-ski conditioning was practiced. When this program was abandoned, three fractures occurred within a year.

Strength, to be sure, is of some importance in skiing, but as Dr. Hans Kraus, a New York specialist in physical medicine and a member of the President's Physical Fitness Council, points out, it is muscular flexibility as much as strength, which protects the skier from injury. There is an old saying in skiing that the best safety bindings are well-conditioned muscles.

Willy Schaeffler, the highly successful coach of national champion Denver University, puts it another way: "Don't get in condition for skiing. Get in condition for living!" It is Schaeffler's contention that there is no need for dull, laborious "living-room" fitness programs in October if you hike, swim, water 243 ski, row, fence or play handball in summer or take a brisk half-hour walk every day when that isn't possible. It should be recognized that muscles *must work* to stay in shape. It does not matter whether this work is in the form of play or calisthentics. Its rewards are more than worthwhile: better skiing and a strong sense of well-being.

5BX PLAN FOR SKIERS

DR. WILLIAM ORBAN, author of the Royal Canadian Air Force 5BX *Plan for Physical Fitness,* developed a series of special exercises for skiers in *Ski* magazine which are demonstrated in the following pages. Here is what he has to say about this program:

> "To help skiers of any age achieve proper conditioning, I have designed a program of four basic exercises in three series—beginner, intermediate and advanced. In addition, there is a bonus exercise. The five exercises have been selected for their contribution to the conditioning of the muscles and joints which play an important role in skiing.
>
> "The first exercise is a mobilizing exercise designed to produce a greater range of movement in the ankles, knees and spinal column of a rotational nature.
>
> "Exercise two will develop the abdominal muscles which are used in the trunk and hip rotation so essential for certain maneuvers in skiing.
>
> "Exercise three is primarily for the development of lower and upper back muscles on which there is an additional demand in the skiing posture. Exercise three, particularly in the advanced series, will also improve the strength of the upper arm muscles needed for pole action.
>
> "Exercise four is the key exercise for strengthening the lower muscles of the limbs used in skiing as well as for strengthening the knee and ankle joints which are so prone to injury. The exercise also provides practice in dynamic balance if hands are kept on hips and an attempt is made to exercise by jumps on a designated mark on the floor.
>
> "Exercise five lays particular emphasis on strengthening the lower leg.
>
> "My exercises are designed to improve physical condition without soreness or stiffness in a minimum length of time when regularly performed. The exercises may be performed by men or women of any age with maximum

benefit as long as the directions for performing them are carefully and accurately followed. If you have any previous history which makes you feel uncertain about following the 5BX program, you should first obtain your physician's approval before starting.

"Physical conditioning will enable you to engage in skiing for more hours per day, more days a week and more years in a lifetime. It will also contribute to the prevention of injuries. Many injuries, particularly of the sprain variety, can be attributed to poor physical condition. Lack of strength in the muscles involved in skiing and lack of strength and mobility in the joints, particularly in the knees and ankles, contribute to the incidence of injuries. Furthermore, lack of organic or muscular endurance increases the onset of fatigue, frequently cited as a prime cause of injuries among weekend skiers.

"The principles of progression and overload have been completely utilized in the program. Progression enables the development of physical condition from a very low level to a very high level by increasing the rate at which each exercise is regularly and gradually performed. Each exercise, while remaining basically the same, increases in intensity (and difficulty because of increased resistance) as you graduate from series to series.

"It is important, therefore, when you undertake the exercises—regardless of your present physical condition—that you start with the first level of the

---

BEGINNERS SERIES: Number one exercise, five repetitions per minute for the first five days, then add three repetitions per day for five more days. Exercise number two, five repetitions per minute for first five days, add three per day for next five days. Exercise number three, five repetitions per minute for the first five days, then add three per day for the next five days. Exercise number four, 25 repetitions per two minutes, then add five per day for next five days.

INTERMEDIATE SERIES: Exercise number one, ten repetitions per minute for five days, add two per day for ten days. Exercise number two, ten repetitions per minute for first five days, add two per day for two weeks. Exercise number three, ten repetitions per minute for first five days, then add two per day for ten days. Exercise number four, 30 repetitions per two minutes for first five days, add seven per day for ten days.

ADVANCED SERIES: Exercise number one, ten repetitions per minute for first five days, add one per day for 30 days. Exercise number two, ten repetitions per minute for first five days, then add one per day for thirty days. Exercise number three, ten repetitions per minute for first five days, then add one per day for thirty days. Exercise number four, 30 per two minutes for five days, then add five per day for 30 days.

245

EXERCISE ONE

BEGINNER: Starting position is with feet parallel and flat on floor about shoulder width apart, hands clasped behind head, elbows back. To perform the exercise turn the upper trunk slowly toward the left, twisting as far as possible without losing balance and without moving the feet. Slowly return to starting position, then twist to the right as far as possible allowing the hips and thighs to follow trunk without moving feet. Returning to starting position completes one repetition. This movement should be slow and performed without any jerking action.

INTERMEDIATE: The starting position is the same as exercise one of the beginner's series except that the arms are held horizontal and at shoulder height to the trunk. Exercise is also performed in the same manner except that when the rotation is made, the head is turned to follow the arm which is moved backward. The arm should be pushed as far back as possible without moving the feet. The rotation should be in a twist from the ankles and hips. One rotation with each arm completes one repetition.

EXERCISE TWO

BEGINNER: Starting position is lying on back, feet straight together with arms stretched to the side, palms flat on floor. The exercise is performed by lifting left and right leg alternately across the body so that the raised foot comes directly above the hand. The other foot and hand maintain contact with the floor during this movement. The second movement of the exercise is raising the left foot to a position over the right hand and returning to the starting position.

INTERMEDIATE: Starting position is the same as the beginner's series. The first movement of this exercise is raising both legs simultaneously so that the left knee is almost directly over the right shoulder. The legs then are returned to the starting position. The second movement of the exercise is raising the legs simultaneously so that the right knee is vertically above the left shoulder before returning to the starting position. These two movements complete one repetition of the exercise.

EXERCISE THREE

BEGINNER: Starting position is lying flat on the back with arms by sides and hands flat on floor. The exercise is performed by lifting the buttocks just high enough to clear the floor. The complete length of the arms, shoulders, head and heels maintain contact with the floor during the entire exercise.

INTERMEDIATE: Starting position for this exercise is lying on the back, arms by sides, hands flat on the floor as in exercise two of the beginner's series. Now move the feet close to the buttocks by bending the knee. The buttocks should be on the floor and the feet flat before the exercise is performed. The exercise is performed by raising the buttocks and forcing the hips upward as high as possible. Feet should remain flat; the head, shoulders and the entire length of the arm should maintain contact with the floor during the entire performance. Each time the hips are raised is one repetition.

ADVANCED: Starting position of this exercise is similar to the beginner's except that the arms are held across the chest with the upper arm horizontal from the shoulder. The exercise is performed by swinging the left arm backwards to rotate the upper trunk, the hips, knee and ankles as far as possible without moving the initial placement of the feet. The first movement is completed by returning to the starting position and bending the arm. The second movement of the exercise is the flinging of the right arm backwards, rotating the trunk and hips to the right and backwards as far as possible. One repetition is completed when the initial starting position is assumed after the second movement.

ADVANCED: Starting position is the same as the beginner's series. Exercise is performed by raising both legs together, then lowering them to touch floor just beyond the fingertip before returning to starting position. The second movement of the exercise is performed by repeating first movement but touching floor to the right. The completion of these two movements is one repetition of the exercise.

ADVANCED: Starting position is the same as in exercise three of the intermediate series. The exercise is performed by raising the buttocks and the shoulders off the floor forcing the hips and chest upwards as high as possible. Force for the movement is applied at the elbows, the back of head and the feet. Only the feet, lower arm and back of head should be in contact with the floor when hips are raised. One repetition is completed when buttocks are lowered to the starting position.

EXERCISE FOUR

BEGINNER: Starting position is feet wide astride with hands on hips. The exercise is performed by alternately jumping from one foot to the other to the outside of two imaginary parallel lines which are a leg-length apart. Cause your entire weight to shift from one foot to the other as you jump from side to side across the parallel line. Each time the foot touches the floor completes one repetition.

INTERMEDIATE: Starting position is hands on hips, feet together. Exercise is performed by jumping from side to side while keeping the knees and feet together. The distance of the jumps should be between one-and-one-half to two foot-lengths apart. Both feet should come in full contact with the floor each time.

ADVANCED: Starting position is the same as exercise five for the intermediate series. It is performed by jumping from side to side, keeping and landing on both feet together. Distance should not be less than three foot-lengths apart. Each jump is one repetition.

BONUS EXERCISE FIVE

STARTING POSITION of a bonus exercise for the ladies but from which men can receive benefit as well. Place hands flat on the wall or immovable object about chest high, then move feet backwards until heels are just making contact with the floor.

EXECUTION is performed by raising both heels together as high as possible before lowering them to the starting position. Raising and lowering of the heels constitutes one repetition.

BONUS: Because of high-heel shoes and the subsequent shortening of the Achilles' tendon, an exercise to produce an adequate mobility in the ankle joint is recommended for women. However, men can gain benefits from this exercise too because it does help to mobilize the ankle joint as well as increase the strength of the muscles of the lower leg. The schedule for this exercise should be as follows: two repetitions the first five days, about five seconds apart and increasing one repetition per day for the next 45 days till the completion of the training schedule. The exercise may be performed as rapidly as desirable after the first five days but up till that time the five second interval should be maintained.

beginner series in order to prevent discomfort. No matter how physically fit you may feel, you are courting trouble with muscle soreness if you undertake a new exercise without specifically conditioning your muscles for it. So perform the allotted number of exercises in the unit of time given for that exercise. This means that if five repetitions of an exercise are suggested for one minute, they should be evenly spaced so as to take the full one minute.

"Time units are established for individuals twenty years or younger. Anyone over twenty years of age should add one second for every year on to the time allotted. For example, if an individual is forty years old, he should add forty seconds to the time allotted to each exercise. Women, in addition to this age factor, should add another fifteen seconds to the time allotted for each exercise. This means that if a woman is forty years old, she should add forty plus fifteen, or fifty-five seconds to each exercise time unit.

248

"In addition to the basic exercises, you should endeavor to strengthen arm and shoulder muscles by practicing regular pushups. To improve heart and lungs, I would heartily recommend a program of running, starting with a quarter mile (one large city block) and working up to the mile distance. Hiking in hill country also benefits both legs and wind.

"For best results with the 5BX program, follow directions carefully. Perform exercises gradually, remembering never to give in to the temptation to skip parts of the schedule or to accelerate repetitions."

WARM-UPS

MUCH of your conditioning effort will be negated if you fail to warm up either before your first run on a warm day or before every run on a chilly day. Usually a few kneebends and body twists are sufficient. The important thing is that you should feel loose before starting down the trail.

Even if you have taken a few warm-up exercises, ski the first few runs cautiously. When muscles are chilled it takes considerable effort to warm them up and you should avoid jarring stops or extreme maneuvers. A series of snowplow turns, which involve more body and leg motion, are better than schusses or long traverses, which usually require the body to be held in one position.

Another way to warm up is to sidestep and herringbone uphill until you feel yourself getting warm.

To keep legs warm on the chairlift, swing the legs to and fro to maintain circulation, being careful to watch that the chair isn't so low over the snow that you'll catch the tips of your skis. Slowly raising your legs and holding them out straight for a few seconds, then slowly lowering them is also a good way to strengthen your legs.

If normal warm-up exercises won't do the trick, by all means go inside to thaw out. If you ski with cold legs, you won't enjoy it very much, and you'll be needlessly risking injury as well.

Start your conditioning program now, warm up, stay loose. It pays off in good health and good skiing.

CHAPTER 29

The beginning

IN THE company of experienced skiers, the beginner may feel somewhat less than heroic. Yet, as he moves from one maneuver to the next and becomes master of his skis, no temporary feeling of inferiority can squelch his sense of accomplishment. The first no-fall downhill run with snowplow turns can be as thrilling to him as a smooth series of wedeln turns to the expert.

One of the achievements of modern skiing is the way it has reduced and simplified the learning process to an absolute minimum. But what remains is important and stays important, even if the skier should reach international racing ranks. Even the best skiers have occasion to use the snowplow and the stem turn. The beginner shouldn't be impatient in having to learn them.

From the very start, a cardinal law of skiing becomes clear: improperly or sloppily executed maneuvers end in falls, either immediately or when the skier gets on more difficult terrain. Even when it doesn't lead to a fall, faulty technique will soon tire a skier, particularly if he is skiing at high altitude. In skiing there is no way to fudge without paying a penalty in one form or another.

At some risk of being repetitious, we would like to repeat again: *RELAX*. The beginner, especially the adult beginner, has a natural fear of sliding down a slope uncontrolled. Yet he must not let this feeling—which is not fully justified if he is in ski school—get the best of him. Tense muscles have a mind of their own, and the very thing the skier tries to avoid actually happens. This is one of the reasons for this chapter—to prepare you for what is coming.

TERMINOLOGY

ONE of the major difficulties that hampers progress is a confusion of terms. Uphill, downhill, inside and outside have a disconcerting way of changing as the turn is made, and sometimes it is hard to tell which is which, particularly on certain types of terrain. A skier who has a clear grasp of terminology, who is not puzzled by terms a ski instructor will use, can learn much faster than one who has to have an explanation. A good way to practice and appreciate these terms is to get on a small slope at home and spell them out to yourself from the following explanations.

Uphill, Downhill

THE ski, edge, pole, arm, leg, and shoulder closest to the top of the hill, regardless of the angle of the skis to the hill, are *uphill*. Conversely, the ski, edge, pole, arm, leg and shoulder closest to the bottom of the hill are *downhill*. The confusion arises on two counts. When a skier makes a turn so that he faces in the opposite direction, everything that was uphill before becomes downhill and vice versa. When he comes straight down the hill and goes into a traverse or a turn, he must determine beforehand which will be the uphill and downhill side of the body.

Inside, Outside

ONCE a turn is started, it is customary to refer to the equipment and parts of the body to be on the *outside* (that is, farthest away from the center of the turn) or the *inside* (closest to the center of the turn). Thus, in a turn to the right, the right ski is the inside ski; in a turn to the left, it is the outside ski.

"Inside" and "outside" reference to edges should not be confused with the inside-outside terminology used in a turn. The inside edges are those on   **251** the big-toe side of the foot, the outside edges those on the little-toe side. This is constant, *regardless* of the location of the skis in relation to the hill.

Fall Line

THE fall line, as one instructor puts it, "is the fastest route between you and the bottom of the hill." By technical definition, it is the fastest and most direct way down. Therefore, if you want to pick up speed, you must get into the fall line. If you want to cut down on speed you must ski at some angle to it. This is known as a . . .

Traverse

ANY time the skier is at some angle to the fall line, he is traversing, regardless of whether he happens to be walking uphill or skiing downhill. In traversing on skis, the edges are the critical element.

Edges

ANY time the skis are not flat on the snow, they are on their edges. The "bite" of the edge is determined by its angle to the snow. The edges are the key to modern skiing, and any exercise or maneuver involving them should be practiced diligently. It will pay large dividends.

Method, Technique, Style and Teaching Devices

THIS is a source of much confusion and the cause of many semantic difficulties. There are frequent references to new techniques when in fact the subject is only a new teaching device or a new style. Unfortunately, ski instruction doesn't follow dictionary definitions too closely, mainly because the origins of much of the language of ski technique are to be found in French or German texts and many of the translations frequently leave a great deal to be desired.

For all practical purposes, *system*, *method* and *technique* mean the same thing, that is, a complete approach to skiing from the most elementary to the most advanced steps. In this way we talk about the Austrian, French or American technique, meaning by this the Austrian, French and American sys-

252

tems of describing the execution of everything from the snowplow to wedeln. These techniques may differ in minor degrees or quite substantially. The important thing is not to confuse technique with style. *Style* is the individual interpretation of a technique. Physiological differences, physical condition and personal idiosyncracies all may account for a difference in style without invalidating the fundamental technique. For instance, with the exception of the French, all ski schools use fundamentally the same technique—that is, a so-called counter-rotational technique. However, there are important stylistic differences between the various national schools, stylistic differences distinctive enough to identify the place where the skier learned to ski.

It is important not to confuse style or technique with *teaching devices*. In order to get across a certain point of technique, the instructor will have numerous teaching devices and exercises. Finding that one explanation doesn't penetrate, he may use a different approach to reach the same objective. This does not mean that he is teaching a different technique. The end result will be the same.

Formal techniques usually only go up to certain levels. They rarely get into refinements (skiing in special snow conditions are rarely spelled out), stunts or specialized racing techniques. However, these exist and better skiers learn them. This explains our approach in this section of the book. Generally, we use the American Technique up to wedeln, then go into a series of refinements as demonstrated by some of the best skiers in the world.

WALKING AND GLIDING

WALKING on skis is really no more difficult than walking without skis. The difficulty the beginner encounters is that the skis are intentionally slippery. To overcome this slipperiness on the level, the skier makes use of his poles and edges.

Walking on skis involves a step somewhat shorter than the one used in normal walking. Again, there is a pronounced shift of weight, from the ski to be moved forward to the ski remaining in place. This weight shift momentarily 253

Paul Valar demonstrates simple walking on skis. Right ski and left ski are alternately weighted.

"sets" the ski, enabling the skier to push off on his step. The skier also makes use of his poles. The pole and arm opposite the forward-moving leg move forward as the leg is moved forward and the pole planted in the snow. This enables the skier to pull against the pole in the first part of the stride and to brace against it when he brings the other leg forward.

If the skier is walking up a slight incline, he can prevent backslip by more bracing against the pole and by slightly edging his skis.

A more vigorous form of walking is gliding. Each gliding step is preceded by the skier going into a slight crouch. As he takes his forward step he rises out of his crouch and propels himself forward and upward, using the pole as an aid. The skis are then allowed to glide for a distance before the next step is taken.

Gliding: (*left to right*) leg and pole push, gliding, leg and pole push.

FALLING AND GETTING UP

ALL skiers fall, even the best of them. In skiing it is not considered a disgrace. You will soon learn to recognize an impending fall. Try if possible to stay on your feet, but when it becomes inevitable relax and enjoy it.

Don't fight a fall to the bitter end. Instead, try to fall backward and to one side, using your seat as a shock absorber.

To get up, simply swing your skis across the slope so that they are at a 90 degree angle to the fall line. Then tuck your legs under your hips and get up. If this is too difficult, use both poles, pushing them into the snow near your hips. Then, with one hand around the handles and the other around the poles near the basket, push down hard and get on your feet.

THE STEP-AROUND

SKIING in the modern sense means turning. The step-around is the simplest way to change directions. It also introduces the important concept of shifting weight from one ski to the other.

255

LEARNING TO SKI

The step-around is accomplished by moving the skis fan fashion, the pivot of the fan being either the tips or the tails of the skis. One ski is moved at a time, either the tip or the tail remaining in place, the skis opening into a V. The other ski is then brought alongside and the sequence is repeated until the desired direction is achieved.

The important aspect of this exercise is the *weight shift*. In order to move a ski, weight must be removed from it and transferred to the other ski. This is an almost automatic reaction, but it must be emphasized in skiing. In the step-around there should be a conscious transfer of weight to the stationary ski before the other ski is moved.

THE SIDE STEP

THE skier soon reaches a point where he no longer can walk up a hill. Back-slip becomes too pronounced and tiring as well. The side step is the simplest way to go uphill.

Sidestepping requires horizontal skis and small steps for easy transfer of weight. Upper ski must move up first.

The traverse side step is a combination of the side step with walking. There is a complete weight transfer to the upper ski, and the motion is unbroken. *From left to right:* upper ski weighted, lower ski weighted, upper ski weighted.

In the side step the skis are placed directly across the fall line and edged enough to prevent them from sliding downhill. The skier then moves the uphill ski uphill for about a foot and then draws the downhill ski alongside it. This is repeated until the desired altitude is gained.

If the slope is very steep, the skier can support himself with his poles. However, care should be taken not to rely on the poles to the point where they substitute for positive weightshift. The weightshift rule applies in side-stepping particularly. There must be no weight on the ski to be moved.

A frequent error in sidestepping is to be too ambitious. Too large steps result in awkward position; this makes sidestepping more tiring than it already is and may lead to a fall.

TRAVERSE SIDE STEP

In climbing longer distances you will soon find the side step excessively tiring. To reduce both the effort and the tedium of climbing, the traverse or diagonal side step will prove somewhat easier.

The traversing side step combines walking and sidestepping. Instead of going straight uphill, the skier walks across the slope, gaining altitude by moving the skis uphill slightly as well as ahead. The skis are edged at all times.

A frequent error in this approach to climbing is to move the ski up the hill too much for comfortable walking. The uphill motion of the ski is usually less than in the straight uphill side step.

LEARNING TO SKI

The purpose of the traverse side step is to gain both altitude and distance. The angle of the climb to the fall line of the slope is governed both by the destination to be reached and the steepness of the slope. If the slope is very steep it may be necessary to make several traverses before the destination is reached.

STRAIGHT RUNNING

STRAIGHT running or schussing may seem simple enough, but it is important to practice it to learn correct body position. In addition, it is an excellent confidence exercise because it gives the skier a feeling for his skis.

In straight running, the skis slide straight down the fall line. There is nothing for the beginner to fear. The slope he will practice on in ski school will be gentle and with sufficient run-out so that he can come to a stop safely.

In straight running the skis are flat on the snow, close together and with the weight distributed equally on both of them. The body should be in a forward leaning position, slightly forward from the perpendicular to the slope.

It is important to assume the correct body position. The best way to do this is to lean the entire body slightly forward from the ankles. Then flex the knees and hips. Do not lean forward by bending from the waist.

Once you are sliding downhill, stay loose. Do not freeze into a position. Raise and lower your body. Let your legs absorb the shock of the bumps. Rock back and forth slightly on your skis. These motions will relax you and give you a feeling for your skis.

THE SNOWPLOW

THE snowplow, while mainly a beginner's tool, is often used by even expert skiers because it is the only way to slow down on skis without changing directions. However, it should be considered more than a brake. Through it the beginner learns the basic elements of edge control, which are so vital to advanced skiing.

Straight snowplow final form.

To get into a snowplow, you can either start from a standing position, pushing off with your poles, or you can get into it from a straight running position. The tails are displaced into a V at equal angles from the fall line. The tips are together and the surface of the skis are at right angles to the lower legs. This means that the skis are edged.

259

Straight snowplow exercise.

From a running position you get into a snowplow by pushing the tails apart with a gentle, brushing motion, being careful not to overedge by pressing the knees together. If you want to slow down more, do not use your edges for this purpose. Instead press the tails further out.

The slowing action from a snowplow does not come immediately and it will take a few yards for the braking action to take effect. So anticipate your need to slow down. A good exercise for getting a feeling of what a snowplow can do is to move from a straight running position into a snowplow and back into a straight running position several times when going down a slope.

HERRINGBONE

THE herringbone is a slightly faster means of walking straight up the hill than the sidestep, providing the hill is not too steep. The skis are formed into a V with the tails of the skis forming the point of the V. The skis are put on the inside edges. Weight is shifted to one ski and backslip is prevented by bracing against the opposite pole. The unweighted ski is then moved forward and the process repeated.

In the herringbone the points of the poles should not be ahead of the skier's boots. If the pole is too far forward, particularly on steeper hills, it will require a rearrangement of the pole before the next stride is taken. This breaks the rhythm of the herringbone stride.

In the herringbone, the pole opposite
the step supports the skier.

LEARNING TO SKI

THE KICKTURN

THE skier is going to find himself in situations where step-around turns are not feasable. These are situations which require the kickturn.

The kickturn is a means of making a 180-degree change in direction from a standstill. The turn starts with a complete shift of weight to the uphill ski. Then the downhill ski is kicked up high enough so that the ski rests on its tail. From there it is swung around so that its tip faces the tail of the uphill ski. Then, in one motion, the uphill ski is brought around and moved alongside the other ski.

Care should be taken to see that the poles are in the right position so that they are out of the way of the skis swinging around and that they provide proper support when the skis are facing in opposite directions. After the leg is kicked up, the support of the body should come from the uphill pole, and

The kickturn: (*left to right*) preparatory, ski on tail, ski set down, swing-around.

the downhill pole should be placed above the skis either before or as the downhill ski is swung around.

Timidity and lack of vigor are the major problems in executing the kick-turn. To get the ski on its tail, the leg should be swung up briskly and the rest of the action should follow quickly.

Combined with traverses, the kickturn is an extremely useful maneuver. The skier who finds himself atop a slope he hesitates to negotiate in the usual way can use the two to make a safe descent.

SKATING

SKATING is a variation of gliding, but with emphasis on the use of the edges. Essentially it is a herringbone used on the level or in downhill skiing. It can be used for increasing speed and is an excellent rhythmic exercise, stressing knee action, edging, and balance.

Skating is best started when you are already in motion, either gliding or straight downhill skiing. Edge one ski slightly, crouching slightly as you put your weight on the edged ski. Push off the edged ski, take an oblique (forward and slightly to the side) step with the other ski and glide on it. Then re-edge the gliding ski and repeat.

Skating calls for practiced reflexes and good judgment of speed. It is best to try the exercise first when gliding on the level or when skiing very slowly downhill. The additional speed of the skis will surprise you at first and you will experience the sensation of the skis catching up with you. Start with very small skating steps at first, gradually increasing the size of the steps as you grow more confident.

Final skating form.

CHAPTER 30

The steered turns

THE FIRST maneuvers learned by most skiers—apart from walking on skis, straight running and learning how to get up from a fall—are the various snowplow, stem or "steered" turns. We have already described the snowplow position. In this position, the ski tips are together in front and the skier spreads his legs out to put the skis in a V-position on the snow. In so doing, the wobbly, beginning skier has set up a solid three-point base under himself. This is also a psychological base of confidence. Confidence and progress in skiing go hand in hand. As the skier progresses, the "V" snowplow or stem position takes on less importance until it is eventually eliminated in parallel skiing. For the beginner who is aggressive, determined or physically well coordinated, the period of snowplow and steered turns may be very brief, perhaps only a couple of days.

THE SNOWPLOW TURN

To execute the snowplow turn, go down the hill in a snowplow position. Then gradually shift the weight toward the ski which will become the outside ski of the turn. The skis will turn in the direction of the weighted ski.

264

Analysis of snowplow turn: the turn starts in the fall line (*top*) and moves out of fall line with weight shift to skier's left ski (*second and third from top*). Second turn in series of two turns starts when skier has outside ski almost in traverse line (*sixth from top*). Uphill ski now becomes outside ski of turn. The shoulder angle of the counter-rotation movement becomes plain as the shoulder moves in the direction opposite the turn (*fifth, sixth and seventh figure from the top*). Skier again reaches fall line position (*seventh and eighth*). Now skier repeats the cycle that started with the top figure, going from the fall line to the traverse line (*bottom figure*).

Analysis of stem turn (p. 268): Figure in traverse position stems uphill ski (*second, third and fourth figures from top*). By the fifth and sixth figures, skier has started to shift weight to outside ski, and shoulder over ski has been brought back to counter-rotated position. Weight shift to outside ski is almost complete (*seventh figure*) as skier reaches fall line.

To assist you in getting weight on the ski, turn the hip back slightly and bow a bit in the direction you want your weight to go. It is also good practice, both to get full weight transfer and to prevent yourself from sitting back, to press the knee of the weighted ski inwards.

Snowplow turns should be practiced in both directions. The most serious error in execution is incomplete weight transfer. To get complete transfer, the knees must be well bent.

Once individual snowplow turns are perfected, turns in both directions can be linked together. This can be done by shifting the weight alternately from one ski to the other. The motion from side to side should be slow and rhythmic.

THE STEM TURN

THE stem turn is essentially a snowplow turn with only one ski in the snowplow position (snowplows are sometimes called double stems). Many ski schools do not teach a stem turn in the formal sense, but rather go on immediately to an elementary version of the stem christie.

Nevertheless, a stem turn is a useful slow speed turn. Its instructional value lies in enabling the skier to go into a turn from a traverse on a steeper slope without the excessive tilting away from the hill that is required when a snowplow is used. It also encourages greater mobility of the skis.

From a traverse position, the uphill ski is stemmed into a half-V position. (Before the ski can be moved, the weight must be taken off it.) With the uphill ski now in position, apply body weight to it by angling your body over the ski. In this way the uphill ski will turn through the fall line and into the new direction. When the new direction is established, the skis are allowed to run together into a parallel position.

If the turn is executed correctly, the skier should enter the traverse in the correct traverse position with a slight reverse-shoulder look and with the weight on the downhill ski. He should be ready to start the next turn.

In all stemmed turns from snowplow to stem christie, it is important not

268

Traversing: Crossing the slope, the uphill ski, hip and shoulder are slightly advanced, skis are close together, more weight on lower ski, upper body is angled over weighted ski.

to try to force the turn by further angling of the ski once the turn has started. If the ski doesn't seem to be turning sufficiently, the fault lies not with the angle of the ski, but in insufficient weightshift to the outside or uphill ski.

TRAVERSING

WHENEVER you are skiing in a straight line other than on the fall line, you are traversing. Basically, this is similar to straight running except that you have to compensate for the slant of the hill. This requires the edging of the skis into the hill so that the skis bite into the snow and cannot slip off the hill.

269

LEARNING TO SKI

To edge the skis, knees and hips should be rolled into the hill. To compensate for this motion, angle the upper body outward and down the hill. This bending of the body is known as *angulation* and is best achieved by turning the chest and hips down the hill. The twisting has the additional advantage of advancing the upper ski slightly, thus keeping it from crossing the lower ski. The amount of angulation depends on the steepness of the slope.

In a traverse, most of the weight should be on the downhill ski to prevent it from straying. Failure to put adequate weight on the downhill ski, usually caused by stiffening the uphill leg or by incorrect body position, will result in a ragged traverse. This can be avoided by pressing the downhill knee down and slightly into the hill while traversing.

SIDESLIPPING

SIDESLIPPING is the basis of a great deal of advanced skiing. It is also an important safety maneuver. Faced with a slope that is too steep, the skier can sideslip down it without the risk of putting his skis into the fall line.

The forward sideslip is started from a traverse with a slight up-unweighting, the angulation is eliminated and this flattens the skis, resulting in a sideslip.

From a standing traverse position, simply straighten up the body slightly. The angling inwards of the hips and knees is reduced, the edges are released and the skis will slide sideways. On more gentle slopes you will not find it quite that easy. Try it first with poles in the snow on the uphill side; as you straighten up push a little with your poles. Then go to a steeper slope and try it without poles.

Sideslipping can also be done with the skis in motion. By sideslipping and traversing the skier can more accurately select the spot where he wants to turn. In practicing sideslipping with traversing, start with a gentle traverse. When you have picked up a little momentum, straighten up. You will find that you'll sideslip much more readily than if you started from a standing position. To stop the sideslipping, simply lower your body into the normal traverse position.

THE UPHILL CHRISTIE

THE uphill christie is not a complete turn. Rather, it is the closing portion of a number of turns. It also provides valuable practice in pushing the heels and, perfected, is a valuable means of stopping at high speeds since the skis are turned *up* into the fall line.

The uphill christie is started from the traverse with a down or up motion to unweight, heel thrust and turning of the skis.

LEARNING TO SKI

The uphill christie is the first of the turns with the skis parallel (a christie or christiania is any turn in which the skis are in a parallel position as the turn is completed). In its simplest form, the uphill christie is a traverse followed by a sideslip accompanied by a pushing of the heels downward and outward. The pushing of the heels is similar to grinding a cigarette into the ground with your heels.

Care must be taken that the hips and knees press uphill while the upper body leans toward the valley as the heel pushing phase begins. If you allow your hips to move out of the hill, weight will shift from the downhill to the uphill ski and loss of control is immediate.

There are a variety of exercises built around the uphill christie. Most of them involve increasing the steepness of the traverse, raising the skier's confidence to negotiate steeper slopes by giving him the ability to come to a stop.

It is not always necessary to come to a stop following an uphill christie. Simply terminate heel push before stopping and resume the normal traverse position.

THE STEM CHRISTIE

THE stem christie combines the elements of the stem turn and the uphill christie. Starting from the traverse, the turn starts exactly like a stem turn. But instead of holding the stem or V-shape until the skis have completed the turn, the inside ski is brought parallel alongside the outside ski as soon as the skis start to turn. The rest of the turn is finished like an uphill christie.

In practicing the stem christie, the skier takes it through various phases. In the initial phases the stem is rather large and is held until the skier reaches the fall line. As the skier progresses, he stems only as long as it takes him to shift his weight to the stemmed ski. Then the inside ski is immediately brought alongside, even though the turn has barely begun.

Before the skier reaches this latter phase, he must introduce *up-unweighting* into his turns. Details of this will be introduced in the next chapter. Insofar as the stem christie is concerned, it simply means that stemming of the uphill

272

ski is accompanied by a slight down motion. Then as the weight is transferred to the stemmed ski, the skier rises in an up motion. The skier remains in a relatively high position until he reaches the fall line at which point he begins to sink to set the edges for the finish of the turn. While the skier is in this down position at the end of the turn, he is also in a position to launch immediately into the next turn, which is what most skiers do.

A beginning stem christie holds the stem into the fall line (*sixth figure from top*). Skis close coming out of fall line (*seventh figure*). Skier sets edges with down motion (*last figure*) to finish the turn in the new traverse.

The critical phase in the stem christie is coordinating the down motion with the stemming motion, the up motion with the shift of weight and the sinking motion with the uphill christie phase. This must be done smoothly and in one continuous motion.

It is during the stem christie stage of learning that the skier must get away from what is called "position" skiing. From the stem christie on, the skier must at all costs avoid getting into a position and holding it until a change is required. Rather the turn must be a continuous motion of extremely fluid execution. This philosophy of "Total Motion" is one of the basic principles of the American Technique. It assumes that every movement in skiing involves the skier's whole body and that it is unnatural to stay in a static position. A skier who freezes into positions has a tendency to become tense and stiff; this throws off his timing and makes his movements into new positions jerky and uncertain.

The stem christie should be developed to the point where little additional benefit can be gained by reducing the stem. As soon as there is smoothness and fluidity in execution, it is time to move on to the parallel christie.

274

CHAPTER 31

Parallel Turns

IN THE advanced stem christie stage, the skier begins to swing his turns. He still starts the turn with a steering motion, but then carries it through to completion by taking advantage of gravity, momentum, the rotational forces generated by his body and the "turn" built into the design of the ski.

In parallel skiing this development is carried one step further. The skis are not steered at all in the sense of being set to point in a new direction. Rather they are swung into the turn from the moment the turn is initiated. This is done by perfecting three concepts that have been encountered casually before: unweighting, edge change and rotational movement.

We have already learned that in order to turn, a ski has to be unweighted. Clearly then, if the skis are to remain parallel, both skis have to be unweighted simultaneously. It is possible to unweight by hopping, and this is exactly what skiers do when they are skiing parallel slowly. However, at higher speeds, hopping is not only expensively time-consuming but also unnecessary. The unweighting motion can be brisk and in some cases barely noticeable.

To start an unweighting motion, sink slowly as the point is approached where you wish to start the turn. When the point is almost reached, rise smartly, pushing against the snow. When the body decelerates its upward motion, the skis begin to unweight. This moment of lightness permits rotary motion to become effective and to permit an edge change.

275

LEARNING TO SKI

Rotary motion can be imparted to the skis by twisting the feet in the direction of the turn. This twisting of the feet can be assisted somewhat by turning the shoulders in a direction opposite to that of the turn. This seeming paradox is explained by Newton's Third Law that every action has an equal and opposite reaction: that is, the turning of the legs is counter poised by the rotation of the upper body in an opposite direction. There are other theoretical ramifications, but we'll leave these for Chapter 33.

As important as rotational power is edge change. As the parallel skier unweights from the traverse position, the skis come off their edges and go momentarily flat on the snow as they are turned. As the tips drift downhill in the direction of the new turn, the skier changes and banks the skis onto the other set of edges. The design of the ski is such that it bites more at the tip than at the tail when the ski is on edge. The result is a carving of the skis on the snow and an arcing turn. Thus the pure parallel turn is born.

In the advanced stages of the stem christie, the skier experiences some of the dynamic aspects of skiing. In parallel skiing he experiences them more purely. Movements are more sharply coordinated. Unweighting, turning action and edge control must be finely synchronized. Beyond that, the skier requires a certain flair, often described as rhythm, but which is also a oneness with his skis and the snow. This flair is not confined to parallel skiers alone, but it is essential if you are to become a parallel skier.

THE PARALLEL CHRISTIE

In the American Technique, the essential philosophy is to reduce progressively the stem in the stem christie so that the skier arrives at the parallel christie more or less automatically. With some skiers it works, with others it doesn't. Usually the major source of the difficulty is the coordination of the edge change with unweighting, as can be seen in the description of the parallel turn.

From a traverse, the skier sets the uphill edge of the downhill ski by sinking and then rising explosively to unweight. As he unweights both skis simultaneously, he changes the edges and starts to twist legs and skis in the direction of the turn. As the weight settles back on his skis, the weight is shifted to the outside ski. As the turn progresses, the skier continues to apply turning power by progressive counter-rotation through the fall line and into the traverse. The finish of the turn should leave the skier in a position where he can start immediately into his next turn.

From the stem christie skier's point of view, the difficulty in moving to parallel is the coordination of unweighting with edge change. In the earlier stem turn, this difficulty was not encountered because the edge was changed before the skier unweighted and shifted his weight to the outside ski. But in parallel, unweighting must be sharply coordinated with the turning of

Analysis of parallel christie: Down motion sets edge of downhill ski (*second figure*) and up motion for unweighting follows (*third figure*). Weight is changed, turn commences, and inside ski is advanced (*fourth figure, fifth figure*) with the angulation and the bringing back of the shoulder.

the skis. Many beginning parallel skiers also have difficulty in discarding the stem itself. This can be avoided by remaining in the traverse position and even intensifying it until the start of the upward unweighting motion.

The angulated or "comma" position of the traverse and the action that follows is a critically important element in the success of the turn. The amount of edging is determined by the amount of angulation—that is, the "comma" position assumed by the body as the legs and hip bend into the hill and the upper body inclines and faces to the outside or downhill. Adequate angulation assures that the weight is on the downhill ski prior to the turn, that the edge is properly set and that the skis are not stemmed at any time during the turn.

The mechanics of angulation play a further role as the turn unfolds. As the skier rises for his unweighting motion, the body will automatically uncoil (de-angulate). This releases the edges. As the upper body continues to counter-rotate toward the outside of the turn and again assumes an angulated position, the inside edges begin to bite. Since the radius of the turn is determined by the amount of edging and since the amount of edging is governed by angulation, the skier can control the radius of the rest of his turn simply by adjusting the amount of angulation.

The pole can be used in the parallel christie, but not in the sense of a vaulting pole. The pole should be planted simultaneously with the end of the

Check and hop: This exercise is a transition from the parallel christie to the parallel christie with check. Emphasis is on displacement of tails downhill, ending in a check, and then the subsequent upward hop.

down motion prior to unweighting. It provides a certain amount of stability and should be viewed as a trigger for the subsequent events.

Parallel Christie with Check

THE parallel christie works well only up to a point. On steeper terrain and in difficult snow conditions, the speed of the skis will be such that the skier will experience some difficulty in setting his edges. In these instances, a check prior to the turn is the proper remedy.

The parallel christie with check is the same as a parallel christie except in its beginning phases. Instead of preparing for the unweighting motion by simply sinking, the skier ends the traverse as in an uphill christie, by sideslipping. As soon as the tails begin to slide out, he drops (bounces is a good word), increasing angulation, and plants his pole. This sets the edges very firmly, checks speed and provides a platform from which to push off into the unweighting phase of the turn.

SHORT SWING

THE American Technique no longer makes a distinction between short swing and wedeln since the two are so closely related. Actually, they are not really different turns from parallel christies, but rather refined applications. However, for reasons of tradition and to demonstrate some aspects of edge application, they are treated separately here, although only wedeln is illustrated.

The definition of a short swing is "consecutive parallel christies without traverse, using the setting of the edges and pole plant." Two items are notable in this definition: the de-emphasizing of the traverse and the prescribed use of the pole plant.

Basically, short swing is a series of parallel christies with check, the heel thrust and finishing edge set of one turn being used as the platform for initiating the next turn. The use of the pole is required in order to bring the heel thrust to a sharp end, leading to a quicker setting of the edges.

279

Analysis of the parallel christie with check: The differentiation from the earlier parallel is apparent in the downward displacement of the tails in eleventh and twelfth figures from top of series.

Hop in fall line: This exercise provides practice in making the quick up and down motion needed in wedeln and short swing, and improves balance through rhythm. Tails are hopped across fall line.

The term short swing readily implies tight radius rather than long, drawn-out turns. The time between checks is clearly minimized, hence there is more precise control of speed. For this reason, short swings are used on steep, relatively narrow slopes.

Throughout the series of turns the orientation of the upper body is essentially down the fall line. There is some counter-rotation of the upper body although the skier is hardly aware of it. The skier feels as though he is skiing with his legs only.

In its extreme form, short swing leads to an actual hopping of the ski tails from side to side, with the body continuing in a straight line down the slope. In this case, the ski displacement is used purely as a braking mechanism and not as a means of turning. At the other end of the scale, short swing can merge into wedeln.

281

Analysis of wedeln: Body form is slightly more smooth than in short swing. Skis are held flatter throughout and poles do not actually have to be placed although characteristic swing of poles remains. Down and up motion and angulation tend to be subdued compared to action of short swing and the parallel christies previously learned.

WEDELN

WEDELN is an Austrian colloquialism meaning wagging, or tail wagging, and this is exactly how it appears to the onlooker. Expertly done, it is smooth, fluid and graceful, the epitome of skiing skill.

By definition wedeln is "consecutive parallel christies without traverse or appreciable edge setting." Its similarity to short swing is apparent, the only difference being that no check intervenes between turns.

Wedeln requires a good deal of coordination if done on anything other than smooth, easy slopes. The skis must never be allowed to get very far out of the fall line. Since there is no check between turns, failure to coordinate will result in the skis getting away from the skier.

Since wedeln turns are done mostly in the fall line, up and down motion and angulation are minimized. The skier seems to be wagging his fanny only, an appearance caused by the fact that he uses only his knees and ankles in bringing about the changes of direction. Clearly, with this minimum of motion edge play has to be extremely subtle.

Although a great deal of advice is dispensed on wedeln, its perfection requires a great sensitivity for the texture of the snow and good coordination. The only way to achieve this is to keep practicing (and to be prepared for quite a few falls), starting with relatively long, linked parallel christies and gradually speeding up their frequency until they are but wiggles on the snow.

Technique doesn't stop with wedeln. For the technically inclined skier, there is the whole field of rotational technique, the esoteric racing turns and acrobatics on skis. But before the skier becomes involved in these sometimes confusing maneuvers, he should first master his basic technique in a variety of snow conditions.

Breaking through "crud."

CHAPTER 32

Special snow and terrain conditions

THE SKIER will encounter few difficulties in average snow conditions. By average is meant a snow surface reasonably firm, but not so firm that it is unyielding.

But conditions are rarely average. Fresh snow will fall, and if there is enough of it, the skier will have to learn to cope with deep powder. It may rain or temperatures will rise above freezing, in which case the soft, wet snow poses its own special problems. And following these conditions, it may freeze, and the skier must wrestle with the problems of ice. And, invariably, there are moguls—whole slopes of bumps—and there are special ways of dealing with these. Only when the skier can operate competently under all of these conditions can he call himself a true expert.

It should be stressed that these conditions don't call so much for special techniques as for adapting the technique you already have to the conditions. You may not always be 100 per cent happy with such conditions, but if you wait for the day when everything is right, you may not be doing much skiing. 285

LEARNING TO SKI

By being able to ski in special conditions you can perfect your technique for those days you consider ideal, and after a while you may find that the conditions you considered the worst are more than bearable after all.

ICE

WITH the heavy traffic on today's slopes, the most commonly encountered snow condition difficulty is ice caused by the scraping away of snow. Ice may also form when temperatures drop below freezing following a day of warm temperatures (a frequent condition in spring). Ice may affect an entire slope; it may also be found in patches where shadows prevent the sun from thawing the snow.

Of the two conditions, patch ice is the more disconcerting simply because it may be unexpected. However, patch ice shouldn't catch you completely by surprise. By looking ahead you can usually predict when you are likely to

Ski champion Othmar Schneider shows how to roll knees and ankles into the hill to stop sideslip down the fall line. Note very little movement in head and shoulders. Only the force from locked knees turns the ski edges into the hill.

encounter a patch of ice: shadows on the slope, a spot where there has been a lot of turning, and the downhill side of moguls where the snow has been badly scraped.

You may be able to avoid these spots completely, but if you can't, simply anticipate them by setting the edges a little harder. If you have to turn on an icy spot, just push the outside knee down harder. If you are surprised by an icy patch, in which case you'll have the feeling that the skis are sliding away from under you, it is probably too late to get your weight forward and more on the downhill ski. It is better then to ride the icy patch through, anticipating the moment when the edges grip again on snow. Prepare yourself to check —the tendency will be for the skis to sideslip on the ice anyway—so that you can reduce the extra speed you have picked up.

There is a notion that you have to edge madly in order to deal with ice. Not so. The contact between edge and snow is so narrow that a greater or lesser amount of edging is not going to make much difference. The skis should remain as close to the horizontal as possible since this is the position where maximum weight can be brought to bear on the edge. In fact, too much edging may bring about exactly what you are trying to avoid. If, through too much edging, the skis start to ride on their sides, they are more likely to slip away from you than if they had not edged enough. It is the amount of weight you can bring to bear on the edge, not the amount of edging, that determines the degree of control you will have over your skis on ice.

Steel edges, of course, are essential. They should be sharp, but they don't need to be super-honed. If you do sharpen them to this state they will wear quickly. A better solution, particularly if you live in ski regions where ice is fairly common, is to buy a slightly narrower and stiffer pair of skis. Narrower skis have the advantage of putting the edge more directly underfoot. A stiffer ski will put the edge in firmer contact with the snow.

If there is one consolation on ice, it is that the skis are easy to turn— perhaps too easy. An icy period is a good time to stay on the easier slopes and to practice turning by pressure of the knees in the direction of the turn. It is one of the better ways to get the feel of wedeln. 287

LEARNING TO SKI

DEEP POWDER

DEEP powder skiing is as much a state of mind as it is a special condition to ski. What is meant here by deep powder is any snow depth over six inches that is also reasonably light; by light meaning any snow that can be kicked without meeting any appreciable resistance. Powder, of course, can be so dry and light that it will virtually hang in the air. And it can be hip-deep.

Special equipment can be of considerable help in dealing with deep powder. If you don't have a pair of flexible metal skis—most "standards" are flexible enough—you should consider renting a pair. It will greatly simplify the problem.

It is best to start on a slope you think you can take straight and that is wide and has a good run-out. Then go to the top and take it straight, at least until about eight inches of tip is clearly visible. This is the first lesson of powder

Powder kicks up well over belt line on a fast downhill run.

skiing—the tips have to plane. In order to make the tips plane you may have to sit back a little bit, particularly in deeper snow.

Planing is necessary so that the tips don't dive when you turn. Unless they are out of the snow, there won't be enough pressure on the skis to keep the tips from diving. There is an additional reason for planing the skis. Much like a water ski, it will float on the snow. This makes it easier to turn.

As you try your first turn in the conventional manner, you will notice that your downhill ski seems to have a mind of its own. This is because you are weighting it too much and pushing the tip below the surface of the snow. Deep snow turns and traverses require that the weight be distributed equally on both skis. Since there is little lateral resistance from the snow in which the skis are floating, try pushing the skis, heel-push fashion, compensating with the upper body only enough to keep your balance. Hold your arms at shoulder level and partly out to the sides to further help you balance.

You will find that you'll turn. However, you will also find that the turns are somewhat slow in coming and that you have to keep your skis close to the fall line to make them turn easily. Once you are any distance out from the fall line, it becomes increasingly difficult to turn.

In deep powder don't unweight by rising sharply. You'll only help to push the skis below the surface of the snow and to compact the snow beneath the skis so that they are difficult to turn. It's best, rather, to unweight by retracting the legs. In this way, the skis float in the loose snow. As the legs are extended again it is easy to push the tails of the skis so that a new direction can be established. The extension of the legs can be quite sharp. The result is a bouncing effect which assists the unweighting motion for the following turn.

One of the great worries of deep powder is the mess that results from a fall. A fall in powder isn't physically dangerous, but the problems of disentangling yourself from your equipment and the snow (which, being light and loose, will have penetrated into every opening in your clothing) can be formidable.

If there is a trick to powder skiing, it is to ski fast enough so that your

289

skis plane. Everything follows from this. Having once mastered powder—the knack seems to come all at once—you'll find it hard to be satisfied with anything less.

SOFT, HEAVY SNOW AND CRUD

You are most likely to encounter soft, heavy snow in late spring, when high temperatures turn the snow to slush, or following a heavy snowstorm under barely freezing conditions. If the soft snow is deep enough, it may be unskiable. You'll have to pole your way through it. Under other weather conditions

Junior Bounous skis through soggy spring snow: Deep position in the first figure is affected by bending ankles and knees. The poles are placed well forward for correct timing to aid in the unlifting. In the second figure, the upper body is pushed straight upward. The legs lift the skis clear of the snow. Generally, the skis are turned no farther than the fall line before coming back into the snow; a common mistake is to try to turn too far. In the third figure, poles are removed from the snow. The turn is cut off quickly and then repeated.

you may encounter a layer of breakable crusted ice over soft snow. This is known as crud. While somewhat risky (the skis can't cut through the snow as easily as in powder skiing) these conditions *can* be skied providing the skier follows a few simple rules.

Approach soft, heavy snow much as you would powder: flexible skis, weight slightly back so that the tips don't dive, weight equally distributed on both skis and skis as much in the fall line as possible. The difference comes in unweighting. In heavy snow, the unweighting motion must be much more emphatic. It may even require a hop on terrain where a light unweighting motion is usually enough.

Let the skis run as freely as they can. Checking may result in a tumble if the heavy snow builds up as the skis slide to the side. Carve the end of the turn by proper angulation rather than by heel pushing.

Keep the skis well waxed. Wet, heavy snow slows up the skis by increasing suction. A good spring wax will prevent this. Skis properly waxed are easier to control and reduce the effort in making turns.

It is important to keep the skis parallel. (And any bad habits you have acquired will show up quickly when you get on soft snow.) Should the skis begin to separate, don't try to force them together while both are still weighted. Instead, momentarily unweight the ski that threatens to depart from the desired direction and replace it parallel to the other ski.

Simply because spring, when you are most likely to encounter wet, heavy snow, is such a wonderful, sunny time to ski, mastery of these conditions is more than worth the effort.

STEEP TERRAIN AND HEADWALLS

SHORT steep places along the trail—sometimes called headwalls—are to be considered not so much as special terrain conditions as a state of mind. The skier with some experience should seek them out rather than avoid them. In easy terrain he can get away with sloppy technique. Steep terrain, which reveals every flaw, will help him to perfect his technique.

291

LEARNING TO SKI

The most important aspect of skiing steep places is maintaining a tight check on speed. This requires a strong edge set and sweeping the skis rapidly through the fall line. One way of doing this is to use a series of short swings; for the skier who is not yet this proficient, the two-pole turn is the easier solution and, incidentally, good practice for mastering the short swing.

The trick is to make an energetic check just before the start of the turn, the type that gives you a bounce as it is completed. As the check is being made, *both* arms should go forward and the poles should be planted at the moment when the check comes to an end and when the knees and ankles are well bent. This creates a strong platform from which the skier can spring up, pulling the skis into the air with the aid of the poles. When the skis are in the air, they are swept across the fall line in a fanning motion, the amount of arc depending on the steepness of the slope. As the skis come back on the snow, the outside pole is withdrawn first and the body moves down to complete the turn and start a new check, both arms again coming forward.

Challenging a headwall: (*from right to left*) arms are extended forward in position for planting both poles; both poles are planted as ski edges are set ready for the unweighting with knees and ankles well bent into a position from which to spring up; in the third figure the poles are carrying some of the weight as the legs have straightened to spring from the snow, and the skis are pulled up with bent knees; in the fourth figure, the skis are back on the snow, the outside pole comes free of the snow before the inside one, and the body moves in a down motion; in the fifth figure, fanning motion is complete. The arms and poles are again started forward, edgesetting starts.

An important point to keep in mind is to make the check energetic without bringing the skis to a halt. The skis must keep moving, since a turn from a standstill is very difficult on steep terrain.

BUMPS AND FIELDS OF MOGULS

A BUMP can be an obstacle or an adventure. The good skier will consider it an adventure. There are so many bumps of one kind or another, the skier must be prepared for them.

Moguls are skier-made bumps and are formed when the snow is not hard-packed. As skiers turn in one spot, they both carve away and compact the snow so that a deep, rounded rut is formed. It is this that is the cause of the bump. As more and more turns are made on the slope, more bumps form, and unless the area cuts them down with snow-grooming machinery they will get progressively worse, sometimes to the point where they are hip-deep.

Unfortunately, it is not always feasible to cut down bumps since they are more frequently found on steep than on gentle slopes. Skiers turn harder and more abruptly on steep slopes, and as a result moguls form more quickly.

If there is a consolation, it is that skis are easy to turn on moguls. When you stand on a mogul, you will find that your skis pivot easily with a simple twisting of the feet. This is the answer to skiing moguls.

Start into a field of moguls in a traverse along the smoothest line. Pay particular attention to the downhill knee to make sure that it remains flexed and flexible so as to be able to absorb the shock of minor bumps in the traverse. When you reach the first big mogul, don't try to avoid it, but ride up on it. When your *feet* reach the top, pivot the skis so that they sideslip easily on the other side of the mogul. The ensuing turn makes itself, due to the convex shape of the mogul. Resume a traverse after the turn is made and turn again in the same manner as soon as you reach the next mogul. If you make it a practice to turn on top of every mogul you encounter, you will soon find that they are less bothersome and that the descent becomes something of a game.

293

In approaching moguls in this way, it is necessary to control speed carefully. Approaching the top of a mogul too fast will throw you into the air with unpredictable results. If you feel yourself approaching a mogul too fast, avoid becoming airborne by lightly tucking your legs before you reach the top of the bump. When you reach the top of the bump thrust your legs in the direction you want to sideslip.

The single large bump poses no particular problem. The skier can slow down and ski across it slowly. The other choices are to pre-jump it or to use the bump deliberately to become airborne.

In jumping, run up onto the bump in a slight crouch and reach forward with the poles. When the poles reach the crest, they are planted and the skier then lifts himself up with the aid of the poles, becoming airborne before he reaches the crest. The reaching for the crest pushes the skier forward so that he is close to horizontal when he becomes airborne.

Another method is the so-called bunny hop, a maneuver for skiers who really want to become airborne. Instead of approaching the bump in a crouch, remain relatively upright with your legs firm, but not stiff. At the point of the

Skiing over moguls: (*from right to left*) approaching in normal position (*first figure*) there is a straightening of the legs as skis cross hollow (*second figure*) to better position the skier for absorbing the sharpness in the approaching mogul; at the peak of the mogul (*third figure*) the legs have bent to the lowest point to absorb shock of bump, and turning power is applied to change

takeoff bounce down and then spring upward as hard as you can. You will be literally bounced into the air. And in the right position, too. Your legs will be slightly tucked. As you near the snow extend the legs slightly and absorb the landing shock with your knees.

For those who wish to take a bump at full speed but without becoming airborne for excessive periods of time, pre-jumping is the correct procedure. Pre-jumping is done by starting the jump before the crest of the jump is reached. This can be done with the aid of the poles, or by quickly tucking the knees under the chest once the arc of the bump has been reached. If the pre-jump is timed correctly the path of flight will closely approximate the contour of the bump. The trick in timing the pre-jump is to go sufficiently high on the bump to produce enough lift to clear the crest. If the jump is too late, the skier will be thrown into the air, if too soon, he will be descending before he clears the crest.

The way to feel easy in the air is to start with small bumps, get the feel of the correct position in the air and, what is probably most important, master landing.

the ski's direction; in the fourth figure, edges have changed and skis are pointing into a new direction; in the last figure, skis are following a round turn and legs are straightened to return to a normal position.

LEARNING TO SKI

In dealing with unusual ski conditions, it is important not to be discouraged if the first few attempts go haywire. When you consider the amount of practice it took to perfect your turns, you will realize that your adaptation to unusual conditions isn't really taking so long. Part of your discouragement and impatience may be the result of thinking that you have mastered ski technique. The grizzled skimeisters, the true experts, know better. Learning to handle new kind of snow and terrain conditions is one of the fascinations of the sport. There is always something new to learn.

A heavily mogulled slope at Sun Valley, Idaho.

CHAPTER 33

Other ski systems

As YOU ski more and attend different ski schools, you become aware that there are techniques and approaches to skiing other than the one to which you have become accustomed or the one described so far in this book. Ski technique is in a continual state of evolution. There are constant refinements of existing techniques, and there are, if your instructor is a strong traditionalist, various heresies. This makes for fascinating and interesting controversy, but you will find it confusing unless you are aware of some of the ground rules of the ski technique debate.

You will recall that in a ski system, method and technique mean the same thing: a complete approach to skiing from the most elementary to the most advanced steps. These systems are usually enshrined in manuals published by instructor associations or national ski schools in varying degrees of detail. For instance, the Austrian manual not only describes the system in precise, step-by-step detail, but it also prescribes practice exercises and details of instruction. In contrast, the American Technique puts most of its emphasis on *final forms*, the way the correct execution is supposed to look, with only incidental details on sequence of execution and none on how these forms are supposed to be taught. What is frequently hailed as a new technique is actually only a different way of reaching a final form.

LEARNING TO SKI

Whatever techniques are labeled—Austrian, American, or French—there is no substantial difference between them. They may vary in emphasis on certain aspects of execution, but fundamentally they are very similar both in sequence of development (snowplow, snowplow turn, stem turn, etc.) and execution. If anything, the difference is more likely to be in teaching philosophy. The Austrians, for instance, put great emphasis on correct position, the Americans on continuous motion; and there are a variety of philosophies in between.

The differences between these schools are being further reduced through the institution of the International Ski Congress. At every congress the various ski nations give demonstrations, discuss techniques and try to arrive at mutually agreeable positions. And, because of the high interest in technique among the world's skiers, changes or refinements in technique are quickly publicized. Outside the official channels of change, there are a number of systems seeking to bypass the traditional sequence of learning. Essentially, these systems

Ski instructors at the Walter Foeger Natur-Teknik Ski School at Jay Peak, Vermont. System teaches parallel skiing from the beginning, without stem.

try to eliminate the stemmed turns on the grounds that they merely cultivate habits which the skier must eventually unlearn to ski parallel.

The idea in itself is as old as parallel skiing. Its basic difficulty is that ski schools usually cannot hold the skier in ski school long enough so that he really masters parallel. Nevertheless, two all-parallel schools of thought have a strong following in the United States and Canada.

The struggles that beginners have when they strap two long boards on their feet are familiar enough. Why not use short skis parallel in the beginning stages, gradually building up to longer skis as the skier becomes more proficient? This is the argument of short-ski entrepeneur Clif Taylor. He sells skis in two-and-a-half, four and five-foot lengths and claims that he can teach you to ski parallel in a day. The first-time-out skier has little difficulty in turning the skis. He simply twists his feet in the direction he wants to go. The little boards meet virtually no resistance from the snow—providing it is hard packed. It is when the skier attempts to graduate to different snow conditions or more difficult terrain that he senses the inherent instability and lack of speed of the shorter skis. And, traditionalists argue, when he attempts to step up to longer skis, he finds he is lacking in certain fundamentals, such as unweighting and traversing. However, the case is not conclusive yet. Short-ski technique is still too new to determine what its future will be.

Another all-parallel approach is the Natur-Teknik, which is fanatically practiced at several Eastern ski areas. Natur-Teknik is actually not as unconventional as it sounds. Skis of normal length are used, and instead of the stemmed turns a series of special hopping exercises are given. These exercises are intended as a substitute for the confidence the skier feels in the three-point support system of the stemmed turns.

Natur-Teknicians are not the only ones to advocate this approach. The French, ever since they discovered parallel skiing, have de-emphasized the stemmed turns, and at various times have acted as though the stem didn't exist. The only difference between the French and the Natur-Teknicians is that the latter refuse to acknowledge the existence of the snowplow; also, their prize pupils end up looking like products of the Austrian technique (they counter-rotate).

299

LEARNING TO SKI

If there is a drawback to the Natur-Teknik, it is the amount of time that the average skier can devote to learning to ski. Even traditionalists agree that if they have a student for a week or more, they can teach him a passable parallel turn. But, they claim, this would require continuous lessons, and it would also leave limited the terrain a skier so taught could ski. Few skiers are willing to put up with this.

If North American skiers start taking ski vacations instead of weekending, there may well in due course be a switch to all-parallel instruction. But despite the lure of "learn to ski parallel in a week," it hasn't happened yet.

Most of the heat of theoretical argument in the ski sport, however, is reserved for the rotation vs. counter-rotation controversy. This is the thirty-year-old difference of opinion about whether ski turns should be taught by rotating the whole body in the direction of the turn, or by twisting the legs and skis while countering this force by reversing the shoulders and upper torso in relation to the turn. The Austrians officially adopted counter-rotation after the war. Thereafter, despite the claims of rotation-defenders that the new system could never be taught to beginners, it was quickly adopted as *the* system by virtually every nation but France. In the United States, the introduction of counter-rotation as a uniform method of teaching helped bring about the formation of the Professional Ski Instructors of America (PSIA) and the formalization of the American technique. The counter-rotational system was also adopted by the Canadian Ski Instructors Alliance (CSIA), which had first been organized in 1938.

When the Austrians adopted counter-rotation, they convinced many that it was the unstoppable wave of the future. But the French refused to let rotation die. They refined it, polished it and eliminated enough weaknesses to make it once again a formidable contender in the technique race.

FROM ARLBERG TO ROTATION

THE first formal, modern ski technique was developed by the Austrian Hannes
300 Schneider. Its fundamental principle was a lateral weight shift from ski to ski,

which was characterized by the simile that executing a snowplow was like "picking up a bucket of water on one side and putting it down on the other." This was not really a rotation even though some rotary motion was implied. In any event, the skier spent his time perfecting and reducing this motion until the stem was all but invisible (hopefully).

The next development was rotation with skis truly parallel, first advocated by Anton Seelos. The key to this development was up-unweighting of both ski simultaneously. The way the Seelos turn worked was as follows:

The skier "wound up" with a slight counter-rotation, sinking, as he counter-rotated. He then rotated in the direction of the turn, rising sharply as he did so. The rising, in its initial stages, put great pressure on the skis, setting the edges. But when the body stopped moving upward, unweighting took place (you can try this on your bathroom scale). The rotation was timed in such a way that unweighting took place at a point where the body was roughly square to the skis. At the moment when the skis were unweighted, the skier stopped rotating and changed edges. The momentum generated by the rotation carved the turn.

The difficulty with this approach was that it put a lot of weight on the uphill ski before the turn was properly started, and there was also the danger of over-rotation, which put the skier on his inside ski in the turn.

Rotation also appeared in the French Technique developed by Emile Allais and others, who had been coached by Seelos. To overcome the turn's drawbacks, some changes had been made. Instead of sinking and rising during counter-rotation and rotation, the skier simply counter-rotated and rotated with the body staying at about the same level throughout the period of rotation. As the upper body approached a position square to the skis, the skier unweighted by dropping and changing edges. The momentum generated resulted in a turn.

Allais added refinements to the sharp drop. Instead of merely dropping, the tails of the skis were actually retracted from the snow by pulling the legs up. It was done very much in the manner in which a horse kicks to the rear, by ducking forward and down and throwing the legs up. Hence the maneuver's name, *ruade*, which is French for horse kick.

301

The French contended that the basis of the turn was the sideslip, and it was this that the French emphasized in their beginning curriculum. It was argued that the object of skiers was parallel skiing and that anything that sidetracked them was undesirable. This included any form of V-shaped stemming. The French did not abandon stem completely, but deemphasized it to such a degree that it became only a last resort to the French instructor. This is still true in French ski instruction.

In the decade after the war, Austrian and French techniques merged in what became known as modified Arlberg. Sideslipping and rotation were adopted and the stemmed turns modified so that there was a logical meshing of the systems. Improvements in equipment made it possible to reduce the amount of rotation required. This was the state of affairs when the counter-rotational revolution struck in the mid-fifties.

ROTATION AND COUNTER-ROTATION BOTH WORK

When counter-rotation became the religion of the day, it brought with it a mechanical explanation of almost devastatingly simple logic. Counter-rotational turns were simply a logical application of Newton's Third Law that every action has an equal and opposite reaction. By turning the shoulders in a direction opposite to the one in which you wanted to turn, the feet would turn in the direction you wanted to go. It was not only simple, but elegant as well.

This neat scheme had only one drawback. For years skiers had been turning their shoulders in the direction of their turns and getting away with it. How come their skis didn't turn uphill instead of downhill?

The question is not nearly as paradoxical as it seems if the turns are analyzed correctly. In execution and theory they are the equal and opposite of each other. Essentially, the rotational skier establishes the direction of his turns first (through rotation) and then unweights and changes edges. The counter-rotational skier unweights first, then changes edges and establishes the direction of his turn. The rotational skier initiates the turn with a swing of his shoulders, the counter-rotational skier does it with his legs.

302

Yes, with his legs! One of the major misunderstandings of counter-rotational technique is the notion that the turning power comes from a reversal of the shoulders. This is not the case, except under extremely favorable circumstances (such as when the skier is completely unweighted and the skis are in the air). The reverse-shoulder appearance of the counter-rotational skier is a consequence of turning with the legs, not the cause of it. The law of equal and opposite reaction is at work all right, but not in the manner most skiers visualize.

Going one step further, the rotational skier establishes angular momentum and lets the momentum pull his skis through the turn. The counter-rotational skier pushes the skis into a turn and uses his upper body momentum to counterbalance this motion.

It is now possible to discuss the pros and cons of these two approaches more meaningfully.

Since the counter-rotational skier directs his skis with his legs—in other words, since the turning power is close to the skis—counter-rotation is quicker and more precise. While the time lag between a rotational and counter-rotational turn is frequently exaggerated by proponents of counter-rotation, it is nevertheless substantial enough to make a difference. No slalom racer uses rotation, and on today's packed ski slopes, frequently moguled, the extra turning speed makes a great deal of sense. Indeed, the very fact that most slopes today are packed and that the weight must be on the downhill ski, speaks strongly for counter-rotation and its angulated position, which makes certain that the weight is in the right place. Furthermore, a coiled, muscularly tensed (not to be confused with muscularly rigid) body will react more quickly and be less prone to injury in the event of a fall. The system is not without its disadvantages. The position of twisting angulation tends to throw the skier's weight on his heels and back, particularly when he rises to unweight. The skier must be constantly on guard against this.

It is when the counter-rotational skier gets into soft or deep snow that the drawbacks of the system become more apparent. Because he pushes with his legs to make the turn, a great deal more muscular effort is required. But

303

Franz Furtner demonstrates the Austrian technique based on counter-rotation. Unweighting in this system is a quick light "kick" which leaves some weight on skis as they start to carve. Austrian instruction is noted for its uniformity.

more important, the skier is driving his skis into the snow at a time when the skis should be floating. The counter-rotational skier adapts to this by minimizing his motions in staying close to the fall line. The rotational skier has much greater liberty in this respect since he is pulling his skis through the turn and it is relatively easy to keep them floating in the snow. Another advantage of rotation is its virtual insurance that the weight will be forward as the skier goes into his turn. Offsetting this, however, is the constant temptation to overrotate and to throw the weight on the inside ski.

Heel push combined with angulation gives the counter-rotational skier precise control over the end of his turn. But the temptation is always there to overuse it. The rotational skier stays square over his skis and carves the end of the turn, which is neater and cleaner than pushing the heels. Carving is also faster, as the racers have recognized.

The point to keep in mind is that rotation, particularly in its modern version, is not without merit just because it isn't as widely practiced. The very best skiers know this and find ways to incorporate it in their technique, even though there is nothing about it in the manuals of the various ski schools.

THE MODERN FRENCH SYSTEM

THE French are rugged individualists and, although they have prominent counter-rotation advocates in their midst, their national ski school rejects the counter-rotational thesis, at least in its fundamental approach to skiing.

The French equivalent to the American version of the parallel christie of the American technique is *christiania leger,* which literally translated means light christie. The *christiania leger* is no longer the sweeping rotation of old; in fact, the French deny that they are using rotation. The phrase they use to describe what powers their turn is *impulsion par projection circulaire,* which, if it isn't rotation in the classic sense, is still turning power originated in the upper body.

The French enter into the traverse in a position square over their skis, square meaning that the uphill parts of the body are advanced only so far as the uphill ski is advanced. If they angulate, they angulate by simply bending at the hip without turning the upper body toward the valley.

To initiate the turn, the skier sinks, dropping his uphill arm until it hangs almost straight down. From the end of the sinking motion, the skier rises sharply in an up-unweighting motion. As he unweights, his arm starts to come forward and he changes edges. The arm continues to come forward as the skis turn toward the fall line and is just below shoulder level as the skis again enter the traverse.

The turn is so simple that one wonders what makes it go. A comparable analogy is a man throwing a ball underhand. As he starts his throw he puts

Georges Deschiens demonstrates the French system which uses a modern version of Emile Allais' rotation technique of twenty years ago.

his weight on the opposite foot (in the skier's case the downhill ski). As he reaches the point where he is about to release the ball, he steps forward and shifts his weight onto his other foot (skier's weightshift to the outside ski). After he lets the ball go, he follows through and pivots (the skier's arm continues forward, the skis turn). Note that everything the skier is supposed to do happens almost automatically with the possible exception of the edge change. But even this is encouraged by the way the skier shifts weight. The arm motion encourages him to bank his turns, thus putting the skis on their inside edges.

While somewhat quicker than classic rotation, the turn still has some of the weaknesses of that turn—the danger of getting the weight on the inside ski, lack of precise control of the entire turn. Nevertheless, the French have found no difficulty in building on this turn an advanced ski system consisting of wedeln and short swing, even though they borrow here from counter-rotational techniques. French wedeln, in practice, is almost indistinguishable from the counter-rotational version except for a more noticeable use of the arms.

SPLIT ROTATION

AMERICAN skiers are not ideologically inclined. They accept new ideas fervently, but they also have the habit of taking the best from all worlds. Savvy American skiers quickly found a way to combine the merits of rotation and counter-rotation in one turn. The result: split rotation.

A skier actually can start a turn with counter-rotation and finish with rotation. Or he can start with rotation and finish with counter-rotation. There is no particular trick to it if you know how to ski both systems. Beyond this knowledge, the split rotation turn has only two requirements: once you start a turn with one system, you must stick with it until the skis start to turn; and you should arrive at the fall line in a relatively neutral position—not too much rotation or counter-rotation—so that you can exercise the option of finishing either in the system with which you started or switching to the other.

307

LEARNING TO SKI

Split rotation is particularly advantageous in heavier and mixed going on steeper slopes. In heavy going on normal slopes, rotation is a steadier way of launching a turn, but if the slope is steep, the skier may feel that the end of the turn will be a little risky unless he has positive control. Therefore, as he reaches the fall line he switches from rotation to counter-rotation, finishing and controlling the end of the turn with heel push and twisting angulation. In contrast, if the space for turning is narrow and possibly icy, the skier will start with counter-rotation, and if the trail opens up into a long, sweeping turn, he will switch to rotation as he passes through the fall line for the carved, sweeping turn that rotation provides.

This mixing of systems has interesting possibilities. If the skier finishes

the turn with twisting angulation, he has already rotated for the next turn. All he has to do is unweight and bank into a rotational turn. This is not technically rotation, but is called *anticipation*. The distinction is made because the anticipation provides no momentum for the upcoming turn as rotation does. The motion simply anticipates the turn and banks the body for the turn that follows. By following through with the outside arm as the French do in *christiania leger,* a strong rotational impetus is given to the skis.

Split rotation is also helpful to skiers who have difficulty in turning in one direction. By alternating rotation and counter-rotation, the skier can always turn in the direction of his strong side. It's not recommended, but it is a wrinkle to the ski game.

Unweighting technique of Americans (*above*), compared to French (*below*) shows extent to which French move center of gravity when starting to make a parallel turn.

CHAPTER 34

Acrobatics

WHETHER YOU call it anticipation or over-rotation, it can be the starting point for one of the most elegant maneuvers in skiing—mambo. Mambo is a game for smooth slopes only. It combines anticipation with counter-rotation and angulation, and requires a fine feel for edges in order to be successfully executed.

My skis point in the fall line.

Mambo is started by running in the fall line. The skier sinks, and as he rises he rotates as far as he can in the direction of his turn. When the skis begin to bank and turn out of

Stein Eriksen demonstrates a mambo turn across the fall line.

I am running in the fall line.

I sink, prepared to rise.

I rise, start to twist.

kis in fall line, hips twist.

My shoulder, hip, arm stop.

My skis turn out of fall line.

reverse, hand back.

I reverse, hand is way back.

I over-rotate.

My arm, shoulder, hip block.

Blocking turns skis.

I continue reversing.

I sink, prepare for next turn.

My reverse continues.

I hold turn into fall line.

the fall line, the skier counter-rotates, angulating as he does so. This assures that the skis will continue to turn until the skier is over-rotated in the new direction. He then changes edges, banking in the new direction, and as the skis turn he again reverses and angulates to maintain this direction until his reverse has reached the point where he is again over-rotated in relation to the next turn.

Mambo has to be executed with smooth vigor so that the over-rotation is sufficient to bank the skis. At the same time the skier must never lose the feel of his edges. He must sense instantly when they are beginning to bank and the skis beginning to turn so that he can go immediately into the angulated reverse position. Balance is maintained throughout by holding the arms high and to the sides. This also helps put more vigor in the over-rotation motion.

Mambo is not for the timid or uncoordinated. The skier who tries it should be prepared to fall—often. But you will also be king of the slope if you master the mambo.

Just about when you think you've seen everything in skiing, along comes a skier like Art Furrer, wonderfully agile and delightfully uninhibited. The

The Crossed Ski Turn. In this Art Furrer acrobatic, the ski on the inside of the turn is moved out over the weighted outside ski as the turn progresses. The final right or left turn should be completed with the lifted ski at right angles to the running ski. The upper body stays in a reverse throughout the turn. This exercise puts a skier's flexibility to the final test. If you can make a turn on a single inside ski and on a single outside ski, your flexibility and timing are such that you can go on to the Butterfly Turn.

The Butterfly Turn. The skier must swing the ski up behind him in a skating motion. In the final position, the ski is cocked with tip pointing back. The timing of quick swing from the snow to a position behind and above skier is crucial.

The Charleston. This exercise is designed to get the skier used to balancing on one ski. Choose a gentle hill. Start down the fall line and, without shifting the central position of the body between the skis, jump rhythmically from one ski to the other; at the same time swing the tail of the unweighted ski out so that it forms an angle to the ski in the snow. The pole on the unweighted side may be used to help the maneuver. The quicker the change can be made, the better. The skier coming down the slopes should look as if he's kicking up his heels in the Charleston dance step.

The Single Ski Christie. In this maneuver, the skier goes down the fall line of a gentle slope. Furrer, at left, lifts one ski and thrusts it out behind him as far as he can. This straight run can be changed into a Single Ski Christie by leaning to inside while extending tip of the lifted ski to the outside to maintain balance, as shown right.

usually conservative Swiss thought so much of Furrer's acrobatics that they incorporated them into the most advanced techniques of the Swiss National Ski School.

If skiing begins to pall or if you feel you know it all, try the Butterfly, the Single Ski Christie, the Charleston and the Crossed Ski Turn. They're guaranteed to put falls back in your skiing.

CHAPTER 35

Teaching children

IF YOU started to ski late in life, you are bound to reflect on the ease with which children ski. They seem to be so fearless and relaxed. They take the most hair-raising tumbles in stride. And they ski so fast. Inevitably you conclude that your own children should have a similar good start. Such intentions are noble and commendable, but before you begin you might contrast their experience with yours when you started out.

A ski school class of adults starts out by lining up raggedly like a squad of recruits. The instructor talks, they listen. If he is a good one, he talks entertainingly. He demonstrates, they watch. One at a time his pupils take their turns; the instructor shouts exhortations and retrieves the fallen while the others maintain their formation. An altogether purposeful and orderly procedure.

All this may be slow but by the end of the lesson, weak knees are trembling, shins are aching and muscles protesting. More to the point, adults must first understand what they are attempting to do before they try it. By the end of their first lesson, most will be able to do a snowplow, perhaps turn a little.

Children won't put up with this. The lecture amusing to adults is to them seemingly endless and mostly incomprehensible. Standing still in the cold is a form of torture, and looking awkward in front of an adult is an embarrassment. The child leaves for the bathroom or, worse, leaves his skis where he threw them and departs in tears, never to return.

315

The problem is simply that this system, tried and sure as it is for adults, is completely inapplicable to children. Children, and especially very small children, don't learn a sport by listening. They learn by doing. Their kinetic sense is superbly educable, but only through observation and imitation. Making a child stand still in the cold can seem like punishment, and he will at the very least be bored.

Today, however, more and more ski schools have classes for children, staffed with specially trained instructors. Where such effort has been made, the results have been startling. Instructors find that children are easier to teach when the classes and the approach are designed with children in mind, children find that the business of learning to ski is a lot more fun than they expected, and parents are amazed by the progress their youngsters make.

Skiing has much to offer a child. To be out of doors, playing in the snow, being warm and dry despite the cold, and going faster than he ever thought possible—no amusement park, television or other game can offer such a thrill. The child's motive is simply *it's fun*. Take away the fun and the most determined parent or the best teacher cannot make him learn. He'll only ski if he enjoys it. Parents who want their children to ski should put aside dreams of eventual Olympic glory, and, if possible, put them in a ski class before they lose patience. (Losing patience seems to be the inevitable result of trying to be both parent and teacher.)

The child should always be warm and dry, and on skis he can manage—always no taller than the child. A good age to start is before he is two, for as soon as a child can walk, he can walk on skis. Faced with snow up to his knees—say five or six inches—he finds that skis are easier than feet. For this reason a child of two is apt to be a more persistent skier than he will be two or three years hence.

When he is ready for ski school, he should know how to cope with bathroom problems, or, if he doesn't, one of the parents should watch from a dis-

Children learn best by imitating an instructor. Here, at the Squaw Valley Ski School, they play a game—skiing under a pole.

creet distance, ready to take him. A pre-schooler's mother who is not sure if her offspring will last should wait, too, just as she would at nursery school. Children who have started school don't usually need backing.

Youngsters are different from adults in their reactions to the ski environment. When a child says he is cold, believe him. A small child's skin area is more than twice as great as an adult's, relative to body weight and volume. His heat loss is tremendous. He makes up for it, partly, by a higher rate of metabolism, but this also means that when he feels tired, he is on the brink of exhaustion. A child cannot warm up by more activity as an adult can. He should go indoors promptly, preferably in front of a fire with something hot to drink, for he is sensitive to cold in a special way. For him, cold registers as pain, sometimes quite intense.

Compared with an adult, a child's arms and legs are proportionately shorter, his center of gravity is lower and his muscles thicker relative to the bone structure. He also has better padding, his joints contain more cartilage and his tendons are more flexible.

All this works to his advantage when he gets on skis. He hasn't far to fall, and when he does he hasn't much momentum. His legs aren't long enough or thin enough to get tangled up. Skis of the proper length produce almost no leverage in any direction, and his flexible joints will give, even at extreme angles, with no discomfort.

With a class of children, the instructor almost never has to say, "Don't do that, you'll hurt yourself." It just wouldn't be true. It takes a freak fall for a child even to bruise. In fact, falling is apt to be such a lark that he may have trouble progressing to anything else. The rare youngster who is afraid of falling can be brought in line with a ski lesson that resembles a tumbling class in which the instructor falls accidentally-on-purpose.

The major cause of anxiety is the ski pole. Not only can poles be used as lances on others and self, they cause most of the black eyes, bruises and tangles that can result in injury. Children have little use for them except in climbing. It is a good idea to take them away for downhill, lending them for slaloms, underpasses, marking fox and geese circles or race courses on the flat. A well-coordinated child without poles will instinctively use his arms to balance.

318

A child has a somewhat different approach to balance anyway. The familiar wide-open stance of the five-year-old is something that should not be changed too soon. Some children go up and down the rope tow slope and never get their feet closer than 24 inches apart. On a steeper slope, when skiing with some speed, the feet will drift closer together naturally. A child may also use that weighty tail of his like a kangaroo's—stuck way out behind to help him steer. You can give him good reason not to do this by clowning a little, showing him how he looks, and then showing him how he should look.

While most children come to ski class because they want to, there are occasional problems. Attitude is important. Some don't want to be in class. They should get gentle encouragement, but don't insist that they either join the class or stay with you. They may go to the bathroom, get warm and come back. Sometimes they stay close enough and when convinced of the fun they are missing, rejoin the class. At the other extreme, competitively-inclined children tend to become discouraged when friends pass into more advanced classes. If nothing seems to happen for a few lessons, parents can help by taking them to a jump or race or anything that will give them fresh spark.

Poor equipment can be extremely discouraging. No adult can learn in boots too big, on skis without edges, or on skis that won't slide in the first place. Children shouldn't be expected to learn under these conditions either.

Riding the rope tow can be a reward for completing the basic lessons.

LEARNING TO SKI

To get them in the spirit of things, children love chants, songs and rhymed teases, and willingly help an instructor to invent new ones. Variations on the theme of "slippery side, slippery side" may forestall the common four-year-old complaint that "my skis are too-o-o slippery."

You may decide to undertake the early stages of getting your child started on skis. Sliding the skis back and forth in place is a good beginning for the first lesson. A little push will get them moving down a barely perceptible slope. Soon they are walking on the flat, taking turns being engine and caboose, busily making train noises. They learn to run by playing fox and geese. In this first lesson, time can always be taken out for digging an important hole, for making "angels" in the snow, and for throwing snowballs.

For downhill running and then snowplows, use a slope of 10 to 15 degrees, about fifteen feet long, flat at the top, and with a long, barely concave runout. Very little ones can be caught in your waiting arms the first few times. Older ones are encouraged to bounce in the knees. "Making a jet" mark is followed by making a series of snowplows.

Climbing is something of a problem. Sidestepping is difficult and unproductive. Herringboning works a little better for some reason, and some children take to it naturally. Others simply have to live with the difficulty of sidestepping.

By the end of their first lesson, children are ready for the long walk to the rope tow. This walk includes long traverses up and down, perhaps a little sideslipping and sidestepping, much waving to the people on the chairlift and a great deal of chattery conversation.

During the second lesson, most children of four and above will begin turning, at least a little, strictly by imitation and correction. The instructor who can ski backward while holding a child in the proper position has a strong advantage. Sometimes it is helpful to put the child between your skis and urge him to push his skis against yours as they turn, open and close.

By the second lesson, they are all sick of sidestepping, eager for the tow and ready to go up. After you have taken up ten or more four-year-olds, you will have learned thirty-six ways in which children can get entangled.

You will also have learned to support them at every point—skis, hips, shoulders, hands, and ankles. There are also those who don't wait for help, who delightedly take hold and zoom up the first time. And there are those who must be chest-carried. Your biceps develop alarmingly, but children love it. An early tow ride gives them a goal to shoot for.

When they can take a slalom set with their poles, it is time to teach them real sideslipping, preferably on a steep, icy bump. After that there is a great deal of follow-the-leader and free-for-all down the hill.

Children who must attend many classes before they can move into intermediate groups should get a real break from time to time. A hike through the woods looking for tracks and birds can be a tremendous adventure. Watching a junior race will sometimes open junior novice eyes to saucer dimensions.

In this respect, activities designed expressly for children can be of great help. Before any such event, class time is spent boning up on the fine points of egg racing or the problems of the obstacle course. For children it is a great deal of fun.

Children of three and older believe in their hearts that they can fly—they have done so in their dreams. On skis they have a good chance to prove it.

Racers come in all sizes.

CHAPTER 36

How to enjoy touring

CROSS-COUNTRY touring, as its well-versed addicts know, is not just a matter of walking on skis. One Norwegian puts it this way: "There is a vast difference between plodding and touring." Plodding is what you do if you don't know the basic touring stride.

The secret of touring lies chiefly in the stride technique that has matured over several hundred years. Like other forms of skiing, this technique has come to a peak of technical progress since World War II.

The touring discussed here should be distinguished from another North American usage of the word. To many Europeans and Americans, touring has often meant "high mountain touring" where skiers trek into a remote basin on soft-flex metal skis with convertible downhill bindings. This is actually "ski mountaineering." It involves untracked snow and, often, back-packing and survival tactics. Touring in the Scandinavian tradition, on the other hand, is more like hiking on skis. The equipment is extremely light in weight, and the object of the technique is to achieve a light, playful stride over moderately rolling terrain on—for the most part—fairly well-defined routes.

The benefit of touring from the beginner's point of view is that it
322 is basically easier to learn than downhill, that is, it can be mastered more

quickly and really enjoyed sooner. Also, learning in the initial stages is more pleasant. The beginning skier who tours first and then learns the alpine way finds that there are no terrors in sliding on skis. And he will have learned other useful basics.

Often, after a taste of both, a skier elects to continue touring. It provides additional opportunities for skiing, along with all the pleasures of hiking.

Touring skis can be used anywhere where there is snow: frozen lakes, snow-covered lumber trails and rolling hills are not simply so much scenery, but invitations. Every tour offers its own particular challenge.

The basic touring stride is a kick-off from one foot and a gliding step with the other. Kick-offs and glides are alternated from one foot to the other to give a smooth and rhythmical stride that calls for no more co-ordination than ascending stairs, nor is it any more tiring than a brisk walk.

The mark of the skilled touring skier is a relaxed, easy stride with rapid, pushing movements plus long glides with the weight balanced entirely on one ski or the other. As in all skiing, relaxed movements are the crux of the technique; you should be able to tour using far less energy than you would trotting on foot over the same terrain. One of the best tricks is to relax the head and shoulders by focusing your eyes about forty feet ahead of you; continual watching of your ski tips, on the other hand, will result in a cramped and tiring position.

The basic term in touring technique is the "diagonal stride." It means that you employ the diagonally opposite arm and leg at one time. The arm plants the pole while the leg on the opposite side starts the kick. The skier thinks of this kick as kicking his weighted ski toward the back, at the same time transferring his weight off that ski onto the other ski as it moves forward on the gliding stroke. The effect of the kick is to propel the skier forward just as surely and smoothly as a blast of burning fuel from a rocket exhaust kicks the rocket forward.

The pole is merely a support in this maneuver. The main force is in the kick. In fact, the Scandinavians practice without poles first to make sure that

These illustrations show two complete paces of the "diagonal stride," the foundation of the whole art of touring. In the first four figures, the skier swings his *left* arm and *right* leg forward. In the last four figures the *right* leg and *left* arm swing forward. This is what is meant by "diagonal"—the diagonally opposite limbs are swung forward at any one time. Let's look at the movement sequence of the leg and arm movements separately. *Legs:* In figure (*1*) the left leg has come even with the right, is still almost unweighted. The right starts its backward kick movement. To get the most out of the thrust, nearly all the weight must be on the right at this point. (*2*) The right leg has three-quarters completed its kick. A gradual shift of weight to the left (gliding) ski has begun. (*3*) The right leg has completed its kick. Its thrust is over. The left knee is now fully bent. (*4*) The force of the kick carries the completely relaxed right leg back. This is the gliding phase: the left leg is now carrying all the body weight. The left knee straightens. The glide should be cut off before speed drops too much. The whole secret in going long distances without getting tired lies in a relatively long glide with a relaxed body. (*5*) The right leg now swings forward again. Weight is still completely on the left ski, even after the right ski comes completely back on the snow. (*6*) The right leg has come even with the left but still is almost unweighted. The left leg starts its backward kick. (*7*) The backward kick of the left

they get the kick motion learned first. Then, and only then, do they add the pole movement.

324   There are many variations of the diagonal stride. The most important of

leg is three-quarters complete. A gradual shift of weight to the right (gliding) ski has begun. (8) The left leg is relaxed and is swinging up. Weight is completely on the right (gliding) ski with the right knee at full bend.

This alternating kick-and-glide should be practiced at first without poles to gain balance and rhythm. The great part of the driving force comes from leg thrusts. *Arms:* Arms should slide by close to the body almost touching the hips. The hand grip on the poles starts from a firm grip during the "pulling" phase and finishes with a light grip when the arm is completely in back of the body. (1) The left arm begins the push phase simultaneously with the kick of the right leg. (2) The left pole push is complete. The right arm continues its relaxed forward swing. (3-4) The left arm, relaxed, swings back and the pole is free to pendulate. The right arm continues its relaxed forward swing. Neither pole is touching the snow. The grip on both poles is relaxed and loose. (5) The right arm pulls down and in on the right pole, planted in line with the toe of the left boot. (6) The right arm completes its pulling movement and the left arm swings forward. (7) The right arm is now pushing. (8) The right arm push is now finished and the left arm is preparing to plant its pole, at the end of the glide.

these is the double-pole stride where the skier plants both poles instead of only one. The Scandinavian cross-country racers have even more subtle techniques, but there is little point in going into them here. However, the   325

The touring skier can combine double-poling and diagonal strides to form what is known as the "double-pole stride", double-poling with one leg kick between pole settings. In practice, the double-pole stride uses more energy than the diagonal stride and can not be used over very long distances. (1) The skier is gliding with skis equally weighted and body relaxed. (2) Both arms and the upper body begin to swing forward as weight is transferred to the right ski. (3) The right leg is weighted and begins its backward kick to drive the skier forward. The skier swings his poles forward to give him time to react after they are planted. (4) The backward

touring skier should be aware of double poling, which is particularly useful to gain speed on gentle downhill inclines by keeping the skis moving in a rhythmic stride.

Cross-country touring is so simple and inexpensive, it is a wonder that more don't try it. A bit of snow in a city park, trails in the woods, a few rolling hills. These are all you need. Along the way you may enjoy the quiet of an isolated cabin and discover the beauties of winter. As they say in Norway, "*God Tur!*" Good touring!

kick of the right leg is complete and the skier is now gliding on his left ski. The glide in the double-pole stride is considerably longer and the skier has enough time to lean well forward before planting his poles. (5) The poles have just been planted and the upper body weight is over the poles. The right leg is coming forward. (6) The right leg has completed its forward swing and is partially weighted. The pole thrust is almost finished. (7) Both skis are equally weighted as the arms swing up in back. (8) The skier is gliding on equally weighted skis with the body relaxed. He can now go into another double-pole stride or into the diagonal stride.

CHAPTER 37

Ski safety and courtesy

SAFETY IS usually something you think about after an accident. Until then, an injury is something that happens to other skiers.

Skiing is not the safest of sports and, let's be honest, part of its appeal are its risks. In our super-tame, super-safe civilization, the taking of physical risks can be a distinct relief. The man-against-nature struggle is a test of nerves, of courage, and it would hardly be a struggle if there were no physical danger involved.

It is not the purpose of this chapter to preach caution—say, to tell you not to ski slopes over your head. Such advice is silly, first because it must be ignored if you are to make progress in the sport, and, second, because most skiers are only too well aware of the risks. Indeed the problem of most beginners is over-fearful caution.

Rather than suggest you avoid all danger, the purpose of this chapter is to make you aware of it so that you can recognize it when you see it. You should be able to look it in the eye, so to speak, and make your own decision whether to challenge it directly or avoid it.

Simply because there is danger, however, does not mean that you must get hurt beyond an occasional bruise. Because you live with danger does not mean that you have to lose to it. Many, many skiers, including a lot who have courted the extreme dangers of the top international racing trails, have never had a serious injury. Contrary to popular belief, well-trained racers seldom suffer serious injury. Why? Because they are in top physical condition, have the best equipment (including the best release bindings properly adjusted), and possess athletic skill and judgment. If they lack any of these, they are not very good racers. To the extent that the recreational skier lacks them, he is less safe on the slopes.

The best means of avoiding injury is to be in good condition. Although sheer physical strength is helpful, it is not critically important. What is important about good condition is that it provide flexibility, mobility and sensitivity to conditions underfoot. Good physical condition enables you to sense impending difficulty more quickly and to make adjustments.

It makes similar good sense to learn to ski properly in a good ski school. Injuries in ski school are miniscule compared with the injuries incurred in free skiing. This is because the instructor knows what he is doing and selects instructional approaches and terrain with safety in mind. But equally important is the fact that in class you are always concentrating on what you are doing. If you carry the habit of concentration over into your free skiing, your chances of injury are greatly reduced.

Statistically, the snowplowing and stem-turning skier is the best candidate for the ski patrol toboggan. The reasons are not difficult to divine. The beginning skier is a great deal less skilled and experienced—he's clumsy—but, more important, the very nature of the stemmed turn invites injury in the event of a fall or entanglement. In the typical beginner accident situation, the skier gets the feeling that he is going too fast. He tries to check his speed by desperately sticking out his skis in a rough stem. The tips cross and he falls, actually quite slowly. At this point his bindings should release *if properly adjusted*, but they may not. In that case, the position of the skier is such that the weight of the body holds the foot firmly on the snow while the body continues to rotate above the leg—to such an extent that either a sprain or a fracture is entirely possible. Of course, the possibility of such an accident is compounded if the skier is on a slope beyond his real capability.

329

There are many ways to reduce the injury potential of this typical situation:

Good bindings, properly adjusted, will release before the twist turns into a sprain or fracture.

Ski school training, with emphasis on learning to fall, is excellent insurance.

Good physical condition will protect muscles and tendons, even though the fall is a bad one.

But above all, what the skier needs in the beginning stages is patience. As the beginner makes the transition to intermediate, he should be carefully on guard against seeking the thrills of more difficult skiing. During this stage the emphasis must be on correct execution.

Short of senseless schussbooming, speed in itself is not the problem; judgment concerning it is. A slope is not like a tilted billiard table but consists of an infinite variety of angles, pitches, bumps, rolls, sidehills and snow conditions. Light, wind, snow, and other skiers are responsible for constant change—even from run to run. The skier who takes a trail for granted, or runs it without being constantly alert, is asking for trouble.

One of the best ways to avoid trouble is to keep looking far ahead. In looking at a slope the skier should think in terms of two or three moves beyond the one he is making. This prevents him from being surprised. He can adjust his speed, change his direction or come to a stop in the event of a hazard.

The experienced skier's difficulties usually begin when either snow conditions or some error in execution separate the skis. The proper procedure is to unweight the straying ski and replace it in its parallel position. In a turn, the situation is somewhat different. If the straying ski is the outside ski, it means you haven't enough weight on it and that you are at least partially riding the inside ski. The answer to this problem is to put the weight where it belongs.

330 The caught edge is the major cause of hard, jolting falls, the type that

11, 12, 13. *Above and right*. Courchevel. At left, testing a potential avalanche slope —
should a slide occur, patrolmen can be located by their floating balloons.

10. *Preceding page*. The Aiguille du Midi tramway at Grenoble.

14. The Gaisberg chairlift, Austria.   15. *Right*. A sidewalk cafe in Lech.

16. *Following double page spread*. The village of Grindelwald in the Bernese Oberland.

17.   Touring in Norway.

produce injuries. Failure to maintain proper edge control is the cause. But what can be done about it once an edge has caught? Generally speaking, the best protection is return to the neutral de-angulated position so that edge pressure is relieved and the body is able to recover equilibrium. If your body twist can be untwisted, if you can turn back toward the ski tips, the chances of a twisting fall and resulting damage are minimal.

Falls are not the only source of injuries. Poles have a way of snagging in brush or branches when skiing near trees. A wrenched and dislocated shoulder can result unless the skier takes prior precaution by taking the poles straps off his wrist. People find an amazing number of ways to jab themselves and others with poles. Front throws have a disconcerting way of mashing thumbs, and edges can cut fingers and slash through expensive stretch pants and into shins. And there is always the possibility of frostbite, just one of the many reasons why you should never ski alone. Your companion can always spot the oncome of frostbite by the greyish-white appearance of the affected area, usually the tip of the nose or the ears.

COURTESY

GENERAL courtesy, which strongly implies awareness of others, not only promotes ski safety but also enjoyment of the sport by yourself and others. There are some helpful rules to follow:

Join the end of the liftline and keep your place. It's not only polite and orderly, but it also prevents needless damage to equipment and possible cuts and bruises as a result of the confusion.

Avoid stepping on the back of the skis of the skier in front of you as you would avoid stepping on his feet. You may not hurt him physically, but you won't do his skis any good.

If you are alone in a busy line, double up with someone in good time by yelling "single." A last-minute rush to join a single can lead to accidents. When sharing a chair with a safety bar that lowers, make sure that you each 331 know when the bar is coming down, or mashed fingers may result. On a T-bar, don't insist on riding with someone a great deal taller or shorter than you.

Treat lifts with respect. Horsing around on a lift may cause the cable to derail, endangering you and the other riders. On T-bars and platterpulls, keep your skis in the tracks and avoid the temptation to run some kind of uphill slalom. On ropetows, release the rope gradually so as not to jerk it when getting off at the top.

Move out of the unloading area swiftly when getting off a lift. Contain yourself and look at the view, adjust bindings and goggles, at a safe distance.

Ski where you belong and in control. If you are trying something more difficult than anything you've done so far, wait until the coast is clear and keep checking that it is. There is nothing more dangerous than the basher who, unable to turn or stop, knocks down skiers like bowling pins.

Ski defensively. The skier in front of you has the right of way since he hasn't got eyes in the back of his head. Use "track," the skier's equivalent of the golfer's "fore," sparingly and be specific—"track right" if you are passing on the right, "track left" if you are passing on the left.

If you stop on the way down, do so only at the side of the hill where you will be out of the way of other skiers. If, for some reason, you have to walk down, walk at the extreme edge of the trail.

Do not jump or turn full tilt into blind areas or blind corners. Use someone as a spotter if you plan to jump. Check your speed when entering a new trail.

Fill your sitzmark, the hole you make when you fall in softer snow. A hole is like a bear trap to the skier that follows.

Respect flags and trail markers put up by the area, its ski school and its

(*Green*) means "easiest" slope or trails in an area.

(*Yellow*) means "more difficult"

(*Red*) means "extreme caution"

(*Blue*) means "most difficult"

(*Red*) means "avalanche danger"

patrol (see illustrations). They are there to tell you something. Learn the meaning of degree-of-difficulty trail markers and their limitations. If you knock down poles on a practice slalom course, replace them.

Put your skis and poles in the racks provided for them instead of leaning them against the nearest building where others can trip on them and gash themselves if they fall.

Be generally considerate, particularly of skiers not as adept as you. Many trails for better skiers terminate on the beginner's slope. Make allowances for this. Stop for those who seem to be in trouble. Be helpful. You may make a friend.

THE SKI PATROL/INJURIES

DESPITE having taken all the necessary precautions, there may come a time when either you or one of your companions is injured sufficiently to require the help of the ski patrol. If you have been wondering what those guys with rust-colored parkas and crosses on their backs do other than ski and go to the head of the liftline, you are about to find out.

The members of the National Ski Patrol System are rightly called the "Good Samaritans of the Slopes." Actually, they do a great deal more than rescue the fallen. They also do their bit in accident prevention—filling holes, smoothing out ruts, flagging soft or bare spots—which is a never-ending chore at busy ski areas.

The majority of patrolmen are volunteers, although most larger areas also employ one or more professionals so that there is always someone at the area who is competent to deal with injuries. Whether volunteer or professional, the patrolman goes through a rigorous training course, and then must keep current with regular brush-up courses. The patrolman has earned his right to wear his parka. Unless you are a doctor, it is best to leave injuries to him.

In the event of injury to a companion or someone you come upon, avoid panic at all costs. With the exception of avalanches, ski injuries are usually not fatal providing you keep your head.

333

By all means summon help, but before you rush off, do several things first.

1. Determine the damage without moving the skier.
2. If it can be done without discomfort, take off the injured skier's skis. Stick the skis, crossed fashion, into the snow about 20 feet above the injured skier so as to warn others of the accident.
3. Keep the injured party as warm as possible to minimize the effects of shock.
4. Stay with him if at all possible, or get someone else to stay with him while you summon help. If you are asked to summon help, don't let the injured skier down. In either event, make certain of the location so that you can direct the patrol as precisely as possible. If you are not sure, fix a prominent landmark and stay alert for location indicators.
5. Get back to the injured party as quickly as possible. For one reason or another, it may take a little while for the patrol to arrive.

After the patrol arrives, let them do their job without any assistance, unless it is specifically requested. If it is a friend, you will want to know where they are taking him and where his equipment will be stored.

AVALANCHES

A MUCH more serious matter than trail injuries, because of the fatal danger, are avalanches. Any reasonably steep slope can avalanche if conditions are right, though some are more subject to avalanches than others. The problem of avalanches need not be of overwhelming concern within a ski area providing that you observe avalanche precautions and warning signs.

However, if you are skiing in the West and Europe, it is the better part of valor to approach any untracked slope with caution. There are hundreds of avalanches in these regions every season. Those that bring death do so because of factors not easily predicted even by experienced mountaineers.

There are two principal types of avalanche: loose snow and slab. Loose snow has little internal cohesion and tends to move as a formless mass, the slide growing in size as it descends. Slab avalanches, on the other hand, are characterized by internal cohesion—a large area of hard snow begins to slide at once from a well-defined fracture line across the slope. Frequently caused by wind-drifting, which often gives the snow a dull chalky color, the slab avalanche constitutes a great winter slide hazard because of its unpredictability.

Elaborate avalanche prevention techniques are common at major ski resorts. Artillery mortars and explosives are often used deliberately to trigger avalanches, clearing and subsequently making the terrain safe for skiers.

Steep gullies and open, treeless slopes are natural avalanche paths; ridges, outcrops and terraces are natural barriers. Other things being equal, a convex-shaped slope is more dangerous than a concave profile. But both can avalanche.

Avalanche danger is high during and after heavy winter storms. It usually declines as snow settles and stabilizes. But cold weather does not readily allow stabilization.

Underlying snow conditions have an important bearing on avalanche danger. Deep snow smooths out irregularities and promotes sliding. Smooth surfaces, such as rain or sun crust, also make good sliding bases. Rough, firm snow, on the other hand, offers a good anchorage for subsequent layers. Wet snow avalanches occur when rain or melting water lubricates and weakens snow layers which already are somewhat unstable.

When Avalanche Conditions Exist

NEVER travel alone.

Pick the route carefully. The safest route is along the top by way of the ridge. The next safest route is along the valley floor *under* the avalanche. Most avalanches occur on slopes of 30 to 45-degrees.

Beware of lee areas, especially convex profiles beneath a cornice.

Never expose more than one member of the party to avalanche danger at once. The other members should watch the person crossing so they can plot his probable course in case a slide is started.

Don't assume a slope is safe just because the first few crossed safely.

Don't camp or stop under an avalanche path. Prolonged exposure is always risky.

335

LEARNING TO SKI

If you must cross an avalanche slope, remove wrist loops of your ski poles. Unhitch Arlberg or safety straps from your skis so you won't be tied to them in a slide.

Close up your clothing, don hat and mittens and raise your parka hood. If buried in the snow, your chances of survival are much better if snow doesn't get inside your clothes to cause chill.

Wear a brightly colored avalanche cord if one is available. Tie one end to your belt and let it trail out behind you. If you bring down a slide, the cord has a good chance of floating to the surface.

Avalanche "busting", in this case by means of a 75mm shell, is resorted to when a huge accumulation of snow on a hilltop presents a serious hazard to skiers in the immediate area.

If You Are Caught in an Avalanche

CALL out so other members of your party can observe your course in case you are buried.

Discard skis, poles, rucksack.

Try to stay on the surface by swimming. Attempt to work to one side of the moving snow. In a large or fast-moving avalanche, such efforts will probably be of little avail, but they may save your life in a smaller one.

If swimming doesn't help, cover your face with your hands. This will keep snow out of your nose and mouth and you will have a chance to clear a breathing space if you are buried. Avalanche snow often becomes very hard as soon as it stops moving and your arms may be pinned when the snow halts.

If you are buried, try to avoid panic. Many avalanche victims have been recovered dead, apparently uninjured and after only a few minutes of burial. The only explanation doctors can offer is that they were actually frightened to death.

In soft snow you may be able to dig yourself out, or at least make room to breathe. Try to keep your sense of direction; actually you might be digging *down* under the impression that it's the way out.

What to do if Your Companions Are Caught

DON'T panic. The lives of your buried companions may depend on what you do in the next hour. Check for further slide danger. Pick a safe escape route in case of a retreat.

Mark the point on the avalanche path where the victim was last seen as he was carried down by the snow. This will narrow the area of search.

Search quickly. If there are only two or three survivors, they must make a quick but careful search of the avalanche before going for help. One man should then be left at the accident scene to continue the search and guide the rescue party. The chances of a buried victim being recovered alive diminish rapidly after two hours.

Search the surface *below* the last seen point for evidence of the victim or clues to his location. Mark the location of any pieces of his equipment you find—these may provide additional indicators of the path taken by the flowing snow.

Begin probing. If the initial search fails, probe with the heel of your ski, an inverted ski pole, or a collapsible probe *below* the last-seen point. Trees, ledges, benches or other terrain features which have caught the snow are likely places.

Send for help. If there are several survivors, send only two. The remaining survivors may search for the victim in the meantime.

If you must go for help, travel carefully, avoiding further avalanche or injuries from skiing too fast.

The victim's chance of survival depends on your getting through. Mark your route, especially if fresh snow is falling, so you can find your way back. Try to avoid complete exhaustion. The rescue party normally will expect you to guide them back to the accident scene.

If the victim is found, apply first aid treatment immediately for suffocation and shock. Free nose and mouth of snow, and administer mouth-to-mouth artificial respiration if necessary. Clean snow from inside clothing and place victim in sleeping bag with head downhill.

It cannot be overstressed that safety in skiing is not a matter of timidity, but calm common sense. The skier who is oblivious to danger isn't courageous; he is stupid.

Part Five

SKI COMPETITION

CHAPTER 38

The fun of racing

HAVE YOU ever been skiing on top of a hill and suggested to a friend that you race to the bottom? You probably have. And when it was all over, there was a lot of good-natured joshing and debate why you won or lost—the equipment you were using, the quality of your technique, and your choice of line down the mountain. It was all great fun, and, surprisingly, the next time you skied, you found yourself skiing just a bit better.

Simply because you have raced a friend down the mountain, you hardly consider yourself a competitor. Yet, essentially, that is what you are. Virtually every racer, no matter how impressive his reputation, starts this same way.

If you enjoy competition, skiing can provide it, no matter how seriously you want to take it or how old you are. Of course, the best competitors usually started to race in their early teens at the latest, but because you have a late start doesn't mean that a national championship is totally out of your reach. For instance, there is a National Veterans Championship classification for skiers over fifty (Class IV). If you entertain hopes for this competition, you should be good. Few oldtimers who ski consistently lose their skill (though they may lack endurance). Most of them ski better than they did in their racing heydays.

Of course, this class of competition may be the farthest thing from your 341

SKI COMPETITION

mind. You may want to race just for the heck of it, either because you enjoy tying a racing bib across your chest, or because you enjoy collecting pins and medals, or because the hill you have to ski on week after week lacks a certain variety. Whatever your motives, there is a type of racing for you.

Let's take a look at racing and see how it evolved.

When racing first started before the turn of the century, it was very similar to what you and your friend were doing. A group of competitors got together on top of the mountain and at a signal all took off at once and headed for the designated finish line. There were no prepared tracks, no flags to mark the course, and, for all practical purposes, no rules. The first man to arrive was the winner. These mass starts were known as *geschmozzle* starts because of the mixups after the starting signals. This kind of racing was colorful, exciting, but, as speeds increased, dangerous. To decrease the danger, racers were started individually and each racer's run was timed. This is the method for competition today. There are a few competitions where more than one

A *geschmozzle* race, 1935. The simultaneous start of racers down the mountain was a popular form of competition in the thirties, but led to many high-speed collisions.

racer starts at a time. One of the most exciting is a dual slalom in which two racers descend parallel courses. Another is the cross-country relays where the first runners of each team start together, leading to some interesting jockeying where the track narrows.

The original races were pure tests of speed over open alpine terrain. It was very dare-devilish (the British were remarkably good at it), but it did little for skiing skill as such. To emphasize the necessity for skill and judgment in maneuvering, Sir Arnold Lunn invented slalom competition, which was originally supposed to simulate skiing through the woods and around obstacles. Sir Arnold utilized the two-pole gate, a series of which were set in various combinations on a hill. Skiing around poles was not new in itself, but the two-pole gates were a distinct innovation since they could be set in such a way as to trap the skier who did not use sound judgment. As skiing skill increased, slaloms became tighter and tighter, until today, in top national and international competition, they are tests in acrobatics as well as skiing skill. This development has been the source of considerable controversy, and the FIS is urging race organizers to experiment with single-pole slaloms, which are claimed to put more emphasis on pure skiing ability.

As downhills became faster, they too became more closely controlled. Today, while still a test of speed, they no longer offer an option of course down the mountain. The course is pre-selected and carefully prepared, and where speed may become excessive control gates are placed in such a way as to slow the racer down. Furthermore, because of the speeds possible in downhill, the courses no longer plunge down what is necessarily the steepest part of the mountain. Rather, the emphasis is on challenging terrain with such problems as bumps, rolls, sudden drop-offs and accuracy of line. No matter what the level of competition, downhill is not a sport for the faint of heart.

Giant slalom was originally developed just before World War II as a compromise event between downhill and slalom. Since that time, however, it has gained a distinct character of its own. Where downhill follows the fall line as closely as is practical within the limits of safety, and where slalom puts the emphasis on turning, giant slalom is essentially a test of traversing at high 343 speed. The turn that follows the traverse should put the racer in such a position that he can traverse at high speed to the next gate. While there are gates in giant slalom, they are not put together in combinations. Thus, at lower levels of competition, giant slaloms are the easiest to set and the easiest to run. Only as the competitive level rises does the event require special skills.

All of this need not worry the recreational competitor. His course will be set up in such a way that he will have little difficulty. Many areas have standard races which require the skier to pass through the course in a given time to win a gold, silver or bronze pin. The most famous of these are the Sun races at Sun Valley, which are held weekly throughout the season. The holder of a Golden Sun is a skier of some distinction. The winner of the Diamond Sun is usually a first-rate racer. Diamond Sun races are held only once every several years.

There are other forms of standard races. One popular version requires that the participants come within a certain proximity of the time posted that day by one of the area's hotter skiers. Another calls for the skier not only to pass through the course in a certain time, but also to perform certain turns correctly. This one is a favorite of some ski schools and recently became a separate style event called the Masters. In Masters competition, competitors have to perform certain required maneuvers and then ski freestyle. They are judged very much the way ice skaters are judged.

Racers for fun can also satisfy their competitive yen in club and costume races, or they can set slaloms of their own. Setting slaloms is not difficult providing you understand how the gates are set up and how they should be placed in relation to the terrain (see illustrations, p. 346). Although FIS rules call for a mimimum gate width of ten feet, six inches, there is no point in setting the gates that tight; between twelve and fifteen feet with plenty of space between gates is more than adequate for recreational or fun-competition slaloms. Most important is that the course result in a smooth rhythmic run.

But there may come a time when "fun" racing no longer satisfies either yourself or your youngster. The first things you should consider are whether you really like to compete and whether you are now a good enough skier.

344

Slalom gate arrangements under competitive conditions. In recreational slalom, gates should not be as close together.

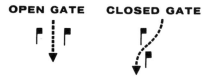

OPEN GATE   **CLOSED GATE**

Open and closed gates are 10½ feet wide for competitive slalom, can be wider for recreational use. Allow 12′ between single or H-gates, 2½′ between flush and hairpin gates, and 5′ for elbows.

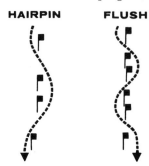

HAIRPIN   **FLUSH**

Hairpin consists of two successive closed gates; third gate makes it a flush. Neither should be set so tightly that rhythm is broken, but both should require proper technique.

ELBOW

Elbow is made up of a closed gate followed by an open gate set off to one side. As in all combinations, approach depends on the location and type of the next set of gates.

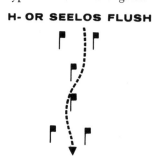

H- OR SEELOS FLUSH

The H- or Seelos flush is a three-gate combination. Slalom gates can always be entered from either direction; choice is with the racer, and is determined by position and figures that follow.

A thirty-five second slalom recommended for intermediates. Note that it is made up of all basic gate combinations, including a trap in the lower section.

These questions may seem obvious, but there are many skiers who force themselves, or their children, into ski racing when they are not instinctively competitive. It is highly doubtful whether ski racing will do anything for skiers who are not so inclined, and in some cases the results can be painful, psychologically and physiologically. The same consideration applies to ski ability. Obviously you should be a good skier if you plan to take up serious racing, but some skiers are so competitive that they race before they are really proficient enough. At worst, this can result in a serious accident. At best, it will be a frustrating experience.

Other prerequisites are physical strength and self-discipline. You don't have to be unusually strong—though it helps. Keep in mind that you will be required to ski hard for three minutes or more with no chance to coast. Before you commit yourself, try to ski fast and hard for two minutes without a stop. It will give you an idea of what you will be up against. You will be surprised how many stops you make on those long, long runs you think you are skiing without interruption. Even the best racers finish races exhausted. Your effort and condition may not have to be as great, but you can't be a weakling either. In most races the strength required is gained by concentrated practice and by physical exercise. The better racers put themselves through some kind of fall

TIPS FOR SETTING SLALOM	TIPS FOR RUNNING SLALOM
1. Don't set gates too tight. 12-15' for open gates, 10-15' for closed gates is sufficient.	1. Strive for precision, not speed, at first.
2. Set gates to maintain smooth, flowing run. Don't set sharp corners that will break rhythm.	2. Study the course. Climb it, memorize it and plan your line of descent.
3. Allow natural check points or gate combinations to hold down speed.	3. Make your turn before entering a gate, not while you are in it.
4. Utilize terrain to require variation in technique and permit alternate lines of approach to gates.	4. Enter a gate slowly, come out fast. Come into a gate high, even if you must use a skating step to gain height.
5. Set gates to test total technique, keeping in mind the skier's ability. Slalom is a test of ability, not endurance.	5. Keep your skies together and don't sit back. Do not over-rotate. Use reverse shoulder to get past flags.

347

conditioning program and do daily calisthenics during the ski season (see Chapter 28). When they ski and are not racing, they either work on improving technique or on gaining strength and endurance. For the latter they might try non-stop runs staying in a tuck position for long periods of time or making as many complete turns as possible down the length of the mountain. Physical strength *is* important, and it relates closely to safe racing.

Self-discipline is probably the last major prerequisite. Everyone sees the magnificent performances that good racers can turn in on occasion, and it sometimes appears to the uninitiated that the whole thing isn't really that hard. This is further reinforced by the attitude of some excellent skiers, who deprecate the difficulty of racing, yet who flounder pathetically through the simplest slalom. The truth is, racing—that is, serious racing—requires a great deal of practice before and between races, practice that is totally unglamorous, often discouraging and a lot of work. And to make it worse, your friends will continually urge you to skip practice and join them for romps in the powder. It takes will power and sacrifice of much "fun skiing" to be a good racer.

What does a racer get out of all this? If he is good enough, a place on the national team, perhaps glory from an occasional important victory, perhaps the ultimate—a medal in the Olympics or the FIS World Championship. There will be travel to exotic resorts, free equipment, free clothing and perhaps world-wide publicity. But don't count on such glory, particularly for a bright youngster who in your eyes has all the makings of a world champion.

The ultimate ski victory: Pepi Stiegler wins a gold medal in the 1964 Olympics.

More important is the old-fashioned Anglo-Saxon notion about "playing the game." There is a lot of satisfaction in doing the very best you can and testing yourself against others in your class. The fact that there are over seven thousand senior racers in the United States, including almost one thousand veteran racers (over twenty-seven), only a handful of whom are national team material, indicates the broad satisfactions of racing.

How is racing organized and run in this country? All amateur racing is controlled by the United States Ski Association (USSA). The USSA is divided into eight geographical regions. In each region, a division of the USSA runs the racing program. If you want to race, you should find out what division you are in and contact that division for membership, classification, a schedule of races, a rule book, and any other information they may have for new competitors. You can often get all of this material through a ski club, providing it is affiliated with the division (some are not).

Racers under nineteen are called juniors; from nineteen to twenty-six, seniors; and from twenty-seven on, veterans. In juniors' and veterans' competition, there are sub-classifications by age brackets. In senior competition, there are three classes based on ability: A, B and C. Classification procedures for new races vary among divisions. Some divisions use so-called classification races early in the season so that would-be racers can run and show if they are good enough to be given a class C race card. In other divisions, a class C card is granted automatically to new racers. In still others, an "unclassified" race card is given to new racers, entitling them to race in certain races to qualify for a class card. In one division there is a class D for new racers, and a system of examiners to study applicants and to decide if they should be given a class C card. Only by writing to your division can you find out exactly what you must do. In most divisions there are also ability classifications for junior racers similar to senior classifications.

For complete information on how to organize your own ski competition, see Appendix F.

349

SKI COMPETITION

The organization of a typical race course. Personnel on the starting platform include: (1) chief starter, (2) assistant starter, (3) start judge, (4) and (5) radio or phone men, (6) start recorder, (7r) racer in gate, (8r) and (9r) next two racers on deck.

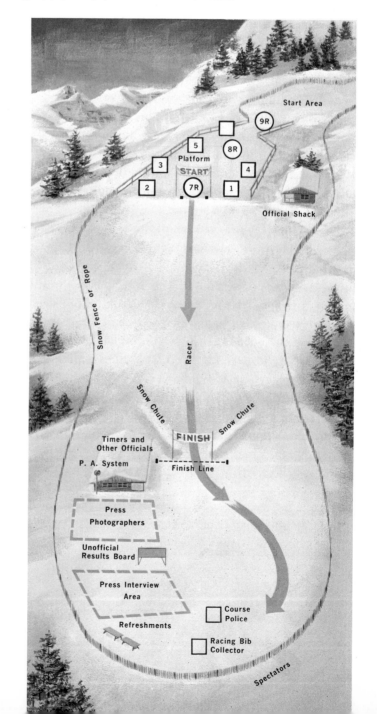

Each division compiles a list of races—so-called sanctioned races—and sends it out to all competitors in its region. Most competitors plan at the beginning of the season what races they will attend.

The races are run in accordance with the rules of the Federation Internationale de Ski (FIS). The FIS supervises the ski events of the Winter Olympics and the World Ski Championships. You should study the FIS rule book (available from your division), particularly the rules pertaining to disqualifications and starts. You should also find out from your division about its promotion policies. In all divisions, promotion from one class to the next is based on some kind of point system. In some divisions, the points are based on placings; in others, on FIS points which are allocated to each racer on the basis of how far he was behind the winner—the winner getting 0.00 points. FIS points become crucial as you climb up the racing ladder. They determine your seeding group. The best fifteen racers, based on FIS points, start first, the actual starting number of the racer being determined by a draw. The next best fifteen racers draw from number 16 to 30, and so on. There is a real advantage in being top-seeded: you don't have to ski through the ruts and the chatter marks made by the other racers. This is particularly crucial in slalom.

For youngsters, getting started in racing should pose no particular difficulty. Virtually every mountain town or ski area has some sort of junior program. Even at places where there is no program, there'll be someone who can take a capable youngster under his wing. If at all possible, parents should avoid getting involved too directly in their child's program. They should by all means help to get the program organized, help out at races by timing, recording, gatekeeping and performing other officiating functions, and provide the necessary transportation. But beyond such involvements, parental emotions and junior's racing don't mix too well. Preferably a good coach, or otherwise an experienced ski instructor, is in a better position to correctly judge the youngster's progress and to determine what he needs in the way of conditioning and practice.

For those out of the junior ranks and not members of a college team, the situation is more difficult. For all practical purposes you are on your own. To **351**

SKI COMPETITION

train by yourself is hard unless you are exceptionally dedicated. The best solution is to find a good club program and join it.

Although you may be advised to the contrary, try to develop a taste for downhill first, particularly if you still harbor hopes for racing prominence. While opportunities for downhill are minimal in B, C and veterans racing, slalom and giant slalom are much more easily mastered if you are a confident downhiller. Most racers who show strength in downhill have relatively little difficulty in becoming proficient in slalom and giant slalom, but only a rare few who are good in the latter two events ever become good downhill racers later. Good downhillers are few and far between. College and national team coaches are always on the lookout for downhill talent.

This does not mean that you should neglect slalom or giant slalom. Most races for lower class racers are based on these events and on-snow practice for slalom is readily obtainable. Almost every area has a slalom hill somewhere. Try to be at the hill during the time when good racers are using the poles to set practice slaloms. Watch them and learn. Ask questions about their equipment, their technique and the course. Ask if you may try the course. Start slowly and try to go the full distance. If you fall, reset the gates you knock

Anderl Molterer of Aspen coaches young hopefuls at a summer racing camp.

down, and try again—more slowly. Before each run, walk up the course, memorizing it. Try to judge the places where your speed will be greatest, decide if you will need to check and how. Occasionally use a stop-watch and time your runs and those of the others on the hill, so that you become familiar with racing for time. Also practice "5-4-3-2-1-Go" starts so that you become accustomed to the countdown.

For additional training, ask your division about any racing instruction schools or camps they may be organizing as an aid to new racers. These schools and camps are often run over part of the Christmas holidays and occasionally on weekends. There are even summer racing camps for youngsters on glaciers. Their cost is usually low and they will give you the opportunity to have your race technique criticized by competent critics. You will also learn about waxing, equipment and race strategy. Some regions have commercial racing schools and some of the larger areas often have a former hot-shot racer on their staff who is also a good instructor. Check on reputations and avail yourself of these opportunities when they arise.

And lastly, having selected the races you plan to enter, be sure to send your entry application and fee in early. Class C races in particular draw many applicants, and the running order is based on the entry date. The earlier your start, the better your chances of finishing first.

There is something about the élan of racers that makes racing great fun, win or lose. It is, of course, more fun to win, and your mind should settle for no less at the start of each race.

Pia Riva at Silver Belt slalom, Sugar Bowl. A fast start may mean the difference between a gold or silver medal.

CHAPTER 39

Learning from the hot-shot racers

IN THE last few years, both the United States and Canada have mounted major efforts to improve their ratings among the ski nations of the world. These efforts are showing some signs of succeeding. A racer with promise, particularly a young racer, no longer needs to struggle along as best he can. There is a program—a system—which will expose him to expert coaching at frequent intervals. Before he has a chance to cultivate bad habits, either in conditioning or technique, there will be someone there to correct him. This system is not perfect, but is improving steadily.

Yet despite these efforts, the Billy Kidds, the Jimmy Heugas, the Jean Sauberts and the Nancy Greenes are few and far between. The lack of a program until a few years ago is in part responsible, but equally important is the matter of motivation. In the eyes of the general public, skiing is less important than, say, football. Not unnaturally, the best athletes drift toward the more glamourous and publicized sports. As an additional handicap, most high school administrators are indifferent if not downright hostile to ski racing. The 355 few high schools that do have ski teams are so circumscribed by unrealistic state high school athletic regulations that they are seldom able to provide a competitive climate suitable for preparing young racers for the more rigorous demands of the senior circuit. The better young skiers usually shun high school teams in favor of freelance competition.

The situation is entirely different in the Alpine countries of Europe. European racers—and particularly the Austrians—consider ski victories in international competition a matter of economic betterment. The racers who can supply these victories or have the potential for doing so are looked on as national heroes, and, by one means or another, are amply rewarded for their sacrifices. This fact is not lost on youngsters with athletic ability, particularly those from the hard and monotonous life of the mountain farms. Ski ability in the Alpine countries is a proven shortcut to the bright lights of the resort hotels in the valleys below.

The wonder then is not that we produce so few true international-class racers, but that we produce them at all. You can be sure that any American who ranks among the top in the world is an extraordinary individual.

What distinguishes the good, competent racer from the great one? A high level of courage, a powerful determination to win and a great deal of natural skiing ability, of course. But beyond these, a winning performance at the international level requires the extra effort for that last foot when it seems a mile, a passion for detail, a highly refined knowledge of all aspects of the sport, sound judgment, and, above all, a frame of mind which Canadian Coach Dave Jacobs calls "mental buoyancy." The latter is probably the most difficult to achieve. The racer must arrive at the starting gate with a certain amount of tension to enable him to perform at his highest level, but too much or too little will reduce his effectiveness.

Racers are well aware of this tension. They think of ways to "psych" their opponents, trying to make them feel overconfident or somewhat less than adequate. Psyching is accomplished by gentle persuasion through tone of voice, careful manipulation of equipment, waxing and clothing and by behavior 356 on and off the course. One of the classic instances of psyching occurred in 1965 at the Three-Nation Team Meet at Vail. The meet was important, but it had been grossly overbilled as a final demonstration of the United States' arrival as a super-ski power. The Austrians and French, whatever they may have felt about it, treated the meet with utmost casualness, and the overanxious Americans were thoroughly deflated. To demonstrate their casual attitude, the French on the last day turned up with baseball caps turned backward, umpire-style, instead of the usual headgear. The Europeans thereupon cleaned up and the Americans never really recovered for the rest of the season.

You can only psych an opponent if he is your equal, and to be his equal may take a good deal of work. Ski racing has developed to a point where as many as a dozen racers are within a second of the winner's time. A few hundredths of a second might separate first and second place.

One would be tempted to describe the winning margin as luck were it not for the fact that certain racers win all season long by just such margins. For example, it was a well known fact that crouching cuts wind resistance

Jean-Claude Killy, a master at "psyching," casually awaits start at 1965 Vail Meet.

The racing crouch or tuck position, as shown here by American Bill Marolt, is key to cutting air drag in downhill events.

and results in greater speed. But it wasn't until 1960, when the French refined the position and developed exercises to enable the racers to hold it longer, that the differences became noticeable. To the unpracticed eye, the French downhill racers were not doing anything especially different from the other downhillers. But their early start in developing the so-called egg position at a time when downhill courses were in a state of flux enabled them to dominate

In the new Giant Slalom turn, the skier comes out of the fall line (*1*), and transfers the greater part of his weight to the uphill ski which carves easily on the snow (*2*). The downhill ski slips away. To maintain his balance on the uphill ski, the skier thrusts his head, shoulders, arms and poles forward in an accelerating movement (*3*). The resulting forward thrust establishes equilibrium and is completed in an energetic burst of speed and determined pole action (*4*). The skier continues his forward projection with double poling which helps both to stabilize and to accelerate (*5*). The upper body has started to swing down hill in typical *serpent* fashion. He snaps into the turn toward the next gate (*6*), continuing the sequence. (Georges Joubert)

downhill for two years. This "domination" averaged about half a second a race.

Racers are constantly looking for such refinements, for ways to cut a few inches off a turn through a gate, to reduce the braking effects of turning, or to get into a faster line. Instructive in this respect is the development of giant slalom. Until the late fifties, giant slalom was approached much like slalom. That is, racers thought of the event as a series of turns. Then came the big change. The Swiss in particular approached GS as a series of traverses linked by turns. They headed straight for the gate, scrambled around it and headed for the next gate. The turns were rough, but the racers more than made up for lost speed in the traverses. They stepped their turns, stepping uphill to start them and on completion stepping uphill again to get a steeper line to the next gate. More recently a GS turn has been developed which commits what used to be a cardinal sin in skiing, getting on the uphill ski in the final phases of the turn. Instead of finishing on the downhill ski, the racer drives forward and over his uphill ski, which, of course, has the higher line. In this way he saves a split second, which previously was spent on a lower line prior to the step up.

SKI COMPETITION

There is no denying that equipment plays a major role in such small but important differences of performance. It isn't merely that skis have become faster through refinements of design, but that they have also become easier to control and to turn. Metal and plastic skis give almost instantaneous edge set and edge release along the entire length of the ski. The racer takes advantage of this characteristic—in fact, the turn which finishes on the uphill ski would be impossible without it.

WATCHING RACES

THE skier who wants to be among the very best must be constantly alert to new refinements in equipment and technique. At least once or twice a season, he should make it a point to race with or watch the top skiers. If he knows how to watch, and knows exactly what he himself is doing and why he is doing it, he will quickly spot what is separating the top racers from the also-rans. There is a definite knack to spectating. The expert spectator can spot new developments long before they have been actually described. Usually, by the time a new development is spelled out, the very best racers are already working on something else.

When you first start watching races, the temptation is to station yourself at a location where you are likely to see the most spectacular action. Actually, for purposes of analysis these are probably the worst places to watch. First of all, the big bumps which usually constitute such spots have a tendency to obstruct your vision of all but a small section of the course. Secondly, the racer's options over these points are usually limited. Except in the degree of perfection with which he can execute them, each racer must do the same thing.

A useful accessory for watching a race is a good stop watch. Time only a short section of the course, preferably one that allows a variety of approaches to a difficult gate or turn. Start the watch a short distance above this point and stop it a little below the key gate or turn that you are watching. This enables you to concentrate on the racer as he passes through the section. When watching the racer, concentrate more on his feet than his upper body.

The clue to what he is doing is more likely to be found there than in his shoulders, unless the turn is of the long, sweeping variety. If you compare carefully the racer on course with those who preceded him, your eye will soon detect subtle differences as to why one is faster than another. Use your watch to confirm your judgment.

In selecting a spot to watch the race, ski alongside the course for the entire distance well before the race. Try to visualize the reason for gates and turns and how they fit in with the course above and below them. Don't ignore flats, particularly if they follow a turn. A flat may be the crucial part of a course. Try to put yourself in the boots of the racer. If you are learning to race, you'll see how far you still have to go. If you are merely a spectator, ski racing will come to mean a lot more than a progression of figures flashing by at high speed.

The study of racing technique has become highly scientific. Here Bernard Perret opens a slalom course with an automatic movie camera attached to his helmet. The films are used for study by Honore Bonnet, team trainer, and French team members.

CHAPTER 40

Langlaufers and yumpers

THE AMERICAN ski heritage is essentially alpine: we use lifts and ski downhill. In North American competition, downhill, slalom and giant slalom are the premier events. It is only in the last few years that Americans have shown renewed interest in the nordic phase of the sport—Scandinavian type touring, cross-country racing and jumping.

The development of lift skiing was too formidable to leave nordic skiing much of a chance. What saved nordic events from oblivion in this country was the spectator appeal of jumping and the faith kept by the college ski teams. College competition has always been four-way (downhill, slalom, jumping and cross-country), and a progression of college coaches not only kept the nordics alive but paved the way for eventual revival. Jumping and cross-country still do not have the stature of the alpine events, but they are gaining in popular appeal.

Part of the gain in cross-country interest can be attributed to the fact that American athletes in general no longer believe in the old cliché that

363

SKI COMPETITION

"Americans aren't cut out for the long distances." American victories in the 5,000 and 10,000 meter events at the Tokyo Summer Olympics proved once and for all that Americans can run just as hard and just as long as anyone else and, furthermore, that such long races have as much spectator appeal as the mile, the pole vault and the sprints.

Much the same is true in cross-country racing. A decade ago, it was not unusual for American langlaufers to be as much as ten and fifteen minutes behind the winners in international 15-kilometer races, the shortest of the cross-country races. The low point came in 1954 when even the Russian and Scandinavian women beat the American men's times over the 10-kilometer distance. Since then, however, there has been a steady narrowing of the gap until today some Americans run as close as two and three minutes behind the winner. A gain of another minute or so would put them within the first ten in the world.

Today's Vasa Race follows practically the same track as Gustav Vasa, the Swedish hero king, used in 1521 (see Chapter 2), although backwards for practical reasons, beginning in Sälen and ending up in the city of Mora. This picture shows the "takeoff" at Sälen.

Essentially, cross-country racing is Scandinavian-type touring at speed. In major national and international meets, the distances are 15, 30 and 50 kilometers (9.4, 15.7 and 31.3 miles respectively), although other distances are not unusual in Scandinavian meets. Juniors usually run less than 15 kilometers. The longest and most unusual cross-country event is the Vasa race in Sweden, which covers 85 kilometers (53 miles) between Sälen and Mora. It is not so much a race as an adventure in mass participation. All the racers start at once, usually five thousand or more of them. The winner finishes in something under five hours. A somewhat similar event, although greatly scaled down, is the Washington's Birthday Inter-Town Ski Touring Race in Brattleboro, Vermont, which covers about seven miles and is co-sponsored by the Brattleboro Outing Club and the Brattleboro Ski Patrol. The event regularly draws over one hundred participants.

The most exciting cross-country event is the relay, usually run in four legs of 10 kilometers and with the first runners from each team starting at the same time. In the Olympics of 1960 and 1964 the cross-country relay was considered the most exciting ski event, both by press and spectators. Both Olympics featured finishing duels right down to the tape.

Cross-country racing is conducted on "tracks" on well-prepared trails which ideally should cover terrain about one-third uphill, one-third downhill and one-third on the level. The tracks, one for each ski, are set into the trail about four to six inches apart. Cross-country racers stick religiously to the tracks unless they are forced to yield to an overtaking runner, who has the right of way.

The training for cross-country racing is highly demanding. It requires year-around conditioning for speed, strength and endurance and must be continued for years to build the necessary stamina. An alpine racer's peak years are between the ages of twenty-two and twenty-six; a cross-country racer's between twenty-eight and thirty-five. This peak period is being lowered somewhat by new training methods, but the fact remains that the very best racers in the world are with few exceptions thirty-years-old and older. American cross-country racers are handicapped for this very reason, inasmuch as

SKI COMPETITION

few can afford to continue participation beyond college age. In any case, in order to be successful, a runner must be able to sustain an average speed of 11 miles an hour or more for up to three hours. Because of the up-down-level nature of the courses, there is not a great deal of difference between the average speed of a 15-kilometer race and one of 50 kilometers, and it is not unusual for one of the longer races to be run faster. For instance, at the 1964 Olympics, the 15-kilometer was won at an average speed of 11 miles an hour, the 30-kilometer at 12.5 miles an hour and the 50-kilometer at 11.5 miles an hour. It is true that these races were run over different courses, but the difference in average speeds is more likely due to snow conditions than the terrain.

Gravity does most of the work for the downhill racer. The cross-country racer relies mainly on his own leg power. For this reason he will sacrifice almost anything for the lightest possible boots, bindings and poles. Every extra ounce is just so much extra baggage.

The cross-country racer, fortunately, does not have to be overly concerned with the strength of his equipment. By alpine standards, the terrain

The start of the 4 x 10 kilometer relay cross-country race at the 1956 Winter Olympics at Cortina. The event was won by Russia.

over which he travels is quite gentle and does not require equipment with high impact strength or the ability to resist great torsional forces.

Cross-country racing skis are feather-light slats. They are made of a large number of wood laminations and incorporate a number of different woods to achieve the desirable characteristics. The lightest weigh less than four pounds a pair and are quite fragile. They should be used only on prepared tracks.

Cross-country skis are extremely narrow—between 2 and 2½ inches—and their tips have low torsional rigidity so that they can follow the terrain without upsetting the balance at the center of the ski. This is an important factor since the racer must have his ski flat on the snow in order to get maximum push from his kick. Although there are various lengths, most racers, almost regardless of height, use a 210 centimeter (6'11") ski. Far more important is that the skis have the right amount of camber and flexibility for the weight of the racer. A ski too stiff will not make full contact with the snow and thus lose the benefit of the wax. A ski too soft will turn up at the tail when weighted, thereby losing tracking stability.

Cross-country racers use relatively gentle terrain which does not require the strong equipment of alpine competition.

SKI COMPETITION

The boots the cross-country racer uses are actually low-cut shoes, quite similar to track shoes. They are made of soft, pliable leather and the soles are formed in such a way that the boots flex easily under the balls of the feet. They are quite narrow so as not to drag on the edges of the track. The boot fits into a binding which is a lightweight version of the light-touring binding. The racer's poles are the same as the tourer's. His clothing is light and loose, usually a knicker outfit of flannel with knee socks.

Because endurance in cross-country racing is so important, the role of technique is frequently underplayed. But perfect execution is important, for the simple reason that basically the same motion is repeated, about five thousand times in the course of a 15-kilometer race. An imperfect kick, which reduces the glide, can be a larger contribution to defeat than lack of good condition.

Related to technique is waxing. Waxing for racing can be a complex business, particularly for the longer races. The ski must not only glide easily, but it must grip well throughout the length of the race. Backslip not only reduces the effectiveness of the kick but is also extremely fatiguing, especially on the uphill sections. The racer who picks the wrong wax may as well not bother to go out on the course.

Although it can take several hours to run off, a cross-country race is exciting sport and is followed avidly by the Scandinavians, who turn out by the tens of thousands to watch the major events. Most of them take their skis to the races and keep moving from key location to key location as the race progresses. Usually the tracks are laid on elliptical or figure-eight trails, and by means of shortcuts spectators can see their favorites several times in the course of a race.

JUMPING

Ski jumping is a complex, demanding and beautiful sport. Almost any moderately-skilled skier can (slowly) negotiate an Olympic downhill course or an FIS World Championship cross-country track. But shot from an Olympic

368

Ole Ellevsaeter of Norway shows good cross-country form. His head, shoulders and body weight are centered over a point between his tracks. His hip rotation is good and without undesirable hip shift.

John Balfanz exhibits near-perfect form on his way to a 250-foot leap.

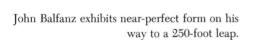

jump, the intrepid intermediate is simply out of his element. He can do nothing to slow down his awesome flight. Yet to a jumper, nothing seems more natural than flight. On any hill over 50 meters, he is literally flying, and not the least of his concerns is that he doesn't fly too far.

Like other ski competitors, jumpers ponder and worry about the hill, the wind, the fog and their own nerves. But their main concerns are to jump farther than the competition and to achieve an esthetic style so perfect as to receive the maximum possible number of style points from the judges. These goals are related. Other things being equal, the most perfect style results in the most perfect jump. On the other hand, given a big hill, a jumper may well outdistance the entire field by two meters on every jump, yet lose the meet because one hand touched the snow each time he landed.

Jumping is the oldest organized ski competition (it celebrated its centennial in 1966). Areas of intensive Scandinavian settlement in this country were producing jumpers before 1887, the year of the first official jumping competition in the United States at Red Wing, Minnesota. The Midwest remains the greatest single source of jumping talent, but other pockets can be found in Northern New England, around Leavenworth, Washington, and Steamboat Springs, Colorado. The United States has always had jumpers on the periphery of greatness, but lack of intensive competition as in Scandinavia—where virtually every village has well maintained jumping facilities—has prevented a breakthrough. However, this, too, is changing. In 1963, John Balfanz and Gene Kotlarek took second and fourth place respectively at the Holmenkollen in Norway, the most prestigious jumping event in the world next to the Olympics and the World Championships. And more talented jumpers are coming along.

There are actually two different types of jumping events: jumping on hills below 100 meters, and ski flying on hills above that length. The present ski flying record was set in 1965 by Germany's Peter Lesser at Kulm, Austria—an incredible 145 meters (476 feet).

The length of a hill is determined by its critical point, that is, the distance that can be jumped on the hill safely. In practice this point is about half-way up the steepest part of the outrun, or landing area. A 90-meter hill should allow safe jumps of up to 90 meters.

For purposes of description, there are seven parts to a jumping hill—the starting point, the in-run (quite frequently a scaffold), the take-off, the knoll (the first section of the jump after the take-off), the straight section (the steepest part of the hill on which the jumper lands after flight), the transition, and the runout section where the jumper can come to a stop. Generally, that part of the jump up to the take-off is called the in-run, the remainder the outrun.

At the starting point, the top of the in-run, a jumper starts by skating one step. Then he drops into an "egg" position almost identical to the racing tuck used in downhill. At the point of take-off, the jumper springs forward over his ski tips and becomes airborne. The take-off is crucial because it determines the success of the entire jump. To catch and ride the air from the very start, the jumper should leave the lip of the take-off with his skis pointed up just slightly. If he springs too late, he will take off with his skis inclined downward, which results in loss of distance and can be dangerous.

In the transition from in-run to flight, the jumper may swing his arms forward or backward. Most jumpers pin their arms to the side as they spring over their skis, a few carry them in front like a diver. Both positions are aerodynamically correct, but the arms-to-the-side position is easier to hold. In flight, the skis are carried horizontal or a little above horizontal to help the jumper ride the air.

The jumper tries to hold a steady, controlled position as long as possible to receive the maximum number of points from the judges. Ideally, the jumper breaks his flight position just as the tails of the skis are about to touch down on the snow. Then he goes into the classic, arms-wide, kneeling Telemark position as he lands. The Telemark position allows the knees and hips to absorb the shock of landing, and should enable him to go from flight to snow in one smooth and continuous movement. After the Telemark landing is completed, the jumper straightens up and rides out the hill, snowplowing or turning to a stop.

371

Jumping style has gone through a series of evolutions, although today's aerodynamic style was anticipated as long as thirty years ago by the late Professor Charles A. Proctor, a jumping enthusiast who also taught physics at Dartmouth College. Another pioneer in this field was a Swiss, Dr. Reinhard Straumann, who analyzed his theories by hanging up jumpers in a wind tunnel. These experiments were finally crystalized by the Finns in 1954. They jumped with extreme forward lean from the ankles and with their bodies arched and their arms pinned to the sides. The more the jumper "kissed his ski tips," the greater his lift. Mastery of the position enabled the Finns to stay ahead of the world for almost six years, until the East Germans broke the Scandinavian monopoly at the Olympics in 1960. Since then, the East Germans, Norwegians, Finns and Russians have been contesting bitterly for world supremacy.

One of the results of the introduction of aerodynamics into jumping was that traditional methods of judging the esthetic qualities of the jump were largely discarded and became the source of considerable controversy. Radicals would like to eliminate judging completely, arguing that the best style will also result in the longest jump. However, style judging is not merely esthetic judgment, but the necessary restraint for safe jumping. Accordingly, jumpers continue to be judged for style, but it is no longer 50 per cent of the total possible score.

Toralf Engan in the three stages of a near-perfect jump. *From left to below:* Inrun just before take-off (judging comment: excellent inrun picture); early flight (judging comment: beautiful curve in body; scissors will cost about one-half point); instant after landing (judging comment: perfect; he is sinking downwards to absorb the shock of landing; this clearly illustrates that Engan is supple on landing).

Jumps are judged for style and distance. In general, good style will result in a longer jump. Markers along the side of the hill indicate length from take-off.

Under the system now in force, the jumper is not judged until he reaches the take-off. From that point on he has 20 points from each of five judges. The judges deduct points for various faults until the jumper has completed his landing. The highest and lowest scores are thrown out and the jumper earns his points on the basis of scores of the three middle judges, 60 points being the maximum possible score for style. The jumper earns additional points, depending on the distance he jumps. On ski-flying hills with a critical point of 90 meters and over, he gets one point per meter; on jumps between 75 and 90 meters, which covers most of the internationally recognized ski jumps, he gets 1.4 points per meter, with more points per meter on smaller hills.

The jumper gets three jumps. The first is for practice, the other two are the actual competition. The total points for the two jumps determine the winner.

374

Jumpers used to be a happy-go-lucky breed of athletes, and they still are to a large degree. However, with competition getting keener all the time, the top jumpers today have to be in training throughout the year. The emphasis is on timing, co-ordination and strength and snap in the legs.

The taste for jumping is acquired gradually. Virtually without exception, big-hill jumpers start jumping on small hills before their teens. They then work up gradually to the bigger hills in about 10-meter steps. Most collegiate jumps are performed on a 40-meter hill.

Since jumping is a matter of going straight down the hill with no turning except possibly at the very end of the out-run, special skis are required. To provide greater speed on the in-run and stability in the air, they are longer and heavier than alpine skis. To enable them to track in a straight line on the in-run and out-run, they are made with three grooves in the running surface.

Despite its risky appearance, jumping is not particularly dangerous—certainly not as dangerous as downhill racing—providing it is done on a properly engineered and prepared hill. There is an occasional serious accident when a jumper drops his tips in flight on a big hill, but most falls look more dangerous than they really are. The jumper's skis are only lightly attached and usually come off easily. Furthermore, the angle of the hill is such that it matches closely the trajectory of a falling jumper, and therefore the impact is not excessive. The most dangerous error, actually, is to overjump the hill and to land in the transition. The impact there is considerable and a fall under these circumstances can be serious.

Jumping is by far the most spectacular spectator event among winter sports, and the pleasure of watching it is enhanced if the spectator has an appreciation of the finer points of the sport.

NORDIC COMBINED AND BIATHLON

THERE are two other nordic events which are recognized Olympic competitions: nordic combined and biathlon.

Nordic combined includes both jumping and cross-country. The com- 375 bined cross-country distance is 15 kilometers, and the jumping is usually done on a 60- or 70-meter hill. The combined competitors are scored in jumping by the same system as in so-called special jumping, and their cross-country time is converted into points. The jumping and cross-country points are then added for the combined score, the man with the most points being the winner. Needless to say, a nordic combined competitor must have the special qualities of both the cross-country racer and the jumper, at least in good enough proportions to have a chance for victory, although most combined competitors are consistently stronger in one event. It is rare, indeed, at any level of combined competition, if the combined winner has won both the jumping and the cross-country. As a matter of fact, it is not at all unusual for the combined winner not to have won either individual event.

Biathlon is a quasi-military event involving rifle marksmanship and cross-country racing. The competitor runs over a total distance of 20 kilometers. At four points along the course he takes five shots at a target at some varying distance for a total of twenty shots. For each miss, two minutes are added to his time. A first-rate biathlon racer can cover the distance, including time out for riflery, in about 85 minutes.

The Biathlon event at the 1964 Winter Olympics.

CHAPTER 41

Great races, great skiers

SKI COMPETITION on an international scale is about as old as skiing itself—that is, skiing as a recognized sport. Almost from its very beginnings, skiing has had international participation, particularly in the alpine events. The young Hannes Schneider, one of the most spectacular competitors of his day, used to cross over into Switzerland regularly to participate in races there. Downhill, of course, was his forte, but he also jumped and raced cross-country.

Even before Schneider's time, ski competition had an international flavor. The first ski competitions in Central Europe invariably featured Norwegian students as well as local talent. The British, who had no skiing of their own to speak of, were regular competitors in alpine races and, until the mid-1930's were among the world's best. And Scandinavian-born jumpers and cross-country racers were invariably the favorites at American meets in the early days.

The oldest premier event in skiing is the Holmenkollen, held outside of Oslo, Norway. It started in 1892 and had foreign participation as early as 1909, the year before the first meeting of the International Ski Congress. The events at the Holmenkollen have evolved as the sport developed. However, 377

Dick Durrance, one of the first great American racers, skiing at Alta in 1939.

although alpine events were added in 1948, the emphasis is still on jumping and cross-country. In those years when there are no Winter Olympics or FIS World Championships, the winners at the Holmenkollen are usually considered the best jumpers and cross-country racers in the world.

While ski competition was always international to some extent, the sport did not command major public interest until well after World War I, actually not until 1924 when jumping and cross-country racing were incorporated in the first Winter Olympic Games at Chamonix, France. That was also the year the International Ski Congress decided that skiing needed an international governing body. The result was the Federation Internationale de Ski, which to this day makes the rules for the sport, compiles seeding lists, selects the sites for World Championships and, through its officials, approves race courses and jumping hills for international competition.

It is indicative of the state of alpine racing in 1924 that the FIS first refused to recognize downhill and the (then infant) slalom. It was not until 1928 that the group tentatively recognized the Ski Club of Great Britain rules for alpine races, and not until 1932 that it sanctioned such races officially. As a result, alpine events were not incorporated into the Olympic program until 1936.

Starting in 1925, the FIS organized so-called FIS Races on an annual basis, at first only in jumping and cross-country, and beginning in 1931 for downhill and slalom. Although the winners of these races were called world champions, the title was not officially sanctioned until 1936 when the name of the races was changed to FIS World Championships. Except in the Olympic years of 1924, 1928 and 1932, they were held annually until 1939. Since World War II, World Championships have been held only on even-numbered years between Olympics.

The Olympics, the most important sports spectacle in the world, bring winners the greatest international renown. And the World Championships, while confined exclusively to skiing, run a close second.

Although the medals at the Olympics and World Championships are the most highly prized in international ski competition, these two meets are not   379 necessarily the ultimate ski racing tests. In these meets, the number of entries permitted each nation is limited: four in the case of the Olympics, five in the case of World Championships. As a result, the major ski nations may leave dozens of racers at home who are more than the equal of racers of lesser ski nations, such as Poland or Bulgaria, who do enter teams in the Olympics and the World Championships but don't bother to participate in the other premier events where participation is virtually unlimited.

From year to year, the entry lists for the Arlberg-Kandahar, the Hahnenkamm, the Lauberhorn and the Grand Prix de Chamonix affect the relative importance of these four races. Occasionally, one or more of the major ski nations will pass up one of these races because of schedule conflicts or for tactical reasons. But usually, these meets can be counted on drawing the very best racers in Europe and the rest of the world. More important, their downhills are run over the toughest courses anywhere.

Of all races, the most important and the oldest is the Arlberg-Kandahar, which is rotated among five key Alpine resorts—St. Anton, Austria; Mürren, Switzerland; Garmisch, Germany; Chamonix, France; and Sestriere, Italy. Started in 1928 by Sir Arnold Lunn and Hannes Schneider, it is to alpine racing what the Holmenkollen is to nordic competition—in effect, a world championship in the years when there is no World Championship or Olympics. Because they are likely to encounter the best competitors in the world at the Arlberg-Kandahar, many racers treasure an A-K pin more than a World Championship or an Olympic medal.

The Lauberhorn, held in Wengen, Switzerland, and the Hahnenkamm, run off in Kitzbuehel, Austria, are the two most important early-season tests. They are usually held in the second half of January, and are looked to for clues as to who is coming up, who is slipping and what is new in equipment and technique. The A-K and the Grand Prix de Chamonix, which usually come in the first half of March, are the climax of the season and provide rugged tests to determine who is best for that year.

National championships are rarely premier events. With the exception of the United States and Canadian championships, these races are open only

Emphasis at the Holmenkollen is
still on cross-country and jumping.

The 1936 Winter Olympics at Garmisch-Partenkuchen marked the first time that the alpine
events were incorporated in the Olympic games. Franz Pfnur of Munich dominated the
combined event that year.

to natives of the country. However, they are watched closely to determine the progress of each nation's second-string racers. Close competition for the established stars of a ski nation is a good sign that that nation will remain tough for the next season.

The most important races in North America, the ones that attract the strongest foreign entries, are the Harriman Cup at Sun Valley, the Roch Cup at Aspen and the Werner Cup, a team race among the leading ski nations of the world. The National Championships, which are circulated among the leading ski areas in the country, have had a checkered history, but are regaining prestige under new United States Ski Association leadership. In Canada, the Du Maurier series, initiated in 1966, is probably the leading national event, although the Quebec Kandahar and the Ryan Cup have traditionally drawn the strongest Canadian fields and, occasionally, strong American and European entries.

Since the Scandinavian phase of the sport came first, it is not surprising that the first ski heroes were Scandinavian. Torjus and Mikkel Hemmesveit were probably the first well-known competitors. Both were superb jumpers for their day. Mikkel immigrated to the United States from Norway in the late 1880's and continued to jump successfully here. In the pre-alpine stage of Olympic and World Championship ski competition, Johan Groettumsbraaten of Norway had a virtual monopoly on international ski competition, winning the 18-kilometer cross-country and nordic combined titles in 1926, 1928, 1931 and 1932. He was also the winner of ten Holmenkollen medals between 1923 and 1931. Such dominance was not seen again until the cross-country feats of Veikko Hakulinen of Finland and Sixten Jernberg of Sweden. Starting in 1952, these two racers completely overshadowed the other great racers of their era for a period of twelve years. Super-stars in every sense of the word, they won more than half of the available medals at all distances in Olympic and World Championship cross-country competition between 1952 and 1964. Only the Russian Pavel Kolchin could come close to challenging them and then only over a period of about four years.

382 Probably one of the most dramatic competitors of the mid-thirties was

Sixten Jernberg after winning the Swedish Championship 15 kilometer race. This was his seventh Swedish Championship in a row.

Birger Ruud, the most successful of three brothers who were Norway's top ski family for a decade. Birger was not only an outstanding jumper, but to this day he is the only competitor who has won Olympic gold medals in both nordic and alpine disciplines. This unusual feat took place in the 1936 Olympics, when he won the downhill over highly touted German, French and Austrian racers and then went on to win the jumping.

The first great alpine racers were mostly Swiss and British. Esmé Mackinnon and Audrey Sale-Baker were probably the first women who could really be called racers. Miss Mackinnon was the first women's world champion, winning both the slalom and the downhill in 1931 and also the Arlberg-Kandahar in 1933. Miss Sale-Baker won the A-K twice, in 1929 and in 1931. Walter Prager and Otto Fürrer were the skimeisters of the late twenties and early thirties, winning between them three world championship titles, five A-Ks and a Hahnenkamm. Following his European triumphs, Prager came to the United States and became coach of the Dartmouth ski team, which swept aside all competition for more than a decade. Fürrer, frequent coach of the American women's team before World War II, was killed on the Matterhorn in 1951. 383

SKI COMPETITION

The racing hero of the mid-thirties was Anton (Toni) Seelos, who revolutionized slalom technique by skiing parallel and with rotation. Seelos was so far ahead of his time that slalom victories of his by 10 seconds or more were not at all unusual. Because of his superiority in this event, the rules were rigged in such a way that he could not (always) also win the combined—in figuring combined, downhill was worth about one-third more than the slalom. Still, Seelos kept winning until he turned pro to coach the French team.

The female counterpart of Seelos was Christl Cranz, who won the World Championship in 1934, 1935, 1937, 1938 and 1939 and the Arlberg-Kandahar in 1937. She also won the alpine combined medal at the 1936 Olympics. No woman racer since has performed as consistently and successfully.

In the last three years before World War II, the great races were dominated by two men—Emile Allais and Rudolf Rominger. It wasn't merely that they took eight World Championship titles between them; they were also important as pioneers of great new alpine techniques. Allais was one of the innovators of the French rotational technique; Rominger was the only skier of his day who was complete master of the counter-rotational system advocated by Testa and Matthias. Of the two, Allais was the more famous. It took almost twenty years for history to prove that Rominger was not a freak, but an extraordinarily skilled and analytical technician.

In the years before World War II, the United States could not boast of any world champions or Olympic medal winners. Except for the women, who campaigned annually in Europe, American skiers were too isolated from world developments in the sport. Nevertheless, as the decade came to a close, America could boast of a small group of racers who might have been the equal of the Europeans had not the war prevented the U.S. team selected for the 1940 FIS World Championships from going to Europe.

The first great American racers were Dick Durrance, Clarita Heath and Marion McKean. Durrance, who spent several years in Germany as a boy, had a distinctive style and unlimited courage. He might well have been a medalist in 1936 had he not been penalized five seconds for straddling a gate in the slalom. The manager of the team failed to protest this penalty

384

Emile Allais, one of the forerunners of the
French rotational technique and a great racer
in the period just before World War II.

Dick Durrance receiving the first Harriman
Cup from Mrs. Averell Harriman, 1937.

and Dick had to settle for eleventh. He was later to distinguish himself by winning the Harriman Cup three times against many of his Olympic rivals.

By 1937 American women had made rapid strides under the managership of Alice Kiaer. Clarita Heath and Sis McKean could be counted upon to finish in the top ten in any European race they entered. Miss Heath was fourth in the World Championship downhill, and in the Arlberg-Kandahar Miss McKean was fourth in downhill, fourth in slalom and fourth in the combined. The following year, Miss McKean was sixth in the World Championship downhill and eighth in the combined.

Meanwhile, back home, other talent was coming along. Gordon Wren and Barney McLean were two youngsters of exceptional ability. A Norwegian-born jumper, Torger Tokle, who was subsequently killed while serving in the Tenth Mountain Division in Italy, was breaking every American record in the book. And a pig-tailed girl by the name of Gretchen Kunigk, who had never been outside of the United States, was beating the European-seasoned American girls with disconcerting regularity.

It can only be guessed what American skiers might have done in the forties had it not been for the war, but there are clues. At the 1948 Olympics, Gretchen Fraser won a gold medal in the special slalom and a silver medal in the combined (an Olympic event no longer held). Gordon Wren, who switched to the nordic events at the last moment, was second in combined jumping (which carried no medal) and fifth in the special jumping. Considering the state of skiing at the end of the thirties, American racers might have developed to the point where they could have been considered among the best in the world. It is unfortunate that the proposition was never put to a proper test.

The discontinuance of international competition from 1940 until 1947 did not affect the Americans alone. James Couttet, who was a mere seventeen when he won his first World Championship downhill title in 1938, really should have been one of the sport's super-stars. Even after the war, he won three A-K's, but the Olympic gold medals that could well have been his escaped him by frustratingly small margins. Nils Karlsson of Sweden may well have been the equal of Jernberg and Hakulinen as a cross-country racer, but he has only one 50-kilometer Olympic gold medal to his credit. Karl Molitor was a six-time winner of the Lauberhorn, but by the time international competition resumed he had passed his peak. The war also cut short the racing careers of Willy Walch, Edi Rominger and many others of great promise.

When ski competition resumed after World War II, it was an entirely different sport. Competition gained in intensity; technique was refined and improved over and over again; coaching and training became major factors; and equipment made extreme high speeds possible. With one or two exceptions, the new heroes of the Olympics, the World Championships, the A-K's and the Hahnenkamms were products of systems whose only objective was to turn out champion skiers, no matter the cost.

Zeno Colo was probably the last of the old school of racers. He trained, all right, but an occasional cigarette and glass of wine before the start were not out of order. Colo defied almost every racing convention. At all times he enjoyed himself, which didn't prevent him from winning the 1950 downhill and giant slalom World Championship titles in Aspen and from taking the A-K in 1949 and 1951 from more dedicated competitors. There was no mistaking when Colo was in town for a race.

Almost matching him for clownishness was France's Henri Oreiller. Oreiller's knowledge of turning was somewhat rudimentary, but for three years after the war he had no equal in downhill. Yet for all his clowning, he was a serious and dedicated skier and an intense competitor. His sense of competition turned him to automobile racing, which caused his death in 1962.

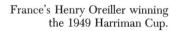
France's Henry Oreiller winning the 1949 Harriman Cup.

SKI COMPETITION

Witnesses to the 1950 World Championships were aware that the old order was changing and that soon a new generation of racers would take over. The harbingers of this change were Christian Pravda and Othmar Schneider of Austria and Stein Eriksen of Norway. Of the three, Eriksen was by far the most dramatic. His technique, while not as polished then as today, had certain distinctive characteristics obvious to the galleries. Eriksen did not disappoint them. In the 1952 Olympics he won the giant slalom, and at the 1954 FIS he took the slalom, giant slalom and combined. If ever a racer was made to heroic proportions, Eriksen was it. Blond-haired, blue-eyed and relatively tall for a racer, he is one of the few competitors who has been able to capitalize on his racing successes in a big way. He is not only a successful ski school director (at Sugarbush), but he draws large crowds wherever he makes public appearances.

Othmar Schneider, now ski school director at Boyne Mountain, Michigan, and Portillo, Chile, while not as spectacularly successful as Eriksen, was and

Mrs. Gretchen Fraser of Vancouver, Washington, the first U.S. competitor to win a ski medal in the Winter Olympics.

Gordon Wren, one of the top American racers of the prewar era.

remains one of the most influential racers in the world. He was really the first modern counter-rotational technician, and won a gold medal in slalom at the 1952 Games. More important has been his subsequent role as teacher, both to recreational skiers and racers.

Christian Pravda was in many respects his equal. With good right he was called "The Old Fox." A master tactician with edge control a particular forte, he became a consistent winner on the professional racing circuit even as he approached the age of forty. His amateur moment of glory came in 1954, when he became world downhill champion.

It took some time for Americans to appreciate these two men, for they had a champion of their own—Andrea Mead Lawrence. Andy had made the 1948 Olympic team at the age of fifteen, then the FIS team for 1950. But it wasn't until a year later that she came into her own. She won the 1951 A-K downhill, the first American to have won this event, and only a momentary disqualifying lapse in the slalom prevented her from taking the combined.

Andrea Mead Lawrence at Cortina. "Andy" won two gold medals in 1952 Olympics.

Othmar Schneider, one of the finest slalom skiers of the modern era.

SKI COMPETITION

The following year, at the 1952 Olympics at Oslo, she won gold medals in slalom and giant slalom.

The next few years were to prove frustrating to American skiers, and nearly every other skier in the world. It was the era of Toni Sailer and Anderl Molterer. When the chips were really down, one of these two could be counted on to produce victories for Austria. And when they didn't win, there was always a youngster named Karl Schranz, who won at the Arlberg-Kandahar with clockwork regularity. Out of ten A-K's between 1953 and 1962, Molterer won three times and Schranz four times, a record that will be hard to equal with ski competition growing more intense all the time.

But the man with "it" was Toni Sailer, probably the greatest pressure skier of all time. Essentially a downhiller, he nevertheless could produce in slalom and giant slalom, which is exactly what he did in the 1956 Games. His

Christian Pravda, "The Old Fox."

Anderl Molterer won a silver and bronze medal for the Giant Slalom and Downhill at Cortina in 1956. Molterer holds eleven Austrian Championships and now competes in professional races.

Karl Schranz of Austria in the starting gate at the 1965 Vail Meet.

Toni Sailer winning the Second Slalom at Cortina in the 1956 Winter Olympics.

sweep of all three alpine events may never be duplicated again as racers become more and more specialized. Even more remarkable, Sailer almost pulled the trick a second time at the 1958 FIS, when he won the downhill and the giant slalom and was nosed out by Josl Rieder in the slalom. What he might have done had he not decided on a movie career is, of course, difficult to say, but everyone who knew him was sure that he had plenty of good races left.

During the Sailer era, American racers had more cause to be frustrated than most other racers. In Bill Beck, Brookie Dodge, Ralph Miller, Buddy Werner and Tom Corcoran, the United States had racers potentially the equal of any in the world. Unfortunately, there was no program to develop these racers to their ultimate potential. Still, they were a remarkable lot. Beck was fifth twice in downhill, in the 1952 Olympics and the 1954 FIS. Dodge came tantalizingly close to a medal in the 1956 Olympic slalom and Corcoran, despite the fact that he was deep in the second seeding, came within four-tenths of a second of an Olympic medal in the 1960 giant slalom.

But the greatest of them all was Buddy Werner. He startled the world at the tender age of seventeen by beating the world's best in winning the Holmenkollen downhill just before the 1954 FIS. But even then he was haunted by bad luck. A training injury put him off the team. Year after year he returned to Europe to do battle with the world's best, until he was one of the world's best. In 1959 he was the world's best downhiller, and also strong in slalom and giant slalom. But bad luck struck again shortly before the 1960 Olympics when an ankle fracture put him out of the Games. He was at a point in his development where a medal was as certain as a medal can be in ski racing.

If Werner was bitter or discouraged, he didn't let on. He gave his all for four more years while the United States Ski Association built a program that made sure that all potential Buddy Werners had an opportunity to develop to their fullest. He campaigned doggedly, sometimes showing flashes of his former brilliance, but most of the time he was giving the benefit of his experience to the up-and-coming racers. Shortly after his retirement from racing in 1964,

392

Billy Kidd and Jimmy Heuga at the 1964
Olympics after capturing the silver and
bronze medals in slalom.

Penny Pitou, winner of two silver medals at
the 1960 Olympics.

Buddy Werner, perhaps the greatest American
skier of the modern era.

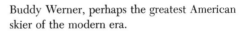

the bad luck that haunted him all through his racing career struck for the last time. He was killed in an avalanche in Europe during the filming of a ski movie.

If medals proved to be elusive to the North American men, they were far from that for the women. Since Olympic and FIS World Championship competition resumed after World War II, Americans and Canadians have failed only twice to bring home medals—in 1950 and in 1956. After 1956, Lucille Wheeler of Canada stunned the world by winning the downhill and the giant slalom in the 1958 FIS. In 1960, it was another Canadian, Ann Heggtveit, who captured a gold medal in slalom at the Squaw Valley Olympics. Ann also was the first North American to win the Arlberg-Kandahar, in 1959. But most of the attention at that time was focused on two plucky American women, Betsy Snite and Penny Pitou, who campaigned in Europe for three years for that invaluable experience that comes only from racing against the world's best week after week. Penny was strong in downhill and Betsy a demon in slalom. There were weeks in Europe when the Europeans wondered if they had any women racers at all. The American girls swept all honors.

There were silver medals in downhill and giant slalom for Penny and a silver in slalom for Betsy at the 1960 Olympics. Combined with Ann Heggtveit's gold in slalom, it was the biggest racing setback the Europeans had ever received.

But 1960 was also notable for the great French renaissance. Using metal skis for the first time in international competition and with their egg position, the French swept to victory in almost every downhill in 1960 and 1961. In the Olympics, the hero was Jean Vuarnet, a journeyman racer from whom little had been expected. Yet there was justice in his surprise victory. He, along with the French ski theoretician Georges Joubert, were primarily responsible for developing the egg position which carried the French to victory.

In 1961, the French had a new hero, Guy Perrillat. Perrillat managed the unprecedent feat of winning every major race he entered that season, some-

Guy Perillat winning a silver medal in the Special Slalom at FIS Championships 1962.

thing that even Sailer had not managed to do. But just as it seemed that French domination was assured, the Austrians staged a strong comeback in the 1962 FIS. The man who led the comeback was Karl Schranz, who was thought to be over the hill after he had failed to crack the first ten in the 1960 Games.

The Olympics at Innsbruck in 1964 brought the long-awaited breakthrough for the American men, and they waited until almost the last day to secure it. After Jean Saubert had won bronze and silver medals against the impressive Goitschell sisters in the slalom and giant slalom, Billy Kidd and Jimmy Heuga came through for silver and bronze in the slalom on tremendous second runs. Kidd lapsed in 1965 against the French and Austrians, but was the toast of Europe in January, 1966, with impressive slalom and giant slalom victories over Austria's Schranz and France's Killy.

Victory in the great races are usually essential for a racer to be ranked among the great. But sometimes—not often—a man's legend is bigger than his records. Such a racer was Toni Matt.

Toni was a good racer, no question about that. He won the Harriman Cup in 1939, the U.S. Nationals in 1949 and several other important races. But this is not what he is remembered for.

In 1939, he stood atop Mount Washington for the third and, as it turned out, the last running of the American Inferno, a four-mile downhill with a vertical drop of over four thousand feet. Part of the course was across the frighteningly steep Headwall of Tuckerman's Ravine. There were no control gates on the Headwall. The race organizers assumed that the racer who treasured his life would throw in a couple of turns to check his speed as all other racers had done in previous runnings.

What prompted Matt to take the Headwall straight is the subject of numerous stories. Toni himself claims that he intended to take it straight. Witnesses to the race claim that he lost control momentarily as he went over the lip of the Headwall and by the time he regained it, he was heading straight down. There is still another version, that he checked as he came to the lone control gate on the lip, looked down the Headwall and took the plunge.

Strangely enough, Matt's schuss received no attention to speak of at the time. Newspaper accounts of the race and an article in the Ski Annual of the following fall merely state that Matt won the race in record time. Perhaps because of this oversight, the story bounced around among skiers of how Toni Matt schussed the Headwall. It soon became a fixture of skier conversation, lovingly passed on from skier to skier until it became the greatest deed in American skiing history.

And maybe it was. No one has done it since.

Tuckerman's Ravine, 1939: Toni Matt's final check turn on the lip of the Headwall.

Afterword

WHAT is skiing?

This may seem like a strange question after so comprehensive a volume. But odd as it may seem, the more you know about skiing, the harder it is to explain it.

Within our limits of space we have tried to give you as complete a picture as possible of what skiing was like in the past and how it is practiced today. We have explained the techniques of skiing. And we have introduced you to the equipment of the sport, to the areas where it is practiced, and to some of its brightest names.

Yet from the very beginning we knew that we could answer only part of the question, "What is skiing?" The dynamics of the sport, its subtle appeals to the senses, cannot be captured on paper. It is like any experience whose symbols are imperfectly understood, perhaps like reading some poem. We can still enjoy the poem's rhythms or the drama of its cadences, and, enjoying these, we catch occasional glimpses of the poem's meaning.

That's how it is with skiing. The rest of the answer to "What is skiing?" can only be found by yourself out on the slopes.

APPENDIX

Appendix A. **SKI AREA GUIDE**

1A. NORTH AMERICA: *UNITED STATES*

NAME OF AREA	LOCATION (NEAREST TOWN) OR POSTAL ADDRESS	KIND OF LIFTS						TOTAL VERTICAL DESCENT	SNOW-MAKING
		GONDOLAS TRAMWAYS	CHAIRLIFTS	T-BARS	PLATTER-PULLS	J-BARS	ROPE TOWS		
ALASKA									
Alyeska	Girdwood		X		X		X	2200'	
Arctic Ski Valley	Anchorage			X			X		
Cleary Summit	Fairbanks			X			X	1200'	
Douglas Ski Bowl	Douglas Island	HELICOPTER SERVICE					X	2700'	
Ski Chalet Tahneta	Mi. 120 Glen Highway						X		
Ullrhaven	Fairbanks						X		
ARIZONA									
Arizona Snow Bowl	Flagstaff		X		X		X	2100'	
Mt. Lemmon	Tucson				X			875'	
Mt. Williams	Williams				X		X	400'	
CALIFORNIA									
Alpine Meadows	Tahoe City		X		X			1600'	
Badger Pass	Yosemite		X	X			X	700'	
Blue Ridge	Wrightwood		X				X	1100'	
China Peak	Huntington Lake		X	X			X	1450'	
Dodge Ridge	Long Barn		X		X		X	1050'	
Donner Ski Ranch	Donner Summit		X		X		X	826'	
Echo Summit	Highway 50				X		X	400'	
Granlibakken	Tahoe City						X	200'	
Green Valley Snow Bowl	Green Valley				X		X	350'	
Heavenly Valley	Stateline	X	X	X			X	3600'	

NOTE: More than 500 ski areas are listed in the following guide. Space limitations do not permit listing of the many smaller rope tow areas. Therefore, all areas included here have a minimum of four rope tows, or at least one T-bar, platterpull or other lift device. The areas listed in **bold face** type have two or more chairlifts or a tramway or gondola lift. North American tourist bureaus are listed separately on page 424.

SKI AREA GUIDE

NAME OF AREA	LOCATION (NEAREST TOWN) OR POSTAL ADDRESS	KIND OF LIFTS						TOTAL VERTICAL DESCENT	SNOW-MAKING
		GONDOLAS TRAMWAYS	CHAIRLIFTS	T-BARS	PLATTER-PULLS	J-BARS	ROPE TOWS		
CALIFORNIA									
Holiday Hill	Wrightwood		X	X			X	1800'	
June Mountain	June Lake		X	X	X		X	2535'	
Kratka Ridge	Angles Crest Highway		X				X	800'	
Lassen Park	Lassen Park			X			X	500'	
Mammoth Mountain	Mammoth Lakes		X	X				2000'	
Mineral King	Porterville								
Moonridge	Big Bear Lake			X			X	900'	X
Mt. Baldy	San Bernardino Freeway		X		X	X		2100'	
Mt. Shasta	Mt. Shasta		X	X			X	1933'	
Mt. Waterman	La Canada		X				X	600'	
Peddler Hill	Jackson			X			X	480'	
Pla-Vada Hills	Soda Springs			X	X		X	370'	
Plumas Eureka Bowl	Portola			X			X	600'	
Poulson's Papoose	Tahoe City			X			X	200'	X
Powder Bowl	Deer Park			X			X	1000'	
Rebel Ridge	Big Bear Lake			X	X		X	400'	X
Sierra Ski Ranch	Twin Bridges			X			X	608'	
Snow Forest	Big Bear Lake		X				X	700'	X
Snow Summit	Big Bear Lake		X				X	1300'	X
Snow Valley	Running Springs		X		X		X	900'	X
Soda Springs	Soda Springs		X	X		X	X	650'	
Squaw Valley	Tahoe City	X	X		X			2700'	
Sugar Bowl	Norden		X		X		X	1600'	
Table Mountain	Wrightwood				X		X	800'	
Tahoe Ski Bowl	Homewood		X				X	750'	
Wolverton Ski Bowl	Sequoia Nat'l Park						X	1000'	
COLORADO									
Arapahoe Basin	Dillon		X		X			1700'	
Aspen Highlands	Aspen		X	X	X			3800'	
Aspen Mountain	Aspen		X					3300'	
Berthoud Pass	Idaho Springs		X	X				685'	X

NAME OF AREA	LOCATION (NEAREST TOWN) OR POSTAL ADDRESS	KIND OF LIFTS						TOTAL VERTICAL DESCENT	SNOW-MAKING
		GONDOLAS TRAMWAYS	CHAIRLIFTS	T-BARS	PLATTER-PULLS	J-BARS	ROPE TOWS		
Breckenridge	Breckenridge		X	X				1900'	
Buttermilk	Aspen		X	X				2250'	
Cooper Hill	Leadville			X					
Crested Butte	Crested Butte	X		X		X		2100'	
Cuchara Ski Basin	Cuchara				X			346'	
Geneva Basin	Grant		X	X			X	1150'	
Glenwood	Glenwood Springs		X					200'	
Grand Mesa	Mesa				X		X	800'	
Hesperus Ski Center	Durango			X			X	600'	
Hidden Valley	Estes Park			X			X		
Lake Eldora	Nederland			X				1200'	
Little Annie	Aspen	Touring by over-snow vehicle							
Loveland	Georgetown		X	X			X	1050'	
Meadow Mt.	Avon								
Monarch	Salida		X	X	X			1000'	
Mt. Werner	Steamboat Springs		X		X	X		2100'	
Pike's Peak	Colorado Springs			X			X		
Purgatory	Durango		X	X				1500'	
Ski Broadmoor	Colorado Springs		X					600'	X
Ski Dallas	Norwood			X				800'	
Ski Idlewild	Winter Park		X						
Snowmass	Aspen		X						
Squaw Pass	Denver			X			X	700'	
Steamboat Springs	Steamboat Springs			X			X	500'	
Stoner	Cortez			X			X	1000'	
Vail	Vail	X	X		X			3050'	
Winter Park	Winter Park		X	X				1700'	
Wolf Creek	Monte Vista				X			700'	
CONNECTICUT									
Mohawk Mountain	Cornwall		X				X	750'	X
Mt. Southington	Southington			X			X	300'	X
Powder Hill	Middlefield		X	X			X	475'	X
Satan's Ridge	New Hartford		X	X			X	554'	X
Tapawingo	Woodbury			X			X	225'	X

SKI AREA GUIDE

NAME OF AREA	LOCATION (NEAREST TOWN) OR POSTAL ADDRESS	KIND OF LIFTS						TOTAL VERTICAL DESCENT	SNOW-MAKING
		GONDOLAS TRAMWAYS	CHAIRLIFTS	T-BARS	PLATTER-PULLS	J-BARS	ROPE TOWS		
IDAHO									
Bear Gulch	Ashton			X			X	600′	
Blizzard Mountain	Moore				X		X		
Bogus Basin	Boise		X	X	X			1500′	
Brundage Mountain	McCall		X		X		X	1550′	
Caribou	Pocatello				X		X	715′	
Kelly Canyon	Ririe		X				X	866′	
Lookout Pass	Wallace				X		X	750′	
Lost Trail Pass	Salmon				X		X	770′	
Magic Mountain	Twin Falls			X	X		X	1000′	
North-South Ski Bowl	Harvard				X		X	500′	
Pine Basin	Swan Valley				X		X	1000′	
Pomerelle	Albion		X		X		X	1000′	
Rupert	Albion		X		X		X	1000′	
Schweitzer Basin	Sandpoint		X					1667′	
Skyline	Pocatello				X		X	1275′	
Soldier Mt.	Fairfield			X	X		X		
Sun Valley	Sun Valley		X					3282′	
Taylor Mt.	Idaho Falls		X		X		X		
ILLINOIS									
Buffalo Park	Algonquin						X	200′	X
Chestnut	Galena		X				X	465′	X
Four Lakes	Lisle						X	85′	X
Fox Trails	Gary						X	135′	X
Gander Mountain	Spring Grove					X	X	200′	X
INDIANA									
Mt. Wawasee	New Paris			X			X	175′	X
The Pines	Valparaiso						X	110′	X
Tamarack	Angola		X		X		X	270′	X
IOWA									
Ski Pal	Mount Vernon						X	250′	X
MAINE									
Agamenticus Mountain	York		X	X			X	500′	X

NAME OF AREA	LOCATION (NEAREST TOWN) OR POSTAL ADDRESS	KIND OF LIFTS						TOTAL VERTICAL DESCENT	SNOW-MAKING
		GONDOLAS TRAMWAYS	CHAIRLIFTS	T-BARS	PLATTER-PULLS	J-BARS	ROPE TOWS		
Bald Mountain	Rangeley			X			X	1200'	
Chrisholm Winter Park	Rumford			X				900'	
Colby College Ski Area	Waterville			X			X	265'	X
Enchanted Mountain	Jackman		X	X				1000'	
Lost Valley	Auburn		X	X			X	236'	X
Mt. Abram	Locke Mills			X				1200'	
Mt. Jefferson				X			X	350'	
Northmen	Caribou			X					
Pleasant Mountain	Bridgton		X	X				1200'	
Poland Spring	Poland Spring			X			X	350'	
Rangeley Saddleback	Rangeley		X	X					
Ski-Way	Mars Hill				X			610'	
Sky-Hy Park	Topsham			X				215'	X
Squaw Mountain	Greenville			X				600'	
Sugarloaf	Kingfield	X		X				2406'	
Sunday River Skiway	Bethel			X				400'	
Titcomb Memorial	Farmington				X		X		
White Bunny	Fort Fairfield			X				300'	
MARYLAND									
Braddock Hts. Ski Way	Braddock Heights			X			X	120'	X
Deep Creek Lake	Cumberland				X		X	500'	X
Oregon Ridge	Cockeysville		X					300'	X
MASSACHUSETTS									
Avaloch Inn	Lenox			X				200'	
Beartown State Forest	South Lee						X	100'	
Benjamin Hill	Shirley			X			X	105'	X
Berkshire Snow Basin	West Cummington			X			X	551'	X
Blue Hills	Canton		X			X	X	350'	X
Boston Hill	Andover					X	X	250'	X
Bousquet's	Pittsfield		X	X	X		X	100'	
Brodie Mountain	New Ashford		X	X			X	900'	
Butternut Basin	Great Barrington		X	X			X	1000'	X
Chickley Alp	Charlemont						X	100'	
Eastover	Lenox		X						

405

SKI AREA GUIDE

NAME OF AREA	LOCATION (NEAREST TOWN) OR POSTAL ADDRESS	GONDOLAS TRAMWAYS	CHAIRLIFTS	T-BARS	PLATTER-PULLS	J-BARS	ROPE TOWS	TOTAL VERTICAL DESCENT	SNOW-MAKING
MASSACHUSETTS									
Hartwell Hill	Littleton						X	175'	
Indian Head	East Pepperell			X			X	320'	
Jiminy Peak	Hancock		X	X			X	750'	X
Jug End	South Egremont			X			X	500'	
Leominster	Leominster			X		X		225'	X
Locke's Ski Tows	Amesbury						X	350'	
Mohawk Mountain	Shelburne			X			X	450'	
Moose	Leicester						X	250'	
Mt. Tom	Holyoke		X	X	X	X	X	840'	X
Mt. Watatic	Ashby			X			X	550'	
Otis Ridge	Otis			X	X	X	X	345'	X
Priest's	Groton						X	145'	
Sawmill Hill	Charlemont					X			
Sea View	Rowley		X				X	166'	
Springfield Ski Club	Blandford						X	400'	
Thunder Mountain	Charlemont		X	X			X	1000'	X
Wachusett	Princeton			X				625'	X
MICHIGAN									
Alpine Valley	Milford		X	X			X	200'	X
Antrim County	Bellaire		X	X	X				X
Apple Mountain	Freeland						X	160'	X
Au Sable Ranch	Gaylord				X		X	300'	
Barn Mountain	Boyne City		X		X		X	355'	
Big-M	Manistee		X	X			X	315'	X
Big Powderhorn Mt.	Bessemer		X	X			X		
Black Mountain	Rogers City				.		X		
Boyne Highlands	Harbor Springs		X	X	X			568'	X
Boyne Mountain	Boyne Falls		X				X	500'	X
Brady's Hill	Lakeview						X	200'	X
Brule Mountain	Iron River		X	X			X		X
Caberfae	Cadillac			X			X	270'	X
Carousel Mountain	Holland		X	X		X	X	311'	X
Chimney Corners	Frankfort						X		
Cliff's Ridge	Marquette			X			X	435'	X

NAME OF AREA	LOCATION (NEAREST TOWN) OR POSTAL ADDRESS	GONDOLAS TRAMWAYS	CHAIRLIFTS	T-BARS	PLATTER-PULLS	J-BARS	ROPE TOWS	TOTAL VERTICAL DESCENT	SNOW-MAKING
Crystal Mountain	Thompsonville		X		X			370′	X
Dryden	Rochester						X	150′	
Eskar	Middleville						X	325′	X
Glacier Hills	Bellaire						X		
Gladstone	Gladstone						X		
Grampion Mountain	Oxford			X	X		X	150′	X
Grand Haven	Grand Haven						X	130′	
Grayling Winter Park	Grayling			X			X	150′	X
Hickory Hills	Traverse City						X	400′	
Houghton Lake	Houghton Lake						X		
Indianhead Mountain	Wakefield		X	X			X	638′	X
Irish Hills	Onsted			X			X	165′	X
Iroquois Mountain	Brimley		X				X		
Jackpine Valley	Blaine						X		X
Lake Valley	Kalkaska						X		
Major Mountain	Clare						X	205′	
Mio Mountain	Mio						X	250′	
Mont Ripley	Hancock			X			X	408′	
Mott Mountain	Farwell						X	200′	X
Mt. Brighton	Southfield					X	X	130′	X
Mt. Frederick	Frederick			X			X	200′	X
Mt. Holly	Holly		X	X			X	200′	X
Mt. Mancelona	Mancelona			X	X		X	300′	
Nub's Nob	Harbor Springs		X		X		X	427′	X
Ogemaw Hills	West Branch			X			X	110′	
Pine Knob	Clarkston		X				X		X
Pine Mountain	Iron Mountain		X				X	375′	
Pinnacles	Gaylord		X					235′	X
Porcupine Mountain	Ontonagon			X			X		
Shanty Creek	Bellaire		X		X			387′	
Sheridan Valley	Lewiston						X		
Silverbell	Pontiac						X	225′	X
Skyline	Roscommon		X				X	220′	
Snowsnake Mountain	Harrison						X	200′	
Snow Valley	Gaylord				X				X
Sugar Loaf	Traverse		X			X	X	400′	

SKI AREA GUIDE

NAME OF AREA	LOCATION (NEAREST TOWN) OR POSTAL ADDRESS	KIND OF LIFTS						TOTAL VERTICAL DESCENT	SNOW-MAKING
		GONDOLAS TRAMWAYS	CHAIRLIFTS	T-BARS	PLATTER-PULLS	J-BARS	ROPE TOWS		
MICHIGAN									
Swiss Valley	Jones						X	200′	
Sylvan Knob	Gaylord				X		X	250′	
Teeple Hill	Pontiac						X		
Thunder Mountain	Boyne Falls		X	X	X		X	450′	
Timber Ridge	Plainvell						X	212′	
Traverse City Holiday	Traverse City			X			X	275′	X
Walloon Hills	Walloon Lake			X	X		X	400′	
Ward Hills	Branch						X		
MINNESOTA									
Afton Alps	Hastings		X	X	X		X	270′	X
Buck Hill	Minneapolis			X		X	X	310′	X
Buena Vista	Bemidji						X	225′	
Cedar Hills	Hopkins						X	150′	X
Detroit Mountain	Detroit Lakes						X		
Giant's Ridge	Aurora			X			X	440′	
Hallaway Ski Hill	Pelican Rapids						X	200′	
Hidden Valley	Ely					X	X	145′	
Lookout Mountain	Virginia		X				X	305′	X
Lutsen	Lutsen		X		X		X	630′	X
Mont Du Lac	Duluth			X			X	310′	X
Moon Valley	Shakopee				X		X	196′	X
Mt. Frontenac	Red Wing			X			X	420′	X
Pine Bend	Twin Cities				X		X	258′	X
Powder Ridge	Kimball			X			X		X
Quandna Mountain	Hill City			X			X	375′	X
Ski Devil	Fertile						X	150′	
Sugar Hills	Grand Rapids		X	X			X	350′	X
Timberlane	Red Lake Falls						X	110′	
Val Chatel	Park Rapids		X				X	275′	
Val Croix	Taylor's Falls						X	258′	
MISSOURI									
Tan-tar-a	Osage Beach			X			X	175′	X

NAME OF AREA	LOCATION (NEAREST TOWN) OR POSTAL ADDRESS	KIND OF LIFTS						TOTAL VERTICAL DESCENT	SNOW-MAKING
		GONDOLAS TRAMWAYS	CHAIRLIFTS	T-BARS	PLATTER-PULLS	J-BARS	ROPE TOWS		
MONTANA									
Bear Paw	Havre				X		X	800'	
Belmont	Marysville				X		X	1500'	
Big Mountain	Whitefish		X	X	X		X	2000'	X
Bridger Bowl	Bozeman		X	X	X			1530'	
Deep Creek	Wise River	X		X			X	900'	
Grass Mountain	Townsend				X		X	565'	
Jack Creek	Ennis					X		1000'	
King's Hill	Neihart			X	X			1000'	
Lionhead	W. Yellowstone		X					1860'	
Lookout Pass	Wallace				X		X	780'	
Lost Trail	Hamilton				X		X	600'	
Marshall Mountain	Missoula				X		X	800'	
Missoula Snow Bowl	Missoula		X		X		X	2600'	
Rainy Mountain	Dillon		X				X	1600'	
Red Lodge-Grizzly Peak	Red Lodge		X		X			910'	
Turner Mountain	Libby			X			X	2165'	
Z-T	Butte				X		X	1000'	
NEVADA									
Lee Canyon	Las Vegas		X				X	1000'	
Mt. Charleston	Las Vegas	X					X	500'	
Mt. Rose	Reno		X	X			X	1500'	
Slide Mountain	Reno		X					2000'	
NEW HAMPSHIRE									
Arrowhead Skiway	Claremont				X		X	650'	
Attitash	Bartlet		X	X				950'	
Black Mountain	Jackson		X	X		X		850'	X
Brookline	Brookline			X			X	600'	X
Cannon Mountain	Franconia	X	X	X				2210'	
Copple Crown	Wolfboro			X			X	500'	
Cranmore Mountain	North Conway SKIMOBILE	X		X				1360'	X
Crotched Mountain	Francestown		X	X				800'	X
Dartmouth Skiway	Lyme			X	X			900'	
Fitzwilliam	Fitzwilliam				X		X	240'	X

409

SKI AREA GUIDE

NAME OF AREA	LOCATION (NEAREST TOWN) OR POSTAL ADDRESS	KIND OF LIFTS						TOTAL VERTICAL DESCENT	SNOW-MAKING
		GONDOLAS TRAMWAYS	CHAIRLIFTS	T-BARS	PLATTER-PULLS	J-BARS	ROPE TOWS		
NEW HAMPSHIRE									
Gunstock	Laconia		X	X			X	1400'	
Intervale	Intervale			X	X			600'	
King Pine Ski Area	East Madison		X			X		300'	
King Ridge	New London			X			X	495'	
Loon Mountain	Lincoln		X						
Meriden	Meriden				X		X	300'	
Mittersill	Franconia			X				800'	
Moose Mountain	Brookfield		X	X			X		
Mt. Sunapee	Newbury	X	X	X	X			1500'	
Mt. Tecumseh	Waterville Valley		X					2020'	
Mt. Whittier	West Ossipee	X		X			X	1650'	
Pat's Peak	Henniker		X	X			X		
Pinnacle Mountain	Keene				X		X		
Purity Springs	East Madison		X			X	X	350'	
Ragged Mountain	Danbury		X	X				1200'	
Snowcrest	Lebanon			X				500'	
Snow's Mountain	Waterville Valley			X				600'	
Spruce Mt. Lodge	Jackson				X			210'	
Temple Mountain	Temple			X	X		X	450'	X
Tenney Mountain	Plymouth		X	X				1300'	
Tyrol	Jackson			X	X			700'	
Wildcat	Pinkham Notch	X	X	X				2050'	
NEW JERSEY									
Craigmeur	Newfoundland			X			X	205'	X
Great Gorge	McAfee		X		X		X	708'	X
High Point	Montague			X			X		X
Pine Hill	Pine Hill			X				127'	
Snow Bowl	Milton			X			X	205'	X
NEW MEXICO									
Angels Fire Ski Basin	Eagles Nest		X						
Pajarito	Los Alamos			X			X	1140'	
Red River	Red River		X		X			1600'	X
Sandia Peak	Albuquerque	X	X	X	X			1750'	
Santa Fe Ski Basin	Santa Fe		X		X				
Sierra Blanca	Ruidoso	X		X				1700'	

NAME OF AREA	LOCATION (NEAREST TOWN) OR POSTAL ADDRESS	KIND OF LIFTS						TOTAL VERTICAL DESCENT	SNOW-MAKING
		GONDOLAS TRAMWAYS	CHAIRLIFTS	T-BARS	PLATTER-PULLS	J-BARS	ROPE TOWS		
Sipapu	Taos				X			437'	
Ski Cloudcroft	Cloudcroft			X				460'	X
Taos Ski Valley	Taos		X	X				2580'	
NEW YORK									
Adirondack Center	Corinth			X				274'	
Allegany State Park	Salamanca			X			X	208'	
Andes Ski Center	Andes		X				X	850'	
Belleayre Mt.	Pine Hill		X	X				1200'	
Big Bear	Vega			X		X	X	1000'	
Big Tupper	Tupper Lake		X	X				800'	
Birch Hill	Brewster			X			X		X
Blue Mountain	Yorkshire		X						
Brantling	Rochester			X			X		
Bristol Mountain	Canandaigua		X	X		X		1050'	X
Catamount	Hillsdale		X	X			X	1000'	X
Catskill Ski Center	Andes			X				911'	
Cockaigne, Inc.	Sinclairville		X			X		425'	X
Colgate University	Hamilton			X				348'	
Columbia Ski Resort	Hurleyville			X			X	410'	X
Concord	Kiamesha Lake			X			X	300'	X
Cooperstown	Cooperstown			X			X		
Davos	Woodridge		X	X			X	380'	X
Delaware Ski Center	Andes			X				1050'	
Drumlins	Syracuse					X	X	100'	
Dry Hill	Watertown			X			X	250'	
Eagle Mountain	Sloatsburg		X	X			X	380'	X
Eagle Ridge	Westfield		X	X				300'	
Fahnestock	Carmel			X	X		X	240'	X
Fawn Ridge	Lake Placid				X			150'	
Glenwood Acres	Glenwood			X			X	517'	X
Gore Mountain	North Creek			X				1000'	
Gore Mt. Ski Center	North Creek		X	X		X	X	1400'	
Greek Peak	Cortland		X	X	X		X	750'	
Grossinger's	Liberty			X			X		X
Grosstal	Allegany		X	X			X	813'	
Gunset Ski Bowl	Richfield Springs				X		X	300'	

411

SKI AREA GUIDE

NAME OF AREA	LOCATION (NEAREST TOWN) OR POSTAL ADDRESS	KIND OF LIFTS						TOTAL VERTICAL DESCENT	SNOW-MAKING
		GONDOLAS TRAMWAYS	CHAIRLIFTS	T-BARS	PLATTER-PULLS	J-BARS	ROPE TOWS		
NEW YORK									
Harvey Mountain	North Creek			X				405'	
Hickory Hill	Warrensburg				X		X	600'	
Highmount	Highmount			X			X	975'	
Holiday Mountain	Monticello				X	X	X	235'	X
Holiday Valley	Ellicottville		X	X			X	700'	
Holi Mont	Ellicottville		X	X			X	560'	
Hunter Mountain	Hunter		X		X		X	1600'	X
Innsbruck USA	Binghamton			X		X		480'	X
Juniper Hills	Harrisville			X				200'	
Kissing Bridge	Glenwood		X	X			X	490'	X
Labrador Mountain	Truxton			X			X	680'	
McCauley Mountain	Old Forge			X					
Moon Valley	Malone		X	X				460'	
Mt. Cathalia	Ellenville		X	X			X	500'	X
Mt. Otsego	Cooperstown			X			X	400'	
Mt. Peter	Greenwood Lake		X				X	340'	X
Mt. Pisgah Ski Center	Saranac Lake			X			X	300'	
Mt. Storm	Stormville			X	X		X	600'	X
Mystic Mountain	Cazenovia			X				590'	
Oak Mountain	Speculator			X			X	650'	
Orange County Park	Goshen			X				150'	X
Paleface	Jay		X	X				730'	
Parkway	Utica			X			X	220'	
Peek 'n Peak	French Creek			X		X		340'	
Petersburg Pass	Petersburg		X					800'	
Phoenicia	Phoenicia						X	450'	
Pines Hotel	S. Fallsburg		X					159'	
Plattekill Mt.	Roxbury			X			X	970'	
Poverty Hill	Ellicottville			X	X			435'	
Royal Mountain	Johnstown			X			X	550'	
St. Lawrence Snow Bowl	South Colton			X				300'	
Scotch Valley	Stamford		X	X			X	750'	X
Scott's Cobble	Lake Placid				X			380'	
Shayne's	Highmount					X		2200'	
Silver Bells	Wells			X			X	400'	

412

NAME OF AREA	LOCATION (NEAREST TOWN) OR POSTAL ADDRESS	KIND OF LIFTS						TOTAL VERTICAL DESCENT	SNOW-MAKING
		GONDOLAS TRAMWAYS	CHAIRLIFTS	T-BARS	PLATTER-PULLS	J-BARS	ROPE TOWS		
Silvermine	Bear Mountain			X		X	X	210′	X
Sitzmarker Ski Club	Colden			X			X	385′	
Skiland	East Berne					X	X	300′	
Ski-Minne	New Paltz			X		X	X	360′	X
Ski Valley	Naples					X	X	560′	
Snow Ridge	Turin	X	X					500′	
Song Mountain	Tully		X			X		600′	X
Sterling Forest	Tuxedo		X		X		X	400′	X
Stony Point	Stony Point		X		X			300′	X
Swain	Swain			X				607′	
Tall Timber	Van Etten			X			X	400′	X
Toggenburg	Fabius			X				580′	X
Van Cortland Park	The Bronx						X	100′	X
Wallkill Park	Goshen			X				133′	
Western Chautauqua	Clymer			X		X		410′	
West Mountain	Glens Falls		X		X		X	1010′	
White Acres Ski Resort	Clayville			X			X	350′	
Whiteface Mountain	Wilmington		X	X		X		2400′	X
Willard Mountain	North Easton			X			X	456′	
Windham	Windham		X	X			X	1500′	X
Win-Sum	Ellicottville		X	X			X	400′	
Woods Valley	Westernville			X			X		
NORTH CAROLINA									
Blowing Rock	Blowing Rock			X			X	350′	X
Cataloochee	Waynesville			X			X	225′	X
Gold Mt. Enterprises	Franklin		X					797′	
Hound Ears Ski Club	Blowing Rock			X				100′	X
NORTH DAKOTA									
Twilight Hills	Bismark				X		X	407′	X
Villa Vista	Arvilla						X	105′	
OHIO									
Alpine Resorts	Morrow		X				X	170′	
Alpine Valley	Chesterland			X			X	240′	X
Boston Mills	Peninsula		X	X			X	240′	X

413

SKI AREA GUIDE

NAME OF AREA	LOCATION (NEAREST TOWN) OR POSTAL ADDRESS	KIND OF LIFTS						TOTAL VERTICAL DESCENT	SNOW-MAKING
		GONDOLAS TRAMWAYS	CHAIRLIFTS	T-BARS	PLATTER-PULLS	J-BARS	ROPE TOWS		
OHIO									
Brandywine Ski Center	Sagamore Hills		X				X	200'	X
Clear Fork Valley	Butler		X	X		X	X	325'	X
Cleveland Ski Club	Lake County		X					127'	
Mont Chalet	Chesterland		X				X	110'	X
Snow Bowl	Cadiz		X						
Snow Trails	Mansfield		X	X			X	275'	X
Valley High	Bellefontaine		X				X	375'	X
OREGON									
Anthony Lakes	Baker		X		X		X	950'	
Hoodoo Ski Bowl	Salem		X				X	1025'	
Mt. Ashland	Ashland			X	X				
Mt. Bachelor	Bend		X	X	X		X	2000'	
Multorpor Ski Bowl	Government Camp		X	X			X	1200'	
Spout Springs	Weston		X	X			X	520'	
Summit Ski Area	Government Camp			X			X	300'	
Timberline	Government Camp		X		X		X	1700'	
Tomahawk	Klamath Falls			X			X	625'	
Williamette Ski Area	Eugene			X			X	800'	
PENNSYLVANIA									
Apple Hill	Allentown			X			X	240'	X
Bear Rocks Ski Slopes	Acme		X				X	350'	X
Big Boulder	Whitehaven		X	X		X	X	450'	X
Black Moshannon	Philipsburg				X			250'	
Blair Mountain	Dillsburg			X			X	400'	X
Blue Knob	Claysburg		X		X		X	1000'	X
Boyce Park	Monroeville			X				169'	X
Buck Hill	Buck Hill Falls			X				300'	X
Camelback	Tannersville		X		X	X		750'	X
Camp T. Frank Soles	Somerset			X				400'	
Charnita, Inc.	Fairfield		X				X	592'	X
Denton Hill State Park	Coudersport		X		X			570'	X
Elk Mountain	Union Dale		X	X		X		1000'	X
Hickory Ridge	Honesdale			X			X	357'	X
Hidden Valley	Somerset				X		X	400'	X

414

NAME OF AREA	LOCATION (NEAREST TOWN) OR POSTAL ADDRESS	KIND OF LIFTS						TOTAL VERTICAL DESCENT	SNOW-MAKING
		GONDOLAS TRAMWAYS	CHAIRLIFTS	T-BARS	PLATTER-PULLS	J-BARS	ROPE TOWS		
Highland	Muncy				X	X	X	275'	
Indian Lake	Somerset				X			250'	
Laurel Mountain	Ligonier			X	X		X	910'	X
Paper Birch	Tafton			X			X		
Pocono Manor Inn	Pocono Manor					X	X	220'	X
Poco-North	Hawley		X	X			X	416'	X
Richmond Hill	Fort Laudon			X			X	125'	X
Seven Springs	Champion		X	X	X		X	634'	X
Sharp Mountain	Pottsville		X	X		X		400'	X
Skimont	Boalsburg			X			X	390'	
Ski Roundtop	Lewisberry		X				X	540'	X
Ski Sno-Hill	Lake Como			X			X	400'	
Timber Hill	Canadensis			X	X			400'	X
White Mountain	Indianhead			X	X		X	380'	
Youngsville Ski Ways	Youngsville			X			X	500'	
RHODE ISLAND									
Ski Valley	Cumberland			X			X	180'	X
SOUTH DAKOTA									
Terry Peak	Lead		X		X			1500'	
TENNESSEE									
Gatlinburg Ski Resort	Gatlinburg		X		X		X	800'	X
UTAH									
Alta	Salt Lake City		X					1800'	
Beaver Mountain	Logan		X						
Blue Mountain	Monticello			X			X	800'	
Brianhead	Cedar Breaks		X	X				600'	
Brighton Ski Bowl	Brighton		X				X	1076'	
Grizzly Ridge	Vernal			X			X	400'	
Snow Basin	Ogden Canyon		X				X	2600'	
Snow Park	Park City		X					600'	
Solitude	Big Cottonwood Canyon		X	X				1900'	
Timp Haven	Provno Canyon		X	X	X		X	1400'	
Treasure Mountains	Park City MINE TRAIN	X				X		2460'	

415

SKI AREA GUIDE

NAME OF AREA	LOCATION (NEAREST TOWN) OR POSTAL ADDRESS	KIND OF LIFTS						TOTAL VERTICAL DESCENT	SNOW-MAKING
		GONDOLAS TRAMWAYS	CHAIRLIFTS	T-BARS	PLATTER-PULLS	J-BARS	ROPE TOWS		
VERMONT									
Birdseye Mountain	Castleton			X	X		X	500'	X
Bolton Valley	Burlington		X						
Bromley	Manchester		X		X	X		1360'	X
Burke Mountain	Lyndonville			X	X			1600'	
Burrington	Whitingham				X		X	240'	
Carinthia	West Dover			X			X	800'	
Dutch Hill	Heartwellville			X		X	X	570'	
Glebe Mountain	Windham			X				302'	
Glen Ellen	Fayston		X	X				2645'	
Goodrich	Northfield			X			X	600'	
Haystack Mountain	Wilmington		X	X				1600'	
High Pond	Brandon			X			X	300'	
Hogback	Brattleboro			X	X		X	500'	
Jay Peak	North Troy	X	X	X	X			1950'	
Killington	Sherburne		X		X			2020'	X
Living Memorial Park	Brattleboro			X				204'	
Lord's Hill				X			X	500'	
Lyndon Outing Club	Lyndonville			X			X	800'	
Madonna Mountain	Jeffersonville		X		X			2150'	
Mad River Glen	Waitsfield		X	X			X	1985'	
Magic Mountain	Londonderry		X	X				1600'	
Maple Valley	Brattleboro		X	X				940'	
Middlebury Snow Bowl	Hancock			X				900'	
Mt. Ascutney	Windsor		X	X				1470'	X
Mt. Mansfield-Spruce Peak	Stowe		X	X				2300'	
Mt. Snow	West Dover	X	X				X	1900'	X
Mt. Tom/Suicide Six	Woodstock				X			600'	X
Norwich University	Montpelier				X		X	500'	
Okemo Mountain	Ludlow		X		X			1950'	
Pico Peak	Rutland		X	X		X		1967'	
Pinnacle Skiways	Randolph				X			550'	
Prospect Mountain	Bennington			X			X	676'	
Skyline	Barre				X			500'	
Snow Valley	Manchester			X		X		586'	
Stowe	(See Mt. Mansfield)								

416

NAME OF AREA	LOCATION (NEAREST TOWN) OR POSTAL ADDRESS	KIND OF LIFTS						TOTAL VERTICAL DESCENT	SNOW-MAKING
		GONDOLAS TRAMWAYS	CHAIRLIFTS	T-BARS	PLATTER-PULLS	J-BARS	ROPE TOWS		
Stratton	South Londonderry		X	X				1200'	
Sugarbush	Warren	X	X	X				2400'	
VIRGINIA									
Bryce's Mountain	Basye		X				X	465'	X
The Homestead	Hot Springs TRESTLECAR			X			X	500'	X
Skyline	Washington			X			X	500'	X
WASHINGTON									
Chewelah Peak	Chewelah		X				X	1400'	
Crystal Mountain	Enumclaw		X	X			X	2400'	
Hurricane Ridge	Port Angeles						X	500'	
Hyak	Snoqualmie Pass		X		X		X	1260'	
Mt. Baker	Bellingham		X				X	1000'	
Mt. Pilchuck	Everett		X				X	1217'	
Mt. Spokane	Spokane		X				X	1523'	
Paradise Valley	Ashford						X	400'	
Satus Peak	Toppenish						X		
Ski Acres	Snoqualmie Pass		X	X			X	900'	
Snoqualmie Summit	Snoqualmie Pass		X		X		X	850'	
Squilchuck	Squilchuck State Park				X		X		
Stevens Pass	Leavenworth		X				X	1800'	
White Pass	White Pass		X		X		X	1500'	
WEST VIRGINIA									
Chestnut Ridge	Morgantown						X		
Oglebay Park	Wheeling				X		X	250'	
WISCONSIN									
Alpine Valley	East Troy		X					260'	
Birch Haven	Baraboo						X	275'	
Bruce Mound	Merrillan						X	325'	X
Calumet Park	Appleton						X	180'	
Camp 10	Rhinelander			X			X	225'	
Cascade Mountain	Portage		X				X	460'	X
Deepwood	Colfax			X			X	293'	X
Delafield Lodge	Delafield						X	200'	
Englewood	Osceola			X		X	X	340'	
Hardscrabble	Rice Lake			X			X	350'	

417

SKI AREA GUIDE

NAME OF AREA	LOCATION (NEAREST TOWN) OR POSTAL ADDRESS	KIND OF LIFTS						TOTAL VERTICAL DESCENT	SNOW-MAKING
		GONDOLAS TRAMWAYS	CHAIRLIFTS	T-BARS	PLATTER-PULLS	J-BARS	ROPE TOWS		
WISCONSIN									
Hidden Valley	Monitowac						X	200'	
Little Switzerland	Slinger		X				X	200'	X
Lockhaven	Spooner						X	250'	
Majestic Hills	Lake Geneva						X	250'	X
Mt. Ashwabay	Bayfield			X			X	317'	
Mt. Fuji	Lake Geneva			X			X	240'	X
Mt. LaCrosse	LaCrosse				X		X	516'	X
Mt. Telemark	Cable		X	X			X	370'	X
Mus-Ski Mt.	Sayner				X		X	200'	
Nor-Ski Ridge	S. Fish Creek			X			X	226'	X
Rib Mountain	Wausau			X			X	680'	X
Sheltered Valley	Three Lakes				X		X	200'	
Ski-Mac	Somerset						X	268'	
Sky Line	Friendship						X	285'	X
Squirrel Hill	Minoqua						X	200'	
Trollhaugen	Dresser			X			X	256'	X
Tyrol Basin	Mt. Horeb		X	X			X	380'	X
View Ridge	New London						X	120'	
White Cap Mountain	Hurley			X			X	350'	
Wilmot Ski Hills	Wilmot		X	X			X	230'	X
Wunderberg	West Bend			X			X	200'	X
WYOMING									
Antelope Butte	Sheridan			X	X			650'	
Fun Valley	Greybull			X	X			650'	
Happy Jack	Laramie			X			X	300'	
Hogadon Basin	Casper			X			X	600'	
Jackson Hole	Jackson	X	X					4135'	
Meadowlark	Big Horn Nat'l Forest				X			600'	
Medicine Bow	Centennial			X				700'	
Pinedale	Pinedale				X		X		
Ryan Park	Saratoga		X		X				
Snow King Mt.	Jackson Hole		X						
Snowy Range	Saratoga		X		X			900'	

1B. NORTH AMERICA: *CANADA*

NAME OF AREA	LOCATION (NEAREST TOWN) OR POSTAL ADDRESS	KIND OF LIFTS						TOTAL VERTICAL DESCENT	SNOW-MAKING
		GONDOLAS TRAMWAYS	CHAIRLIFTS	T-BARS	PLATTER-PULLS	J-BARS	ROPE TOWS		
ALBERTA									
Canyon Ski Lodge	Red Deer			X				465′	X
Edmonton Ski Club	Edmonton						X	200′	X
Happy Valley Ski Ltd.	Calgary				X		X	300′	X
Lake Louise	Lake Louise	X			X			200′	
Marmot Basin	Jasper			X				1000′	
Mt. Norquay	Banff		X	X	X		X	1500′	
Pigeon Mountain	Cranmore				X			800′	X
Sunshine Village	Banff		X	X				675′	
Turner Valley	Calgary			X					
Whistler Mountain	Jasper			X				1500′	
BRITISH COLUMBIA									
Apex Alpine	Penticton			X	X		X	1200′	
Bear Mountain	Dawson Creek			X			X	410′	
Big White	Kelowna			X				1350′	
Borderline Ski Club	Osoyoos			X			X		
Garabaldi Lifts Ltd.	Vancouver	X	X	X				4300′	
Green Mountain	Vancouver						X	1900′	
Grouse Mountain	Vancouver		X	X			X	900′	
Hollyburn Ridge	Vancouver		X	X				1800′	
Kimberley Ski Club	Kimberley			X				2500′	
Lac Le Jeune	Kamloops			X				800′	
Mt. Beecher Ski Club	Courtenay		X			X		3100′	
Mt. Seymour	Vancouver		X		X		X	500′	
North Star Mt.	Kimberley			X				1600′	
Pine Woods Lodge	Manning Park			X			X		
Prince Rupert Ski Club	Prince Rupert			X					
Red Mt. Ski Club Soc.	Rossland		X		X		X	2790′	
Revelstoke Ski Club	Revelstoke			X			X		

SKI AREA GUIDE

NAME OF AREA	LOCATION (NEAREST TOWN) OR POSTAL ADDRESS	KIND OF LIFTS						TOTAL VERTICAL DESCENT	SNOW-MAKING
		GONDOLAS TRAMWAYS	CHAIRLIFTS	T-BARS	PLATTER-PULLS	J-BARS	ROPE TOWS		
BRITISH COLUMBIA									
Silver King Ski Club	Nelson			X				1000'	
Silver Star Mt.	Vernon			X	X			1000'	
Snow Valley	Fernie			X			X		
Taber Mountain	Prince George			X			X		
Tod Mountain	Kamloops	X	X					3100'	
MANITOBA									
Falcon Lake	Falcon Beach						X	140'	
Holiday Mountain	La Riviere			X			X	300'	X
La Riviere	La Riviere				X		X		X
Mt. Agassiz	McCreary			X			X	500'	
NEWFOUNDLAND									
Smokey Mt. Ski Club	Labrador City			X			X	500'	
NOVA SCOTIA									
Alpine Ski Trails	Wentworth Valley			X			X	600'	
Wentworth Valley	Route 4			X			X	860'	
ONTARIO									
Alice-Hill Park	Pembroke			X			X	210'	
Bay Motor Hotel	Owen Sound		X	X				225'	X
Beaver Valley	Flesherton-Markdale			X		X	X	550'	
Bethany Ski Club	Bethany			X			X		
Blue Mt. Winter Park	Collingwood		X	X	X		X	800'	X
Britannia Hotel	Huntsville				X		X	175'	
Caledon Ski Club	Caledon				X		X		
Candiac Skiways	Dacre			X			X		
Cedar Springs	Burlington			X			X		X
Chedoke	Hamilton			X				150'	X
Chicopee	Kitchener						X		
Craigleith	Collingwood			X			X	700'	
Devil's Elbow	Bethany			X			X	325'	
Devil's Glen	Glen Huron			X			X		
Don Valley	Toronto				X		X	100'	X
Fort William	Fort William		X				X		X

420

NAME OF AREA	LOCATION (NEAREST TOWN) OR POSTAL ADDRESS	KIND OF LIFTS						TOTAL VERTICAL DESCENT	SNOW-MAKING
		GONDOLAS TRAMWAYS	CHAIRLIFTS	T-BARS	PLATTER-PULLS	J-BARS	ROPE TOWS		
Georgian Peaks	Thornbury		X	X	X		X	810'	X
Haliburton Highlands	Haliburton		X					237'	
Happy Hills	Orangeville				X		X		
Hidden Valley	Huntsville		X	X			X	360'	X
Hockley Valley	Orangeville				X		X		X
Honey Pot	Maple				X		X		X
Horseshoe Valley	Craighurst		X	X				187'	
Hotel Bernard	Sundridge				X		X	175'	
Kirkland Lake	Swastika					X			
Laurentian	North Bay			X			X	325'	
Limberlost Resorts Ltd.	Sinclair			X			X	250'	
Loch Lomond	Fort William			X			X	775'	
London Ski Club	London						X	100'	X
Mansfield Skiways	Alliston			X			X	375'	X
Moose Mountain	Beardmore			X					
Mount Baldy	Port Arthur		X				X	600'	
Mount McKay	Fort William		X				X	450'	X
Mount St. Louis	Barrie			X			X	318'	
Mountain View	Midland				X		X	150'	
Muskoka Sands	Gravenhurst			X				800'	
Nacona	Napanee				X		X	160'	X
Old Smokey	Kimberley			X			X	265'	
Onaping	Onaping			X			X	280'	
Oshawa	Oshawa			X			X	300'	X
Pinery Park	Grand Bend				X				
Port Arthur	Port Arthur		X				X	550'	
Rainbow Ridge	Bracebridge			X			X	225'	X
Raven Mountain	Kirkland Lake			X				525'	
St. Bernard	Haileybury			X					
Saulte Ski Club	Saulte Ste. Marie			X			X	225'	
Searchmont Valley	Saulte Ste. Marie			X	X		X	650'	
Skee-Hi Ltd.	Thamesford			X			X	150'	X
Snow Valley	Barrie			X			X		
Talisman	Kimberley		X	X			X	600'	X
Tally-Ho Winter Park	Huntsville				X		X	210'	

SKI AREA GUIDE

NAME OF AREA	LOCATION (NEAREST TOWN) OR POSTAL ADDRESS	GONDOLAS TRAMWAYS	CHAIRLIFTS	T-BARS	PLATTER-PULLS	J-BARS	ROPE TOWS	TOTAL VERTICAL DESCENT	SNOW-MAKING
ONTARIO									
Timmins Ski Club	Timmins			X			X	350'	
Toronto Ski Club	Richmond Hill						X	80'	
Twin Hearths	Orangeville			X			X	200'	
Valley Schuss	Orangeville			X	X		X	350'	
QUEBEC									
Avila Ski Center	Piedmont		X	X		X		590'	X
Bellevue	Morin Heights			X		X		300'	
Big Hill	Prevost			X			X		
Bromont	Bromont		X	X				1100'	X
Camp Fortune	Ottawa		X	X	X	X	X	600'	X
Castel-Mont Joye				X					
Chantecler	Ste. Adele-en-Haut			X	X			280'	X
Chateau Lac Beauport	Lac Beauport			X	X		X	550'	
Cochand's	Ste. Marquerite		X	X	X		X		X
East Angus	East Angus			X				325'	
Edelweiss Valley	Wakefield			X	X			600'	X
Far Hills Inn	Val Morin			X			X		
Glen Mountain	Knowlton		X	X				1050'	
Gray Rocks Inn	St. Jovite			X				550'	X
Hills 40 & 80	Ste. Adele			X				350'	
La Reserve	St. Donat		X		X			1000'	
La Tuque	La Tuque			X				475'	
Laurentide Inn	Ste. Agathe		X	X	X				
Manoir St. Castin	Lac Beauport		X	X				550'	X
Manor House	Ste. Agathe			X				150'	
Marquis Hill	St. Sauveur			X			X	250'	
Montagne du Manoir	Lac Beauport		X	X			X		
Mt. Adstock	Thetford Mines		X	X			X	1100'	
Mt. Alouette	Ste. Adele			X				500'	
Mt. Avalanche	Ste. Agathe			X				450'	
Mt. Blanc	St. Faustin			X	X			715'	
Mt. Carmel	Valmont			X			X	225'	X
Mt. Castor	Ste. Agathe			X				270'	

NAME OF AREA	LOCATION (NEAREST TOWN) OR POSTAL ADDRESS	KIND OF LIFTS						TOTAL VERTICAL DESCENT	SNOW-MAKING
		GONDOLAS TRAMWAYS	CHAIRLIFTS	T-BARS	PLATTER-PULLS	J-BARS	ROPE TOWS		
Mt. Chevreuil	Ste. Agathe		X	X				757'	
Mt. Christie	St. Sauveur			X			X	400'	X
Mt. Echo	Sutton		X		X			1500'	
Mt. Fugere	Ste. Agathe			X	X			400'	
Mt. Gabriel	Mt. Gabriel			X				560'	
Mt. Garceau	St. Donat		X	X	X			950'	
Mt. Habitant	St. Sauveur			X				550'	X
Mt. Mars Ski Club	Port Alfred			X			X	525'	
Mt. Orford	Magog		X	X					
Mt. Plante	Val David			X				100'	
Mt. St. Anne	Quebec City	X	X	X				2050'	
Mt. Ste. Agathe	Ste. Agathe		X		X				
Mt. Ste. Castin	Lac Beauport			X	X				
Mt. Sutton	Sutton		X	X				1500'	X
Mt. Tremblant	Mt. Tremblant		X	X	X		X	2400'	X
Morin Heights	Morin Heights			X		X		300'	
North Hatley	North Hatley			X				545'	X
Petit Chamonix	Matapedia			X				400'	
St. Sauveur Des Monts	St. Jerome		X	X		X	X	700'	
Summit Sauvage	Val Morin			X				420'	
Sun Valley	Ste. Adele		X	X	X			475'	
Up-Hill	St. Sauveur		X	X				700'	

SKI AREA GUIDE

NORTH AMERICAN TOURIST BUREAUS

The following state-administered or state-supported agencies help promote the sport of skiing through advertising or public service programs:

COLORADO—Colorado Winter Sports Committee, 308 State Capitol Bldg., Denver, Colorado

MAINE—Maine Dept. of Economic Development, 211 State House, Augusta, Maine

MASSACHUSETTS—New England Council, Statler Office Bldg., Boston, Massachusetts

MICHIGAN—Michigan Tourist Council, 138 Steven T. Mason Bldg., Lansing, Michigan 48926

MINNESOTA—Department of Business Development, Publicity and Promotion Division, State Capitol, St. Paul, Minnesota 55101

NEVADA—Department of Business Development, State Capitol, Carson City, Nevada

NEW HAMPSHIRE—New Hampshire Division of Economic Development, 201 State House Annex, Concord, New Hampshire

NEW MEXICO—New Mexico Dept. of Development, 302 Galisteo, Santa Fe, New Mexico

NEW YORK—New York State Dept. of Commerce, Adirondack Mt. Authority, Albany 1, New York; New York State Conservation Dept., Department of Parks, Albany 1, New York

OREGON—Oregon State Highway Dept., 101 Highway Bldg., Salem, Oregon

PENNSYLVANIA—Bureau of Travel Development, Room 281, Dept. of Commerce, Harrisburg, Pennsylvania

UTAH—Ski Utah Associates, Capitol Building, Salt Lake City, Utah

VERMONT—Vermont Development Dept., State Office Bldg., Montpelier, Vermont

CANADIAN GOVERNMENT TRAVEL BUREAU, 680 Fifth Avenue, New York, N.Y. 10019

ALBERTA—Alberta Travel Bureau, Edmonton, Alberta, Canada

BRITISH COLUMBIA—British Columbia Government Travel Bureau, Victoria, British Columbia, Canada

ONTARIO—Ontario Dept. of Tourism & Information, 185 Bloor Street, Toronto 2, Ontario, Canada

QUEBEC—Dept. of Tourism, Fish & Game, Parliament Bldg., Quebec City, P. Que., Canada

Appendix A. **SKI AREA GUIDE**

2. EUROPE

NAME OF AREA	NEAREST MAJOR CITY	BASE ALTITUDE	NUMBER OF LODGES	NUMBER OF BEDS	NUMBER OF LIFTS
AUSTRIA	For information and travel folders, write: Austrian State Tourist Department, 444 Madison Ave., New York, New York 10022; 332 S. Michigan Ave., Chicago 4, Illinois; 105 Montgomery St., San Francisco 4, California; 195 S. Beverly Drive, Beverly Hills, California.				
VORALBERG					
Brand	Bregenz	3,401	9	—	4
Grosswalsertal & Fontella	Faschinajoch Bregenz	3,756	9	—	5
Kleinwalsertal		—	—	—	—
Riezlern	Bregenz	3,556	58	—	17
Lech-Oberlech am Arlberg	Innsbruck	4,740–5,580	22	—	10
Schruns	Bregenz	2,264	55	—	8
Tschagguns	Bregenz	2,264	—	—	—
Gaschurn	Bregenz	3,210	—	—	—
Gargellen	Bregenz	4,670	—	—	—
Partenen	Bregenz	3,450	—	—	—
St. Anton im Montafon		3,139	—	—	—
Zürs am Alberg	Innsbruck	5,655	8	—	8
TYROL					
Ehrwald, Lermoos	Innsbruck	3,265	56	—	8
Gerlos & Gmünd	Salzburg	4,090	11 plus 500 private beds		5
Hopfgarten	Innsbruck	2,200	20	—	5
Igls	Innsbruck	1,880	215	—	17
Mutters	Innsbruck	2,950	—	—	—
Axams-Lizum	Innsbruck	—	—	—	—
Kitzbühel	Kitzbühel	2,500	134	—	21
Hintertux	Innsbruck	4,900	16	—	6
Lienz	Lienz	2,225	20	—	4

SKI AREA GUIDE

NAME OF AREA	NEAREST MAJOR CITY	BASE ALTITUDE	NUMBER OF LODGES	NUMBER OF BEDS	NUMBER OF LIFTS
TYROL (Cont.)					
Mayrhofen	Innsbruck	2,070	63	—	5
Ober-Gurgl	Innsbruck	6,320	11	—	7
St. Anton am Arlberg	Innsbruck	4,280	162	—	12
St. Christoph am Arlberg	Innsbruck	5,905	5	—	5
St. Johann	Kitzbühel	2,160	121	—	18
Kirchberg		2,750	—	—	—
Seefeld	Innsbruck	3,870	135	—	10
Sölden-Hochsölden	Innsbruck	4,470–6,790	34	—	11
Wildschönau	Innsbruck		36	—	10
Niederau		2,870	—	—	—
Oberau		3,070	—	—	—
Affach	—		—	—	—
Zell am Ziller	Innsbruck	1,890	30	—	5
SALZBURG					
Badgastein	Salzburg	3,550	123	—	9
Bad Hofgastein	Salzburg	2,850	89	—	6
Dieten am Hochkönig	Salzburg	3,540	5	—	2 Summer skiing on glacier
Mittersill, Pass Thurn	Salzburg	2,590–4,180	29 plus 100 private beds		
Krimml, Gerlosplatte	Salzburg	3,520 5,580	43 plus 300 private beds		6
Muhlbach	Salzburg	2,820	12	—	8
Mitterbergalp am Hochkönig		4,930	—	—	Summer skiing on glacier
Obertauern	Salzburg	5,705	41	—	16
Saalbach Hinterglemm	Salzburg	3,290	78	—	23
Zell am See	Salzburg	2,490	103	—	9

NAME OF AREA	NEAREST MAJOR CITY	BASE ALTITUDE	NUMBER OF LODGES	NUMBER OF BEDS	NUMBER OF LIFTS
CARINTHIA					
Heiligenblut	Klagenfurt	4,270	6	—	9
Kanzelhöhe	Villach	4,920–	17	—	4
Gerlitzen		6,260			
STYRIA					
Bad Aussee	Salzburg	2,130	59	—	4
Haus im Ennstal	Salzburg	2,530	17	—	7
Mariazell	Vienna	2,850–	65	—	5
		4,260			
Ramsau	Salzburg	3,940	32	—	7
Schladming	Salzburg	2,460	25	—	8
Tauplitz-	Salzburg	2,920	27	—	9
Tauplitzalm		5,440			
UPPER AUSTRIA					
Ebensee am	Salzburg	1,460	27	—	7
Traunsee					
Feuerkogel		5,248			
Hinterstoder	Salzburg	2,130	13	—	6
Obertraun	Salzburg	1,680–	24	—	9
Hallstatt		6,890	—	—	—
Spital am Pyhrn	Linz	2,120	15	—	5
LOWER AUSTRIA					
Lilienfeld	Vienna	1,230	15	—	6
Puchenstuben	Vienna	2,850	17 plus 390 private beds		8
Semmering	Vienna	2,750	—	—	—

SKI AREA GUIDE

NAME OF AREA	NEAREST MAJOR CITY	BASE ALTITUDE	NUMBER OF LODGES	NUMBER OF BEDS	NUMBER OF LIFTS
FRANCE	For information and travel folders, write: French Government Tourist Office, 610 Fifth Ave., New York, New York; 18 South Michigan Ave., Chicago, Illinois; 323 Geary St., San Francisco, California; 9418 Wilshire Blvd., Beverly Hills, California.				
HAUTE SAVOIE					
Chamonix-Mont Blanc	Geneva	3,415–12,605	112	3,000	26
Châtel	Geneva	3,960	17	300	8
Les Contamines	Geneva	3,841	22	500	8
La Clusaz	Geneva	3,432	24	500	19
Les Gets	Geneva	3,867	30	650	18
Megève	Geneva	3,672	93	1,875	24
Les Houches	Geneva	3,326	26	547	5
Morzine	Geneva	3,300	55	1,200	16
St. Gervais	Geneva	2,970	65	1,205	15
Samoëns	Geneva	2,706	23	800	6
SAVOIE					
Courchevel	Geneva	6,105	60	4,500	25
Méribel	Geneva	5,280	26	382	8
Notre Dame de Bellecombe	Geneva	3,742	12	250	10
Pralognan-la-Vanoise	Geneva	4,653	8	580	7
Tignes	Geneva	6,930	19	298	12
Val d'Isère	Geneva	6,105	45	1,000	28
Valloire	Grenoble	4,719	21	380	11
DAUPHINE REGION					
Alpe d'Huez	Grenoble	6,128	42	1,000	9
Chamrousse	Grenoble	5,445	16	750	12
Les Deux Alpes	Grenoble	5,478	24	300	14
Montgenèvre	Briancon	6,138	12	290	7
Le Sauze	Grenoble	4,620	13	320	7
Serre-Chevalier	Briancon	4,455	20	350	15
Villard-de-Lans	Grenoble	3,465	29	500	11

NAME OF AREA	NEAREST MAJOR CITY	BASE ALTITUDE	NUMBER OF LODGES	NUMBER OF BEDS	NUMBER OF LIFTS
COTE D'AZUR REGION					
Auron	Nice	5,280	13	279	17
Valberg	Nice	5,610	10	183	7
LES PYRÉNÉES					
Barèges	Lourdes	4,092	17	410	6
Font-Romeu	Toulouse	5,940	19	700	6
Superbagnères	Luchon	5,940	2	195	14
LE MASSIF CENTRAL					
Le Mont-Dore	Clermont-Ferrand	3,465	60	1,200	11
LE JURA					
Métabief	Geneva	3,333	18	300	12
Les Rousses	Geneva	3,795	15	315	16

GERMANY	For information and travel folders, write: German Tourist Information Office: 500 Fifth Ave., New York, New York 10036; 11 So. La Salle St., Chicago 3, Illinois 60603; 323 Geary St., San Francisco, California 94102.

NAME OF AREA	NEAREST MAJOR CITY	BASE ALTITUDE	NUMBER OF LODGES	NUMBER OF BEDS	NUMBER OF LIFTS
UPPER BAVARIA					
Garmisch-Partenkirchen	Munich	4,200	60	8,870	30
Berchtesgaden Land	Munich	5,600–7,200	54	3,800	12
Ruhpolding	Munich	1,950–5,100	—	800	5
Bayrischzell	Munich	2,406–5,400	—	1,226	8
Rottach-Egern	Munich	2,220–5,400	—	605	5
Schliersee	Munich	2,400–5,700	—	2,600	6
Grainau	Munich	3,000–8,400	—	600	4
Mittenwald	Munich	2,760–7,200	—	1,000	3

429

SKI AREA GUIDE

NAME OF AREA	NEAREST MAJOR CITY	BASE ALTITUDE	NUMBER OF LODGES	NUMBER OF BEDS	NUMBER OF LIFTS
UPPER BAVARIA					
Oberammergau	Munich	2,550–5,400	—	2,600	4
Bad Reichenhall	Munich	1,410–7,500	—	3,000	4
ALLGAU REGION					
Oberstdorf	Munich	2,529–7,215	—	1,650	8
Hindelang-Bad Oberdorf	Munich	2,550–6,740	—	1,350	9
Kleinwalsertal (Riezlern, Hirsch-egg, Mittelberg)	Munich	3,300–6,600	—	1,400	14
Pfronten	Munich	2,700–6,000	—	1,600	6
UPPER VALLEY (BAVARIA)					
Reit im Winkl	Munich	3,600–6,400	—	620	7
THE HARZ					
St. Andreasberg	Hannover	2,250–2,692	—	391	3
SAUERLAND					
Winterberg	Bonn or Cologne	2,010–2,526	—	303	4
BLACK FOREST					
Feldberg-Schwarzwald	Freiburg	3,000–4,500	34	800	5
Todtnauherg	Freiburg	3,063–4,500	—	200	2

NAME OF AREA	NEAREST MAJOR CITY	BASE ALTITUDE	NUMBER OF LODGES	NUMBER OF BEDS	NUMBER OF LIFTS
ITALY	For information and travel folders, write: Italian State Tourist Office: 626 Fifth Ave., New York, New York 10020; 333 North Michigan Ave., Chicago 1, Illinois; St. Francis Hotel, Post St., San Francisco 2, California.				
DOLOMITES					
Belluno Nevegal	Milan	4,839– 5,192	—	—	5
TURIN					
Sestriere	Turin	6,000	15	—	11
Ala di Stura	Turin	3,608	8	—	3
Bardonecchia	Turin	4,303	19	—	7
Cesena	Turin	4,429	15	—	3
Chiomonte	Turin	2,453	3	—	4
Claviere	Turin	5,774	8	—	3
ALESSANDRIA					
Limone Piemonte	Genoa	3,608	21	—	6
VERCELLI					
Alagna Belvedere	Milan	3,906	10	—	4
Alpe Mera	Milan	5,151	6	—	8
Breuil-Cervinia	Milan	6,574	20	—	7
NOVARA					
Macugnaga	Milan	4,353	25	—	4
BERGAMO					
Foppolo-Montebello	Milan	4,970	7	—	6
SONDRIO					
Aprica	Milan	3,874	20	—	6
Bormio	Milan	4,019	32	—	6
Madesimo	Milan	5,032	11	—	6
AOSTA					
Cogne	Aosta	5,032	10	—	—
Courmayeur	Milan	4,029	67	—	3
Gressoney La Trinité	Milan	5,337	6	—	1

431

SKI AREA GUIDE

NAME OF AREA	NEAREST MAJOR CITY	BASE ALTITUDE	NUMBER OF LODGES	NUMBER OF BEDS	NUMBER OF LIFTS
TRENTO					
Canazei alla Marmolada-Alba Penja	Trent	1,465– 5,220	31	—	10
Madonna di Campiglo	Trent	4,993	29	—	6
San Martino di Castrozzo	Trent	4,737	28	—	8
Vigo and Pozza di Fassa	Trent	4,330	18	—	4
BOZEN					
Alpe di Siusi-Seiseralm	Milan	6,135	22	—	17
Corvara-Kurfar	Milan	5,144	13	—	7
Val Badia (3 Villages)	Milan	4,921	22	—	9
Monte San Vigilio	Milan	5,000	5	—	4
Ortisei-St. Ulrich	Milan	4,048	31	—	7
Passo Gardena-Grödner Joch	Bolzano	6,958	3	—	4
Santa Cristina	Milan	4,685	10	—	5
Selva Gardena	Milan	5,127	37	—	15
Solda	Milan	6,233	22	—	5
BELLUNO					
Cortina d'Ampezzo	Belluno	4,016	71	—	17
Penavena-Belvedere and Croce D'Aune	Belluno	3,412	4	—	4
Sappada	Belluno	4,101	28	—	6
VICENZA					
Asiago	Vicenza	26	—	3,283	6
UDINE					
Tarvisio-Camporosso	Udine	14	—	2,463	4
PISTOIA					
Abetone-Monte Gomito	Florence	22	—	6,207	7

NAME OF AREA	NEAREST MAJOR CITY	BASE ALTITUDE	NUMBER OF LODGES	NUMBER OF BEDS	NUMBER OF LIFTS
FROSINONE					
Campocatino	Rome	2	—	5,905	6
RIETI					
Terminillo	Rome	11	—	5,577	6

SWITZERLAND	For information and travel folders, write: Swiss National Tourist Office, 10 West 49th St., New York, New York 10020; 661 Market St., San Francisco, California 94102.				
Adelboden	Berne	4,452–7,216	18	1,300	13
Andermatt	Lucerne	4,738–9,842	22	700	8
Arosa	Zurich	6,200–9,166	66	3,804	10
Champéry	Geneva	3,460–6,000	14	513	9
Château-d'Oex	Geneva	3,300–5,800	20	500	8
Montana-Crans	Geneva	4,987–7,800	60	3,000	14
Davos and Surroundings	Zurich	5,120–9,262	110	5,000	21
Diablerets, Les	Geneva	3,816–10,000	10	500	3
Engelberg	Lucerne	3,347–7,500	20	2,000	11
Flims	Zurich	3,800–8,775	30	1,300	12
Grindelwald	Berne	3,468–11,342	34	1,477	17
Gstaad	Geneva	3,450–7,080	15	937	20
Kandersteg	Berne	4,000–6,050	20	850	5

SKI AREA GUIDE

NAME OF AREA	NEAREST MAJOR CITY	BASE ALTITUDE	NUMBER OF LODGES	NUMBER OF BEDS	NUMBER OF LIFTS
SWITZERLAND					
Klosters	Zurich	3,967–7,553	32	1,500	9
Lenzerheide-Valbella	Zurich	5,000–7,970	13	850	9
Leysin	Geneva	4,050–7,100	40	2,000	13
Murren	Berne	5,450–7,100	13	650	17
Pontresina	Zurich	6,000–10,013	28	2,000	11
Saas Fee	Geneva	5,906–13,000	30	1,500	9
St. Moritz	Zurich	6,135–10,013	52	4,176	11
Verbier	Geneva	4,921–9,000	37	1,100	20
Villars-Chesieres	Geneva	4,300–7,300	33	1,500	16
Wengen	Berne	4,260–11,342	28	1,500	17
Zermatt	Geneva	5,315–10,284	76	4,000	17

434

Appendix B. GLOSSARY

(For convenience, this glossary is divided into five sections: Technique, Equipment, Area Terms, Competition and General. Terms listed in each of these areas are in alphabetical order.)

TECHNIQUE

ABSTEM—A stemmed turn in which the lower ski is stemmed instead of the uphill ski, as is currently customary.

ANGULATION—A body position in which the knees and hips are rolled into the hill in order to edge the skis. The upper body is angled outward and down the hill to compensate for this action. Also called comma position.

ANTICIPATION—Rotation of the upper body in the direction of the turn prior to unweighting and edge change. Distinguished from rotation inasmuch as anticipation can be followed by counter-rotation or a reversing of the shoulders as the turn is carved.

CATCHING AN EDGE—Accidental catching of the edge of a ski, often resulting in a fall.

CERTIFICATION—The method used in the United States and Canada to distinguish fully competent instructors. A certified instructor has passed both written and practical examinations administered by a board of examiners who are experienced ski instructors. In order to remain certified, an instructor must repass the certification examination every two years.

CHECK—Any maneuver to slow down the skis.

CHRISTIE—A contraction of the word Christiania; any turn in which the skis are in a parallel position as the turn is completed.

COMMA POSITION—*See* Angulation.

COUNTER-ROTATION—A means of initiating a turn by pushing the tails of the skis to the outside of the turn. This results in the shoulders turning in a direction opposite to that of the turn. Also referred to as Gegenschulter and Reverse Shoulder.

DOUBLE STEM—A running position in which the tails of both skis are pushed out into a V position. Commonly called snowplow.

DOWNHILL SKI—The lower ski or the one that will become the lower ski in any ski turn.

DOWN UNWEIGHTING—The removal of the body's weight on the snow by "dropping" the body sharply.

EDGE SET—Increasing the holding action of the edges. The skier may set edges or create a "platform" before the turn by increasing the weight applied to the edges by rising quickly, for instance.

EDGING—A means of controlling the sideward slippage of the skis by setting the skis at an angle to the snow so that they "bite" the surface.

FALL LINE—The shortest distance down the slope; the steepest gradient.

GARLAND—An exercise in which the skis are alternately slipped downhill and traversed across the hill.

435

GLOSSARY

GEGENSCHULTER—A German term meaning reverse shoulder.

GELÄNDESPRUNG—A German term meaning terrain jump; an aerial maneuver to clear obstacles by springing into the air.

HEEL THRUST—The pushing of the tails of the skis down the hill in order to complete a turn or to check speed.

HERRINGBONE—A climbing step in which the skis are edged and held in a V position in order to prevent them from slipping back.

INSIDE SKI—The ski which is on the inside of the turn or will become the inside ski in any turn.

KICK TURN—A means of reversing direction on skis when in a stationary position.

MAMBO—A series of turns using both over-rotation and counter-rotation to produce a light, dance-like movement on easy slopes.

METHOD—See Technique.

OUTSIDE SKI—The ski which is on the outside of the turn or will become the outside ski in any turn.

PARALLEL CHRISTIE—A turn in which the skis remain parallel throughout the turn.

PRE-JUMP—A maneuver in which a skier jumps before he reaches the crest of a bump so that his trajectory follows the contour of the bump.

REUEL CHRISTIE—Frequently, but incorrectly, called Royal Christie. An advanced maneuver in which the outside ski is lifted off the snow and carried behind the skier as the turn is made on the inside ski.

REVERSE SHOULDER—See Counter-Rotation.

ROTATION—A means of initiating the turn by a rotation of the shoulders in the direction of the turn.

RUADE—A parallel turn made by diving forward and unweighting the skis by retracting the tails by pulling up the legs in the manner of a horsekick.

RÜCKLAGE—A German word meaning backward lean.

SCHUSS—Skiing down the fall line without turns or checks.

SHORT SWING—A continuous series of parallel turns with checks.

SIDESLIP—Sliding of the skis sideways by flattening the skis.

SNOWPLOW—A basic means of checking speed accomplished by opening the tails of the skis into a V position and edging the skis. Also called a double stem.

SNOWPLOW TURN—A turn made out of the snowplow position by shifting the weight to the ski which will be on the outside of the turn.

SPLIT ROTATION—A turn which is initiated with rotation and completed with counter-rotation, or vice versa. See also Anticipation.

STEERED TURNS—Turns of the stem variety in which one of the skis is pointed in the new direction in the initiation phase of the turn.

STEM—The basis for a series of turns in which the tail of one ski is pushed out so that the turn is started from a half-V position.

STEM CHRISTIE—An advanced form of a stem turn in which the ski is stemmed only slightly and in which the other ski is immediately brought alongside so that most of the turn is completed with skis parallel.

436

STEM TURN—A turn in which the uphill ski is stemmed and then weighted, and then held in that position until the arc of the turn is well established. The turn can be finished either in the stemmed position or the skis can be brought back to a parallel position in the completion phase.

STYLE—The individual interpretation of technique.

SYSTEM—*See* Technique.

TECHNIQUE—A formal exposition of ski instruction from the beginning stages to the advanced maneuvers. Also called a teaching system or a teaching method. Hence American Technique, The Official Modern Austrian Ski System, the French Method.

TRAVERSE—Skiing across the slope at some angle to the fall line.

UNWEIGHTING—A means of reducing the weight on the skis prior to turning so that the skis turn more easily.

UPHILL CHRISTIE—A turn "into" the hill with skis parallel. The completion phase of all "christie" turns.

UPHILL SKI—The upper ski or the one that will become the upper ski in any ski turn.

UP-UNWEIGHTING—Unweighting by means of rising sharply. When the rising motion slows or stops, the skis are unweighted.

VORLAGE—Forward lean or shifting the weight forward prior to a turn.

WEDELN—A series of parallel turns made in the fall line with a minimum of edge set.

WEIGHT SHIFT—A transfer of weight from one ski to the other, specifically from the downhill ski to the uphill ski in the initiation phase of steered turns.

WEIGHTING—The application of weight to the skis in order to set the edges. Usually accomplished by angulation or by rising sharply.

EQUIPMENT

ARLBERG STRAP—A leather strap attached to the ski and wrapped around the boot to prevent the ski from running away when the binding releases.

BASE—A protective layer of lacquer or plastic covering the running surface of the ski and designed to make the ski slide easier.

BEAR TRAP—Any non-release binding, specifically toe irons.

BOOTLOCK—A type of binding which grips the boot by spring pressure and usually consists of both a toe and heel unit. The springs are adjustable and usually require metal boot plates for proper functioning.

BUCKLE BOOTS—Boots that use specially made buckles instead of laces for closure.

CAMBER—The arch built into a ski so that the ski can distribute the skier's weight over the entire length of the ski.

CHATTER—The tendency of skis not to grip on snow or particularly ice when put on edge, caused either by the inability of the ski to damp vibration or by the skier not weighting the ski properly and sufficiently.

DAMPING—The quality in a ski which prevents it from vibrating excessively after it is deflected by a bump. Skis insufficiently damped have a tendency to be unstable.

437

GLOSSARY

Double Boot—A ski boot with a soft inner boot for improved fit and warmth built into a stiff outer boot which provides control over the skis and support for the ankle.

Edges—The strips of metal, usually made of hard steel, on the outer edges of the running surfaces of skis.

Flexibility, Flex—A quality of skis whose significance depends on the type of snow on which the skis will be used. A ski must be flexible enough throughout its length to absorb bumps and to get a maximum amount of edge on the snow, yet stiff enough so that it provides a grip on hard snow and ice.

Front Throw—A device for tightening the cable assembly which holds the boot to the skis. It can be of the release type.

Groove—The channel which runs almost the full length of the running surface of the ski and which is essential to keep the skis running straight when they are flat on the snow.

Heel Release—A device that enables the heel to release from the ski in the event of a fall directly over the tips of the skis. A heel release can be affected by a heel unit, whose releasing mechanism is at the heel, or through a front throw which will open when cable tension reaches a certain point.

Long Thong—A binding consisting of a long leather strap fastened to the ski and then wound around the boot in a special pattern to provide maximum support and to transmit every foot motion to the ski. Usually used in connection with a turntable.

Notching—Two vertical notches in the sole spaced to engage two projections in the toe unit so that there is sufficient grip to assure release.

Polyethylene—A plastic available in various degrees of hardness and used for the running surfaces of skis. It is very fast on snow. Usually on skis under the trade names of Kofix or P-Tex.

Release Binding—Any heel or toe release or a combination thereof that releases the skis from the boot in the event of a bad fall.

Safety Binding—A misnomer for a Release Binding. A release binding does not automatically guarantee a degree of safety unless it is properly adjusted.

Shimmy—The tendency of the skis to wander from side to side when skiing straight and with the skis flat on the snow.

Shovel—Area near front tip of the ski.

Side Camber—The slight arc built into the sides of skis to assist in turning.

Step-in Binding—Usually, a release binding consisting of an integral toe and heel unit which snaps the boot in place as the skier steps on the ski.

Tail—Rear end of the ski.

Toe Irons—A non-release binding which holds the toes of the boots rigidly by means of two metal brackets fastened to a base plate.

Toe Release—Any unit which holds the toe of the boot to skis but releases in the event of a twisting fall.

Torsion—A quality in skis that determines the ability of the skis to twist in the vicinity of the tip when passing over uneven terrain. Also referred to as torsional stiffness.

TOURING ADAPTER—Special metal plates used to adapt a release binding for cross-country touring allowing free heel movement.

TRACKING—The quality of skis in maintaining a given direction without shimmy.

TURNTABLE—A swiveling heel binding for attaching long thongs that enables the toe release to function. There are also turntables which allow for release in an overhead fall.

WARP—A twist in a ski.

SKI AREA TERMS

AERIAL TRAMWAY—A large lift in which two large cabins are suspended from heavy cables. As one cabin goes up, the other comes down, jig-back fashion. Usually only found in very large areas with steep approaches to the top of the mountain. An aerial tram car may accommodate as many as a hundred or more passengers.

BASE—A firm layer of hard-packed snow covering the bare ground. Necessary to prevent ski bottoms from being damaged by rocks and dirt.

BOILER PLATE—A covering of solid ice resulting from a hard freeze following thawing conditions or rain.

BREAKABLE CRUST—A condition in which the surface of the snow freezes into a crust when there is loose snow beneath it. This condition is most frequently encountered in spring and following warm wind on new snow.

CHAIRLIFT—A form of uphill transportation in which a series of chairs are suspended permanently from a continuously moving cable. Each chair can accommodate one to four skiers, depending on design.

CORN—A type of snow found in spring or warm weather and formed by alternating thawing and freezing. This action removes the sharp edges off the snow crystals and gives the skier the illusion that he is skiing on ball bearings.

CRUD—*See* Breakable Crust.

FROZEN GRANULAR—A type of snow often confused with ice, but which is often made up of crystals of frozen snow.

GONDOLA—A lift consisting of a series of enclosed cars or cabins suspended from a continuously moving cable. Unlike a chairlift, the cabins are loaded while they are stationary and then are clamped on the cable by means of a special mechanism.

J-BAR—A lift in which a series of J or L-shaped bars are suspended from a continuously moving cable. The skier leans against the bar and is pulled uphill.

LIFT LINE—A line of skiers waiting to load onto a ski lift. Also the straight cut through the trees where the lift ascends the mountain.

MASHED POTATOES—A type of snow that gets wet and heavy as a result of warm weather.

MOGUL—A bump formed by the turning action of skiers. Usually found in quantity on steeper slopes, particularly following a heavy snowfall.

PACKED POWDER—A condition of snow which is packed either by skiing across it or by machinery. Packed powder is firm, but has a soft, almost fluffy surface which makes it ideal for skiing.

439

GLOSSARY

Piste—A term used in all Alpine countries of Europe meaning a hard-packed trail or slope.

Platterpull—*See* Pomalift.

Pomalift—A lift consisting of a series of steel bars, usually retractable, that can be suspended from a continuously moving cable. The bars have discs attached. The skier straddles the disc and is then hauled uphill.

Powder—Light, dry snow.

Rope Tow—A form of uphill transportation consisting of a continuously moving rope. The skier is pulled uphill by grasping the rope.

Sitzmark—A hole made in the snow by a skier's fall.

"Ski!"—A warning that a loose ski is coming down the hill.

Snowcat—Actually a tradename for Tucker over-the-snow vehicles, but used generically by skiers to designate all over-the-snow, tracked vehicles.

Spring Conditions—A catch-all phrase used in snow reporting to designate constantly variable conditions due to freezing temperatures at night and above-freezing temperatures throughout most of the day.

T-Bar—A lift consisting of a series of T-shaped bars suspended from a continuously moving cable. The T accommodates two skiers who lean against the bar and are pulled uphill.

Teleferique—*See* Aerial Tramway.

"Track Left" or "Track Right"—A warning a descending skier shouts to someone in his path whom he intends to pass, "left" or "right" indicating on which side the skier will pass.

COMPETITION

Alpine—All competitive events whose basic element is down-mountain skiing; downhill, slalom, giant slalom.

Biathlon—A nordic event combining cross-country racing and rifle marksmanship in which the competitor is penalized from one to two minutes on each errant shot, depending on how close to the mark he comes.

Closed Gate—A gate whose line between the two poles is in the fall line.

Combined—The result of two or more races arrived at by converting the results of each into points and then adding them together. *Also see* FIS Points.

Cross-country—A race in which competitors cover a set distance in which the terrain usually consists of one-third uphill, one-third downhill and one-third on the level. Cross-country events are usually run at distances of 15, 30 and 50 kilometers. There is also a 4 times 10 kilometer relay.

Downhill—A race essentially down the mountain in which control gates are used only to check unsafe speeds and to guide the racer around dangerous obstacles.

Elbow—A slalom figure in which a closed gate is followed by an open gate set off to one side.

FIS Points—A mathematical system used to convert times and distances to points, both to determine the skier's ranking in the combined standings and to determine his seeding position. The systems differ for Nordic, Alpine and Four-Way competition, but basically points are determined by the percentage by which competitors trail the winner.

FLUSH—A slalom figure made up of three or more closed gates in succession.

FOUR-WAY COMPETITION—Ski competition that involves downhill, jumping, slalom and cross-country.

GATE—Any arrangement of two flags or poles through which a skier must pass in a race.

GESCHMOZZEL START—A start in alpine racing no longer used. All racers started at once.

GIANT SLALOM—A form of alpine racing in which the racer passes through a series of gates which are connected by relatively long traverses. Giant slalom combines elements of both slalom and downhill.

HAIRPIN—A slalom figure made up of two successive closed gates.

H-GATE (Seelos Flush)—A three-gate slalom figure in which a closed gate is sandwiched between two open gates.

JUMPING—A nordic form of competition in which competitors jump on a specially prepared hill both for distance and for style.

LANGLAUF—The German word for cross-country.

NORDIC COMBINED—Competition involving both jumping and cross-country racing, the winner being determined by adding the point totals earned in each event.

OPEN GATE—A gate whose line between the two poles is across the fall line.

RACE CIRCUIT—A series of races, generally a series of key races throughout the season in which ambitious racers are expected to participate.

RACING EDGES—Edges made of somewhat softer steel than those usually found on recreational skis. The steel is softer so that the edges can be sharpened more readily.

SEEDING—A method of classifying racers in a given race according to ability. Racers are usually seeded in groups of fifteen, each racer's group being determined by the number of FIS points he has. Within each group, a racer's starting number is determined by draw.

SKI FLYING—A form of jumping on hills where distances of 100 meters or more can be reached.

SKI MEISTER—A German term meaning ski master; in four-way competition the competitor who has the best combined score in downhill, slalom, jumping and cross-country.

SLALOM—An alpine form of competition in which the racer must run a course designated by a series of gates set in various combinations so as to test his technique, speed and agility. Failure to pass through the gate properly results in disqualification.

GENERAL

AMERICAN PLAN—A method followed by some lodges and hotels in which the per day cost includes both meals and lodging.

CHARTER FLIGHT—A flight (usually to Europe or major resort) in which a bona fide group charters a plane for the purposes of skiing. Charter flights result in a per seat cost about 40 per cent lower than the lowest regular air fare.

EUROPEAN PLAN—A method followed by most lodges and hotels in which the per day cost includes only lodging, meals (if available) being to order and charged separately.

EXCURSION FARE—A fare usually lower than economy fare, but which requires that the passenger return within a set period of time, usually two to three weeks.

441

GLOSSARY

HIGH SEASON—A time of the year when the resorts are busiest, specifically the two weeks over Christmas-New Year's, from mid-February to mid-March, and over Easter if Easter falls within the ski season. European hotels usually raise their rates during these periods.

KANONE—A German word meaning cannon, a somewhat dated designation of a "hot" skier.

LOW SEASON—That part of the ski season when most resorts are relatively quiet, usually before Christmas, in January and in late spring.

MODIFIED AMERICAN PLAN—Hotel accommodation includes room, breakfast and dinner, but not lunch. Favored at many ski resorts.

PACKAGE TOUR—An arrangement whereby the skier pays for everything—transportation, lifts, rooms and meals—at one time. Some package tours are somewhat less comprehensive.

POWDERHOUND—A skier who loves and seeks out deep powder skiing.

SCHUSSBOOMER—Also known as a boomer, a skier who skis recklessly and indiscriminately.

SNOW BUNNY—A new or beginning skier, so named because he is invariably as white as a snowshoe rabbit.

442

Appendix C. SKI ORGANIZATIONS

CASA (Canadian Amateur Ski Association)—The Canadian equivalent of USSA. It makes the rules for the sport throughout Canada, sanctions races, promotes safety on skis, and raises funds for the Canadian teams.

CSIA (Canadian Ski Instructors Alliance)—The Canadian organization for ski instructors. CSIA determines the technique that will be taught by Canadian instructors and publishes a manual to that effect. It also certifies instructors through boards of examiners who give written and practical examinations.

FIS (Federation Internationale de Ski)—This is the world governing body of skiing. Through its committees and its annual congress it makes the rules for the various ski competitions, determines eligibility, approves courses for international competition (through its technical delegates), sanctions events eligible for FIS points, selects the sites for the quadrennial FIS World Championships, and approves the courses for Olympic competition.

NSAA (National Ski Areas Association)—A professional group for ski area managers in the United States. It deals with such common area problems as trail marking, safety and legal matters.

NSPS (National Ski Patrol System)—A volunteer organization of skiers who patrol the slopes and render first aid to the injured. NSPS is organized along the regional lines of USSA and each region has several sub-regions. Members must be experienced skiers and highly proficient in first-aid skills. (Address: Boston Building, Denver, Colorado.)

PSIA (Professional Ski Instructors of America)—An association of professional ski instructors in the United States. This group is responsible for the American Technique and other matters of concern to professional ski instructors. PSIA does not certify instructors. This is left to divisional certification groups whose geographic locations roughly correspond to those of the amateur divisions (see USSA).

SIA (Ski Industries of America)—A professional group which consists of manufacturers, distributors and importers of ski clothing and equipment. SIA conducts several trade shows annually in the spring, studies tariffs, and generally promotes the sport.

USSA (United States Ski Association)—The major ski organization in the United States which implements the FIS rules in this country, raises funds for the national teams, sanctions national championships and other major races, nurtures neglected phases of the sport and concerns itself with almost every aspect of skiing. Much of its work is done through committees which recommend action to the national conventions. A great deal of its work is done at the national headquarters (Address: Hotel Broadmoor, Colorado Springs, Colorado), the remainder through its eight regional divisions, whose addresses are given below:

AD, USSA (Alaska Division)—100 East Fireweed Lane, Box 434, Anchorage, Alaska. Covers Alaska only.

CD, USSA (Central Division)—205 East Front St., Traverse City, Michigan. Covers Michigan, 443

SKI ORGANIZATIONS

Wisconsin, Minnesota, Illinois, Indiana, Kentucky, Tennessee, Iowa, Nebraska, North Dakota and South Dakota.

FWSA (Far West Ski Association)—Box 2431, San Francisco, California. Covers California, Arizona and Nevada.

ID, USSA (Intermountain Division)—Box 2203, Salt Lake City, Utah. Covers Utah, western Wyoming, southern Idaho.

ND, USSA (Northern Division)—Box 81, Kalispell, Montana. Covers Montana.

PND, USSA (Pacific Northwest Division)—114 East Yakima Ave., Box 434, Yakima, Washington. Covers Washington, Oregon and Idaho as far south as Sun Valley.

RMD, USSA (Rocky Mountain Division)—520 Boston Building, Denver 2, Colorado. Covers Colorado, New Mexico and eastern Wyoming.

USEASA (United States Eastern Amateur Ski Association)—98 Main St., Littleton, New Hampshire. Covers entire Eastern Seaboard as far west as Ohio.

Appendix D. A CHRONOLOGY OF SKI DEVELOPMENTS

1850–51—The organization of first "snowshoe" clubs reported among prospectors in the "Lost Sierras" in California.

1853—First downhill races by snowshoers in Onion Valley, California.

1856—"Snowshoe" Thomson, a Norwegian immigrant, makes the first of his 90-mile mail runs on skis between Placerville, California, and Genoa, Nevada, setting off a "snowshoe" rage. He continued the runs until 1869.

1860—Sondre Nordheim makes the first officially measured jump (30.5 meters) in Morgedal, Norway.

1866–1875—Peak of racing enthusiasm in California. Races are of the downhill type with money prizes for the winners. "Dope" (wax) becomes a factor in racing.

1868—The first public discussion of ski technique (in Norway) following the use of the Telemark turn by the skiers of Telemark in a competition with skiers from Kristiania (Oslo).

1877—Kristiania (Oslo) Ski Club founded.

1882—Nansen Ski Club, Berlin, New Hampshire, becomes first ski club in America organized along modern lines and remains the oldest ski club in this country with a continuous history.

1887—First jumping competition in the United States at Red Wing, Minnesota, won by Mikkel Hemmestveit, a Norwegian immigrant.

1888—Fridtjof Nansen, a Norwegian, traverses southern Greenland using skis. The event itself and the book he subsequently published resulted in a tremendous interest in skiing throughout Europe. The two combined are usually considered responsible for opening the alpine skiing era.

——Skis first reported used in New York City during blizzard of '88.

1891—Group of eleven clubs forms the Central Ski Association, an unsuccessful forerunner of the National Ski Association (now United States Ski Association).

1892—First Holmenkollen meet (jumping and cross-country).

——First German books on ski technique.

1894—Fritz Huitfeld produces the first toe irons, a significant invention which made positive control over the skis feasible, and which greatly speeded the development of skiing on the more difficult Alpine slopes.

1896—The Austrian Mathias Zdarsky publishes the first methodical analysis of the stem turn and its application to Alpine skiing. The method advocated by Zdarsky involved a single pole.

1903—Ski Club of Great Britain founded.

1904—National Ski Association founded at Ishpeming, Michigan. Carl Tellefsen is elected its first president.

——Montreal Ski Club, Canada's first, is founded and a few days later conducts first Canadian jumping meet.

1905—Zdarsky sets first slalom course. This required the competitors to go around a single pole, not through a gate made up of two poles.

445

A CHRONOLOGY OF SKI DEVELOPMENTS

1907—First United States cross-country championships held at Ashland, Wisconsin, won by Asario Autio.

—Hannes Schneider starts the ski school at St. Anton, Austria.

1909—Dartmouth Outing Club is founded and Fred Harris is elected first president.

1910—First International Ski Congress is held at Kristiania, Norway.

—Alpine skiing takes on a distinct identity of its own with the publication of ski technique books in English and German.

1911—First Dartmouth Winter Carnival.

—First ski factory in the United States is opened by C. A. Lund in St. Paul, Minnesota. It remains in continuing operation as the Northland Ski Company.

—The stem christiania is first described as such by Carl Luther, a German writer, although Hannes Schneider had developed the turn as early as 1908.

1913—Dartmouth defeats McGill in the first inter-collegiate ski meet at St. Saveur, Quebec.

1917—First community winter carnival held at Newport, New Hampshire.

—First Canadian cross-country championships are staged by the Montreal Ski Club.

1920–24—Hannes Schneider formalizes his technique into an instructional system, which subsequently became known as the Arlberg Technique. It was the first truly Alpine technique and advocated the abandonment of the Telemark.

1921—Canadian Amateur Ski Association formed. First Canadian national championships in jumping and cross-country held.

—First modern slalom set at Mürren, Switzerland, by Arnold Lunn. The following fall, the first systematic exposition, complete with diagrams, of two-gate slalom was published by Arnold Lunn.

—Dr. Arnold Fanck, a German documentary film maker, makes the first ski movie. Hannes Schneider is the major participant in the film.

1922—United States Eastern Amateur Ski Association formed.

—The first Vasa race is held in Sweden.

1923—First American slalom set by Prof. Charles Proctor of Dartmouth College.

1924—First Olympic Winter Games held at Chamonix, France, with Nordic ski events only.

—The International Ski Congress is made into a permanent organization: the Federation Internationale de Ski (FIS); Col. Ivar Holmquist is named first president.

—Cash prizes outlawed by NSA in American amateur competitions.

1925—NSA recognizes USEASA as an affiliate.

1926—First modern downhill race in the United States held at Mt. Moosilauke, New Hampshire, and won by G. Michelson of the University of New Hampshire.

—First ski shop opened in the United States by Oscar Hambro in Boston.

—NSA recognizes U.S. Western Ski Association as affiliate.

1927—First snow train in North America from Montreal to the Laurentians by the Canadian Pacific Railroad.

—Central U.S. Ski Association founded. Recognized as an affiliate of NSA in 1928.

1928—First Arlberg-Kandahar race held at St. Anton, Austria.

—Second Olympic Winter Games held at St. Moritz, Switzerland. Ski events are confined to Nordic competition.

—FIS provisionally recognizes Ski Club of Great Britain downhill and slalom rules.

1928–30—Rudolf Lettner of Salzburg, Austria, develops and perfects the attachment of steel edges to skis.

1929—First ski school in the United States organized at Peckett's in Franconia by Sig Buchmayr.

—First ski train in the United States runs from Boston to Warner, New Hampshire.

—An experimental downhill race is run in connection with the 1929 FIS World Championships at Zakopane won by B. Czech of Poland.

1930—The first speed trials inaugurated, the so-called Flying Kilometer, at St. Moritz, Switzerland. Gustav Lantscher of Austria is the winner at an average speed of 66.4 miles an hour. (Ralph Miller of Dartmouth College was clocked at over 109 miles per hour at Portillo, Chile, in 1955, but this speed was unofficial because there was no electric timing. The figure has been approached both by American and European racers in speed trials at Cervinia, Italy, and at Portillo since that time.)

—Pacific Northwest Ski Association formed and recognized by NSA.

—California Ski Association, predecessor of the Far West Ski Association, recognized by NSA.

—FIS gives full recognition to downhill and slalom.

1931—First official FIS World Championships in downhill and slalom at Muerren, Switzerland, won by Walter Prager and David Zogg, downhill and slalom respectively; and Esme Mackinnon, both women's downhill and slalom.

1932—Third Olympic Winter Games held at Lake Placid, New York, with downhill and slalom still excluded from the ski events.

—The first rope tow installed by Alex Foster at Shawbridge, Quebec, Canada. This invention was to have a major effect on the development of skiing in North America.

—First Quebec-Kandahar is held at Mt. Tremblant, Quebec.

1933—First National Downhill Championship is held at Mt. Moosilauke, New Hampshire, and won by Henry Woods.

—Hollis Phillips wins first American Inferno race at Tuckerman's Ravine on Mt. Washington, New Hampshire.

1934—The first rope tow is installed in the United States on Clint Gilbert's farm at Woodstock, Vermont.

—Dick Durrance wins second American Inferno race.

—First public ski shows held at Madison Square Garden and Boston Gardens. These events draw thousands.

—Otto Furrer becomes first three-time winner of Arlberg-Kandahar.

1935—American women participate for the first time in FIS World Championships at Muerren, Switzerland.

—First U.S. National Downhill and Slalom Championships held at Mt. Rainier, Washington, and won by Hannes Schroll.

—First counter-rotational technique is introduced by Toni Ducia and Kurt Reindl, two Austrians who worked as trainers for the French team.

—The first Kandahar cable binding holding the skier's heel to the ski is introduced.

—First snow reports published in New York City.

A CHRONOLOGY OF SKI DEVELOPMENTS

1935—The first overhead cable lift, a J-bar, is built at Oak Hill in Hanover, New Hampshire, by the Dartmouth Outing Club. The lift is still in operation.

1936—First issue of *Ski* magazine published in Seattle by Alf Nydin.

—Fourth Olympic Winter Games at Garmisch-Partenkirchen includes downhill and slalom for the first time. The rotational technique of Toni Seelos receives first world-wide attention when, as forerunner, he beats the slalom gold medalist by over five seconds.

—Development of Mt. Mansfield begins after arrival there of Sepp Ruschp from Austria.

—Sun Valley opens for its first season, installing the first two chairlifts ever made.

1937—First American ski team visits Chile.

—First chairlift installed in the East at Belknap, New Hampshire.

—First parallel technique introduced to North America by Fritz Loosli.

—Dick Durrance wins first Harriman Cup race at Sun Valley.

1938—First aerial tramway in the United States installed at Cannon Mountain, Franconia, New Hampshire.

—First skimobile built at Cranmore Mountain at North Conway, New Hampshire.

—First Canadian chairlift built by Joseph Ryan at Mt. Tremblant, Quebec.

—National Ski Patrol established with Minot Dole named as chairman of national committee.

—First certification examination of ski instructors held at Woodstock, Vermont. Sepp Ruschp becomes the first certified instructor in the United States.

—Canadian Ski Instructors Alliance formed.

—Arlberg-Kandahar cancelled when Germany annexes Austria and Hannes Schneider is imprisoned by the Nazis.

1939—Hjalmar Hvam introduces first workable release bindings.

—Hannes Schneider arrives in the United States and takes over leadership of the ski school at Mt. Cranmore. Schneider also developed the first groomed slope by cutting down trees and completely clearing the south slope of Mt. Cranmore.

—Toni Matt schusses Headwall of Tuckerman's Ravine in third and last American Inferno race.

—First National Women's Downhill and Slalom Championship at Stowe, Vermont, won by Marian McKean and Grace Carter Lindley, respectively.

1940—First T-bar in the United States installed at Pico Peak, Vermont.

1941—87th Mountain Infantry Regiment activated at Fort Lewis, Washington, and trains on Mt. Rainier; later merged into the 10th Mountain Division, which trained at Camp Hale.

1946—Aspen Skiing Corporation formed under Walter Paepcke.

—Platterpull (Pomalift) developed in Europe by Jean Pomagalski.

—First successful metal skis made (but never marketed) by the Chance Vought Aircraft Corp. The skis were designed by Wayne Pierce Jr., Art Hunt and Dave Richey, who subsequently developed another metal ski design, the Alu-60.

1947—First double chairlift installed at Berthoud Pass, Colorado.

A Chronology of Ski Developments

—Howard Head begins first experiments with metal skis, ironically using a somewhat similar approach to that developed by Hunt & Co. for Chance Vought.

—First Learn-to-Ski Week promoted by Sun Valley.

1948—Gretchen Fraser becomes first American to win Olympic medals (gold in slalom, silver in alpine combined) at fifth Olympic Winter Games at St. Moritz, Switzerland.

—KLM runs first ski flight to Europe.

—First chairlift in Midwest is built at Boyne Mountain.

—*Ski* magazine evolves out of merger of *Ski Illustrated* (the changed name of the original *Ski* magazine), *Ski News* and *Western Skiing*. The new magazine is published by William T. Eldred.

—Nicholas Stumpf of Switzerland becomes the first non-Scandinavian to finish in the first three in the Nordic Combined in the Holmenkollen.

—A sharp swing toward reverse shoulder technique is noted among the younger racers of Europe.

1949—Mad River Glen, Vermont, and Squaw Valley, California, are opened.

1950—First post-war FIS World Championships are held at Aspen (alpine) and Lake Placid (jumping) and Rumford, Maine, (cross-country).

1952—Andrea Mead Lawrence wins gold medals in giant slalom and slalom at sixth Olympic Winter Games at Oslo, Norway. This is the first Winter Olympics at which giant slalom is recognized as a separate event.

—First artifically made snow is used at Grossinger's resort in New York; Fahnestock, New York, two years later, becomes first ski area to make snow on regular basis.

1953—Modern Austrian Technique using counter-rotation is introduced in Austria by Prof. Stefan Kruckenhauser.

1954—NCAA recognizes skiing as an inter-collegiate sport.

—Ski Hall of Fame dedicated at Ishpeming, Michigan.

1955—Modern Austrian Technique is first internationally demonstrated at International Ski School Congress at Val d'Isere, France.

—Hannes Schneider dies.

—First buckle boots introduced by Henke.

—First stretch pants introduced by Bogner.

—First polyethylene base introduced by Kofix.

—First Hart metal skis introduced.

1956—Toni Sailer wins downhill, slalom and giant slalom at Cortina d'Ampezzo, Italy, the only time that a skier has made a "grand slam" of all three Alpine events at an Olympic Winter Games.

—Austrian Technique makes heavy inroads in American skiing after its introduction here.

1958—Buddy Werner becomes first American male racer to win a major European race when he wins combined at the Lauberhorn.

—Lucille Wheeler of Canada wins gold medals in giant slalom and downhill at the

A CHRONOLOGY OF SKI DEVELOPMENTS

FIS World Championships at Badgastein; Sally Deaver of the United States wins silver medal in giant slalom.

—First gondola installed at the Wildcat area in New Hampshire.

1959—Buddy Werner becomes first American male to win a major European downhill, winning at the Hahnenkamm in Kitzbuehel, Austria.

1960—French become the first team to use metal skis successfully in winning several major European downhills prior to the Olympics.

—Eighth Olympic Winter Games at Squaw Valley, California. Canada's Ann Heggtveit wins slalom; Penny Pitou wins silver medals in downhill and giant slalom; and Betsy Snite wins a silver medal in slalom. France's Jean Vuarnet wins men's downhill on metal skis.

1961—Professional Ski Instructors of America (PSIA) organized at Whitefish, Montana. Bill Lash of Salt Lake City is named first president.

—Christian Pravda wins first professional ski race at Aspen, picking up $1500 in prize money. The pros have raced annually since that time, but have had difficult going against the more spectacular amateurs.

—Ski Industries of America (SIA), the first nationwide trade organization, opens New York City offices.

1961—Bob Beattie, University of Colorado ski coach, is named head coach of the U.S. Alpine team for the 1962 FIS World Championships. Two years later he became the first American coach to succeed himself when he was named to lead the 1964 Olympic team.

1962—Joan Hannah places third in giant slalom and Barbara Ferries third in the downhill at the FIS World Championships in Chamonix, France.

—Chuck Ferries wins Hahnenkamm slalom.

—NSA changes name to United States Ski Association (USSA).

—PSIA formulates American Ski Technique.

1963—National Ski Areas Association (NSAA) founded.

—Jim Balfanz and Gene Kotlarek finish second and fourth, respectively at Holmenkollen, the highest placing Americans have achieved in major international Nordic competition.

1964—Billy Kidd and Jimmy Huega become the first American men to win Olympic medals for skiing, being second and third, respectively, in the slalom at the ninth Olympic Winter Games at Innsbruck, Austria. Jean Saubert ties for second in the giant slalom and places third in the slalom.

—Buddy Werner killed in a Swiss avalanche shortly after announcing his retirement from racing.

—Uniform trail marking system adopted by NSAA.

1965—First American International Team Races (a memorial to Buddy Werner) held at Vail, Colorado, and won by Austria (men) and France (women).

—David Jacobs named first full-time Canadian ski coach.

1966—The first FIS World Championships (alpine) are held in the southern hemisphere, at Portillo, Chile.

450

Appendix E. BOOKS, JOURNALS AND FILMS

No attempt is made here to present a complete bibliography of ski literature and ski films. Only those books which have had unusual influence on the skiing of their time or which are unique for one reason or another are listed below. For those interested in delving further into ski literature, Baker Library at Dartmouth College has the most comprehensive collection of ski books and journals in the United States. Unfortunately, there is no such repository for ski films.

BOOKS

ALLAIS, EMILE, GIGNOUX, PAUL, and BLANCHON, GEORGES, *Ski francais.* Grenoble, France: B. Arthaud, 1938.

BILGERI, GEORG, *Der Alpine Skilauf.* 1910.

BRADLEY, DAVID, MILLER, RALPH, and MERRILL, ALLISON, *Expert Skiing.* New York: Grosset and Dunlap, Inc., 1960. (Revised edition, 1964.)

BRANDENBERGER, HUGO, *Methodik des Skilaufs und Skimechanik.* Rapperswil, Switzerland: Verlag Gasser & Co., 1958.

CALDWELL, JOHN, JR., *Cross Country Skiing.* Brattleboro, Vt.: Stephen Greene Press, 1964.

CASEWIT, CURTIS, *Ski Racing: Advice by the Experts.* New York: Arco Publishing Co., 1963.

CAULFIELD, VIVIAN, *How to Ski.* 1910.

COUTTET, JAMES and GIGNOUX, PAUL, *Christiania Leger.* Paris: Libraire Hachette, 1961.

FOEGER, WALTER, *Skiing for Beginners: The Natur Technik Method.* New York: Ronald Press, 1963.

ISELIN, FRED, and SPECTORSKY, A. C., *Invitation to Skiing.* New York: Simon & Schuster, 1947. (Revised editions, 1958, 1966.)

JOURBERT, GEORGES, and VUARNET, JEAN, *Ski 1957.* Bourg, France: Editions Bressanes, 1957.

KRUCKENHAUSER, STEFAN, *The New Official Austrian Ski System* (translated by Roland Palmedo). New York: A. S. Barnes & Co., 1958.

LUNN, SIR ARNOLD, *The Story of Ski-ing.* London: Eyre & Spottiswoode, 1952.

LUTHER, CARL L., *Der Moderne Wintersport.* 1911.

MATTHIAS, EUGEN, and TESTA, GIOVANNI, *Natürliches skilaufen.* Munich, Germany, 1936.

MICOLEAU, TYLER, *Power Skiing.* New York: Ronald Press, 1949.

NANSEN, FRIDTJOF, *Paa Ski Over Grönland.* Oslo, Norway, 1890. (German and English editions, 1891.)

PALMEDO, ROLAND, *Skiing: The International Sport.* New York: Derrydale Press, 1938.

————, *Ski New Horizons.* New York: Pan American Airways, 1961.

PFEIFFER, J. DOUGLAS, *Skiing with Pfeiffer.* Riverside, Calif.: A to Z Printing, 1958.

PROCTOR, CHARLES N., *Skiing.* New York, 1936.

REINDL, KURT and DUCIA, TONI, *Le Ski d'Aujourd'hui.* 1935.

BOOKS, JOURNALS AND FILMS

RICHARDSON, E. C., SOMERVILLE, CRICHTON, and RICKMERS, W. R., *Ski Running*. London: 1905.

SCHNEIDER, HANNES and FANCK, ARNOLD, *Wunder des Schneeschuhs*. 1926. English edition, *Wonders of Skiing*, New York, 1937.

SCHNIEBS, OTTO, *Skiing for All*. New York, 1936.

Ski Magazine, editors of, *Ski Pointers by the Experts*. New York: Harper & Row, 1961; Universal Publishing & Distributing Corp. (paperback), 1964.

TAYLOR, CLIF, *Ski in a Day*. New York: Grosset & Dunlap, 1964.

ZDARSKY, MATHIAS, *Lilienfelder Schilauf Technik*. 1896.

JOURNALS

American Ski Annual (no longer published).

British Ski Year Book, published annually by the Ski Club of Great Britain.

Der Schnee Hase, published annually by the Swiss Academic Ski Club.

Der Sport, published three times weekly in Zurich, Switzerland.

L'Equipe, published weekly in Paris, France.

Ski Magazine (incorporating *Ski Life*), published eight times a year between mid-September and March by Universal Publishing & Distributing Corporation, 800 Second Ave., New York, N.Y.

Skiing, published six times a year between October and March by Ziff-Davis Publishing Company, 1 Park Avenue, New York, N.Y.

FILMS

BARRYMORE, RICHARD (lecture films).

JAY, JOHN (lecture films).

MILLER, WARREN (lecture films).

Die Weisse Kunst, directed by Arnold Fanck with Hannes Schneider.

Fox Chase in the Engadine, directed by Arnold Fanck with Hannes Schneider.

Ski Country, USA, by Summit Film Productions for United Airlines.

Ski Total, distributed by the French Government Tourist Office.

Sun Valley Ski Chase, available from Dartmouth College Films, Hanover, N.H.

Appendix F. HOW TO ORGANIZE A SKI COMPETITION

Each year the importance of efficient ski race management grows as the number of races increases. Every winter, there are about 500 sanctioned races in the U.S. and 250 in Canada, to say nothing of a host of unclassified club races. The sanctioned races alone take in about 20,000 competitors in downhill, slalom, giant slalom, cross country, jumping and biathlon (shoot and ski). Fortunately, organizations like the United States Ski Association and the Canadian Amateur Ski Association (the groups which govern and give official status to races in North America) have established some guidelines for holding ski races. Under USSA rules, a sanctioned race is one that affects a racer's class rating—A, B, C, junior, veterans. Each division has slightly different requirements for classification. But generally a racer must attend a specified number of sanctioned races to qualify for a class card and move up to a higher rating. All the divisions use the FIS (the international governing body of ski racing) point system to rate the racers and results. As a result, a competitor can travel from one division to another and race in his established class.

A club or group of clubs interested in sponsoring a *sanctioned* race should start planning six months to one year before the event. The first step is to select a race chairman. He is the key person in organizing and administering the race. Certainly he should be familiar with racing, but if the division officials feel that he needs assistance, they may assign a technical advisor to work with the club. There is often a charge for the advisor's time spent at meetings and the race.

Some time early in the planning, the site of the race must be selected by the sponsoring group. Because ski races are usually held on weekends when areas are most crowded, it is important to consider only those areas that have sufficient trails to be devoted exclusively to the race.

Other factors to consider in selecting the area are: availability of the trails for practice prior to the race; adequate lifts or snow vehicles to take racers uphill between runs; proper snow equipment and vehicles to prepare the course; facilities for the extra ski patrol needed for the race; and nearby housing accommodations for racers, officials and spectators.

When a site is selected the group can apply to the competitions committee of the local USSA division for official sanctioning of the proposed race. Tournament rules and regulations vary slightly from division to division, but usually you will need to provide detailed information on the who, what, when and where of the race. There is also a fee, usually ranging from $25 to $100.

Once the application is approved, the committee chairman can start gathering personnel to prepare and run the race. Several race officials may be appointed by the competitions committee. For instance, in the Rocky Mountain Ski Division of USSA (whose rules and regulations are drawn upon for much of this article), the referee, chief of course, course setter, chief timer and jumping judges must be certified officials. This means that they have special training or experience for handling these jobs.

HOW TO ORGANIZE A SKI COMPETITION

Officials drawn from the organization sponsoring the race are: chief starter, start judge, start secretary, judge of finish and forerunners. You'll need many other people to gather equipment for the race, handle entry blanks, supervise gatekeepers, recruit course police and ski patrol. At the race itself, people will be needed to distribute number bibs, collect number bibs, record results, calculate results, operate radios and telephones and public address systems, assist starters and timers and serve refreshments. Many of these posts will require one or more relief men, especially if it is very cold.

Sub-committees must be appointed to handle prizes, programs, publicity, housing, entertainment and the banquet after the race. Keep in mind that more people will be needed after the race is finished to clean up the course and remove ruts and hazards, return borrowed equipment, write thank you notes, and so on.

Prior to the race, however, one of the most critical jobs is gathering equipment. Items of equipment start with slalom poles which should be bamboo, eight or nine feet long, one-and-a-quarter inches in diameter and painted red, blue and yellow. You should have two spare poles for every three gates set on the course. Blank express-type tags can be used to number the gates from the top of the course to the bottom. Tape the tag on the outside gate. Slalom flags should be the same color as the poles.

Other special items of equipment include: four phones or radios and spare batteries, six timing watches, officials' arm bands, pinnies or number bibs for each racer and for the fore- and post-runners. (Incidentally, arrange with the area to have some identifying insignia for racers to wear during the practice period before the race. Area management and lift operators should also be supplied with a list of racers and officials who will be using lift facilities.) You'll need vegetable coloring or other water-soluble fluid to mark the slalom gate positions for the first run (blue) and changes for the second run (red). To handle poor snow conditions, such as extremely wet snow or cold sugar snow, have several hundred pounds of rock salt and ammonium chloride available. Of course, first aid equipment and toboggans should be available at three positions on a downhill course and two positions on all other courses. Each gatekeeper will need a rake or shovel to repair the course. They should also be outfitted with fluorescent-colored vests (which may be obtained at army surplus outlets) to signify their positions as gatekeepers.

Paper work and office supplies needed at the race include: entry blanks, racing order sheets, time sheets and cards, gatekeeper's cards, at least five clipboards with plastic top cover sheets, two typewriters, an adding machine, a computer, paper, pencils, carbon paper, paper clips, a stapler, Mimeograph machine with stencils and paper. Signs needed are: start and finish markers, a blackboard and chalk to mark race results, a blackboard and chalk for last minute information for racers and officials, cardboard and felt-tipped markers for posting announcements.

Some of these items, such as official forms, watches and arm bands, can be bought or rented from your division office. Others may be borrowed from other clubs or the area management.

The starting area should have a shack for officials and racers. If this isn't available, you'll need to bring a tent for this purpose. The area around the start should be level and elevated. If crowds are likely to be a problem, have extra bamboo poles and rope or snow fences to hold them back. If the area doesn't have a starting gate, use two-by-fours set two feet apart and about two-and-a-half feet above the snow.

The finish gate should be large and highly visible. Plan to construct snow chutes two or three feet high on either side of the finish to protect fallen skiers.

Between the start and finish is the weightiest problem for the officials—safety. This is where the advice of a technical advisor or experienced racer will be most valuable. The International Ski Competition Rule Book gives specific descriptions of the terrain requirements for all the races. Trail and snow preparation is spelled out thoroughly. Follow this advice closely and go beyond it by exaggerating the possibility of open or hidden dangers on the trails. Wherever an obstacle might pose a safety problem, build a snow or straw safety wall, barrier or net.

Certain safety factors of a race are, however, left to the judgment of the racing officials. For instance, the rule books say nothing about a downhill race in 35 degree below zero weather or winds up to 50 m.p.h. or fog, flat light or poor visibility. These are problems which rest on the shoulders of the key people who run the race. They need to have the courage to cancel a race or stop or delay a race to remove hazards or allow time to make it safe rather than take a chance on accidents.

A course that can break up or become hazardous or rutty after only 15 or 20 racers is inadequate. Rolling equipment, tramping and chemicals, properly used on a race course should enable it to hold up for 80 or more competitors.

Weather conditions and course preparations are particularly important in junior races. Older competitors are seasoned to the difficulties of racing. One bad experience may be enough to make a youngster drop out for good. For junior races, take extra safety precautions and keep the atmosphere happy.

One safety feature to check on the day of the race is protective headgear. All competitors in downhill and giant slalom events must wear a race helmet bearing the approval decal of the Snell Foundation. This means it has been tested for impact safety.

Announce and post unofficial results as soon as they are available. While these may be changed later, you'll make the race more exciting by giving racers and spectators some reference immediately. You'll need two or three people to work out these calculations.

Be prepared to act promptly on protests. The referee and his committee should use the FIS rules as a guide in disqualifications. Whenever there is a doubt about a dispute, allow the racer a re-run. You can make the final decision later.

Always have some kind of an award ceremony, a banquet if you have time, or presentations immediately after the race near the course or in the base lodge. Prizes may be trophies; medals or diplomas and should not cost more than $5 to $8.

A final word on holding a better ski race. Even if you follow all of the above advice to

455

HOW TO ORGANIZE A SKI COMPETITION

the letter and carry out every procedure, your image will be muddied if the race doesn't START ON TIME. The time schedule below will guide a race chairman to that critical moment when he gives the signal to GO.

CHECK LIST FOR SKI RACE PLANNING

Six months before race:

1. Name race committee chairman.
2. Select committee members who are potential race officials.
3. Investigate sites for race.
4. Prepare application for sanctioned race.
5. Appoint sub-committees.
6. Assign duties.

Six weeks before race:

1. Check equipment available.
2. Distribute press releases.

Four weeks before race:

1. Check arrangements with area.
2. Check progress of committees.
3. Mail entry blanks to clubs and other potential racers.

Three weeks before race:

1. Notify all officials and committee chairmen of time schedule and duties at the race. Be sure they contact all workers.
2. Check snow cover at race site.
3. Check equipment procurement.
4. Install wiring for phones.
5. Obtain prizes.

Two weeks before race:

1. Check progress of all officials.
2. Mail second press release.
3. Check arrangements for spectator control and first aid.
4. Check office supplies, race forms.

One week before race:

1. Arrange to pick up equipment borrowed from division headquarters or other ski clubs.
2. Transport some equipment to the area.
3. Check on press representation.

Two days before race:

1. Check snow report.
2. Arrange for preparation of the course with snow vehicles and/or chemicals.
3. Arrange to mark the course and the practice areas.
4. Hold a meeting to have draw for positions in the first event. Print race order sheets.
5. Check the order of time cards.

One day before race:

1. Hold a meeting of the racers.
2. Check course conditions.
3. Arrange for distribution on the numbers either at the draw for second and third events or on the start.

Day of race:

1. Recheck communications system several hours before.
2. Recheck condition of course.
3. Check classification cards and distribute numbers.
4. Check helmets for Snell OK.
5. Check on refreshments.
6. An hour and a half before race, brief officials.
7. Half an hour before race, officials in positions and police the course.
8. Ten minutes before race, forerunners on the start.
9. Start the race—on time.
10. Have five racers lined up and ready to go at all times. In a giant slalom and downhill, allow one to two minutes interval between racers. In a slalom the course should be cleared before another racer starts. In cross country, racers can start every 30 seconds.
11. Announce and post results as soon as they are available. Post disqualifications and reruns.
12. Be prepared to act promptly on protests.
13. Have bibs collected at finish.

After the race:

1. Check gatekeepers' cards.
2. Make final computation of results and post them.
3. Distribute press releases.
4. Clean course, collect equipment.
5. Hold banquet and awards.
6. Mail results to clubs, papers.
7. Return borrowed equipment.
8. Send thank-you notes to all who assisted.
9. Hold post-race meeting of officials to get suggestions for future races.

457

HOW TO ORGANIZE A SKI COMPETITION

INFORMATION

For a rule book on ski racing, write to your local division headquarters. The International Ski Competition Rule Book is available from the United States Ski Association, The Broadmoor, Colorado Springs, Colo. The National Collegiate Skiing Rules can be obtained from the National Collegiate Athletic Association Bureau, Box 757, Grand Central Station, New York, N.Y.

PHOTO CREDITS

All photographs and diagrams in this book have appeared in *Ski* magazine. Photographers and agencies are credited as follows:

Australian News & Info. Bureau, 234
Dick Barrymore, 224 (top)
Morton Beebe, 200, 212, 214, 215, 216, 217 (top)
The Bettman Archive, 24
Bildbericht, St. Anton, 35
Adrian Bouchard, 397
Canadian Gov't. Travel Bureau, 217 (bottom)
Les Caron, 134
Hanson Carroll, 2, 5, 177, 345
Louis Cochaud, 30
Commissariat Général, Switz., 162, 221
Consulate General of Japan, N.Y., 233
Knut Eduard, 369 (top)
Jim Elder, 357 (left), 391 (top)
Jack Fields, 203
Finley, 211
Foto Rio, 390 (left)
French Gov't. Tourist Office, 226 (left)
John Fry, 36
Otto Furter, 222
Ernest Gay, 204, 210
Gay-Couttet, 361
General Electric, 25 (right)
Joern Gerdts, 146, 193, 194, 388 (right)
Otto Giese, 342
Mladen Grcevic, 230
Helmut Gritscher, 236
Grundig, 209 (bottom)
Judson B. Hall, 152
Homberger, 50, 114
C. Hugel, 145, 224 (bottom)
Hunter Mt. Ski Bowl, 241
John Jay, 228
Kaiser Aluminum, 171 (bottom)

Leonard Kamsler, 180
Alexis Kelner, 191
Knudsens Fotosenter, Oslo, 381 (top)
M. Lacy, 197
Tony Lane, 106
James Laughlin, 378
Fred Lindholm, 7, 10, 47, 188, 284, 294, 310, 311
Fletcher Manley, Jr., 72
Kim Massie, 49 (left), 51, 142, 150, 171 (top), 231 (bottom), 290, 372, 373, 376
Bob Mesterton, 389 (right)
Peter Miller, 49 (right)
Milton Photos, 41
N.Y. State Dept. of Commerce, 179
Oregon State Highway Travel Div., 209 (top)
Oslo Ski Museum, 1, 15, 16, 18, 19, 23, 28
Panagra, 235
A. Pedrett, 34
Photo Constantini, 389 (left)
Photopress Grenoble, 354, 395
Polish Information Bureau, 231 (top)
Charles Pottsmith, 182
Pressus Bild, Stockholm, 364
Dick Rowan, 201
Paul Ryan, ii, 54, 132 (top right, bottom left and right), 136, 139, 155, 353
Barcus Salmon, 219
Sante Fe Railway News Bureau, 196
Sheedy & Long, vii
Carl Shiraishi, 132 (top left)
Dick Smith, 174
Bob & Ira Spring, 225
John M. Stephens, 198
Stowe News Bureau, 393 (bottom)

PHOTO CREDITS

460

INDEX

INDEX

INDEX

INDEX

468

INDEX

INDEX